DISLOCATIONS

General Editors: August Carbonella, *Memorial University of Newfoundland,* Don Kalb, *Central European University & Utrecht University,* Gerald Sider, *The Graduate Center & The College of Staten Island, CUNY,* Linda Green, *University of Arizona*

The immense dislocations and suffering caused by neo-liberal globalization, the retreat of the welfare state in the last decades of the twentieth century and the heightened military imperialism at the turn of the twenty-first century have raised urgent questions about the temporal and spatial dimensions of power. Through stimulating critical perspectives and new and cross-disciplinary frameworks, which reflect recent innovations in the social and human sciences, this series provides a forum for politically engaged, ethnographically informed, and theoretically incisive responses.

STRUGGLES FOR HOME

Violence, Hope and the Movement of People

Edited by
Stef Jansen and Staffan Löfving

Berghahn Books
NEW YORK · OXFORD

Published in 2009 by

Berghahn Books
www.berghahnbooks.com

© 2009, 2011 Stef Jansen and Staffan Löfving
First paperback edition published in 2011

Library of Congress Cataloging-in-Publication Data

Struggles for home : violence, hope and the movement of people /
edited by Stef Jansen and Staffan Löfving.
    p. cm. -- (Dislocations ; 3)
Includes bibliographical references and index.
ISBN 978-1-84545-523-1 (hbk) -- ISBN 978-0-85745-150-7 (pbk)
 1. Assimilation (Sociology) 2. Home--Psychological aspects. 3. Identity
(Psychology) 4. Emigration and immigration--Psychological aspects. 5.
War--Social aspects--Case studies. I. Jansen, Stef. II. Löfving, Staffan.

JV6342.S78 2008
304.8--dc22

2008033846

British Library Cataloguing in Publication Data

A catalogue record for this book is available from the British Library

Printed on acid-free paper.

ISBN 978-1-84545-523-1 (hardback)
ISBN 978-0-85745-150-7 (paperback)
ISBN 978-1-84545-860-7 (ebook)

CONTENTS

INTRODUCTION

Towards an Anthropology of Violence, Hope and the Movement of People

Stef Jansen and Staffan Löfving

The idea for this book grew out of our attempts to grapple with some sharp contradictions encountered in our respective ethnographic engagements. As anthropologists working in the post-Yugoslav states and in postwar Central America, we have been struck by a disturbing discrepancy in discussions of violence and the movement of people. On the one hand, there are the naturalised assumptions in both political and scholarly discourse that the cure for the ailment of violent displacement lies per definition in renewed territorialised belonging (i.e., usually, refugee return). Yet, on the other hand, we found that the realities of people and the places which they more or less temporarily inhabit do not always resonate with such assumptions. People's 'place in the world' after war and repatriation continues to be violently challenged.

In the post-Yugoslav states, Stef Jansen worked with people of different nationalities who, whether displaced or not, were confronted with 'ethnic cleansing' – that is, with hegemonising nationalisms that violently aimed to fix national belonging in discrete homelands. Yet, hundreds of thousands of persons left or aspired to leave those territories *after* the military conflicts, including persons who vigorously supported the legitimacy of the newly established 'ethnically cleansed' political units. Particularly for the inhabitants of a semi-protectorate such as Bosnia-Herzegovina, such discrepancies were sharpened by the foreign-led neoliberal emphasis on entrepreneurialism in postwar reconstruction, as became all too clear when this editor was asked to speak at a careers fair organised by students in the town of Tuzla. During this rather surreal experience, a student came to talk to him. She was a displaced person with a sociological profile perhaps most likely to respond favourably to the foreign-led discourses of post-socialist 'transition': young, highly educated, ambitious, independent. Yet she was deeply aware of the radical contradiction that underlay her predicament in a context where emancipatory politics had largely been colonised by nationalism. The very Western governments enticing her to make return to her prewar place of residence feasible through forward-looking, risky economic initiative were simultaneously engaged in tightening immigration policies to prevent her from doing precisely what she had reluctantly come to associate with such future-oriented action: emigration to a Western state.

The other editor of this book, Staffan Löfving, has long nurtured an interest in social and political movements in Central America and grappled with the paradigmatic changes from movement as contentious politics to movement as migration evident over the last fifteen years. In the autumn of 2006, a peasant woman in the village of Panimatzalam, Guatemala, told him about the relative wealth of two neighbouring families that had members working as undocumented immigrants in the USA. Money was remitted on a monthly basis and their household economies flourished. To her, these families seemed to represent both a problem and a promise. In fact, her own son had recently embarked on a journey to the Mexican border, hoping to hook up with acquaintances in Los Angeles. To pay the US$6,000 fee to the *coyote* – the trafficker – she had been forced to mortgage her house and thus suffered from an increased cost of living. Moreover, she had not heard from her son for a month and an agonising worry permeated her life. A less salient theme, yet unmistakably present in the woman's story, was the social implications of the fact that many young and able-bodied villagers were now lost to 'the community'. Family members who remained were exposed to charges of having failed their community obligations – accusations that increased when someone actually made it into the USA. Migration for work or away from military violence was anything but new to her family's history, but the distances covered, the dangers implied in challenging ever stricter border controls, the economic risk, and the lonely and antisocial nature of this endeavour – all these factors added up to a greater danger than earlier movements. Yet, the possible reward for taking the risk was also perceived as unprecedented.

People's movement through rather than simply away from violence, their 'search for cool ground' (Turton 1996), for places to (re)make home (or, as we argue here, to struggle for it), challenge both popular and scholarly notions of migration and the discourse on violence and place on which they are based. This book investigates such struggles for home. Through ethnographic case studies from Palestine, Bosnia-Herzegovina, Cyprus, the Angolan–Zambian borderland, Southern Spain, Sri Lanka and Guatemala, we trace contestations of emplacement through an analysis not only of memories of social and geographical belonging but also of forward-looking practices of attachment to and detachment from place. We investigate how discourses of localised belonging may on the one hand facilitate, yet on the other hand prohibit, the making of home. Crucially, this implies a critical approach to the power relations that shape particular places. The chapters in *Struggles for Home* explain, first of all, how home is attached to or detached from particular places through relations of power that attribute certain qualities to them, such as security, familiarity, wealth or freedom. But we aim to go beyond this insight, arguing that unequal social relations are also crucial in how places afford people what could be called transformative power. Our ethnographic studies show that over and above – and sometimes in spite of – the abovementioned qualities, both the subjects of our research and the anthropologists themselves recognise how struggles for home involve a contest over how places are endowed, to different degrees, with hope, with a capacity to control and to project a sense of possibility. Through such a political anthropology of home, we hope to insert a sensitivity to transformation (and to the power to transform) into discussions of movement and place.

Movement

The growing anthropological interest in mobility[1] represents a welcome development for a discipline that, while it may have had an early interest in people on the move, has nevertheless contributed to dominant notions of culture and identity as being closely attached to specific territories.[2] Recent developments in the field are providing an adequate response to changing and contradictory social realities that result from accelerating and increasing human mobility and its significance, including for those who do not migrate. Contemporary anthropology offers means to critically engage with the territorialising efforts of nationalist movements, transnational capitalist restructuring, and migration policies. Issues that tended to be obscured by the previous methodological and epistemological focus on the normality of boundedness and fixity are now addressed in novel ways. Conceptually, researchers expose the contingency of 'belonging' by de-essentialising notions of 'identity', 'nation' and 'home', and by investigating their relationship to territory. Politically, moreover, the new anthropology of mobility represents a potentially liberating reaction against a history of oppressively essentialist-collectivist ideologies of home, such as nationalism, and of the normative anthropological approaches to 'community' and 'culture' that are congruent with them (see Gilroy 2000).

A useful starting point from which to approach our contribution to this new anthropology of mobility may be the debate in the *Journal of Refugee Studies* (1999) around Gaim Kibreab's critique of Liisa Malkki's 1995 study *Purity and Exile*, amongst people who sought refuge from large-scale anti-Hutu violence in Burundi. Malkki's ethnographic work focused on refugees in two sites in Tanzania: a refugee camp – run by the Tanzanian authorities in alignment with international humanitarian organisations – and a nearby town. One of Malkki's main arguments revolves around the stark differences between camp informants and town informants in the way they related to nationhood, to 'home' and 'homeland', and in their experiences and understandings of exile. Camp refugees overwhelmingly experienced their predicament as that of a nation in exile. Through what Malkki calls 'mythicohistorical' remakings of the world, exercises of a deeply moral nature, they essentialised nationhood along the lines of a dominant national cosmology, constructing their own Hutu-ness in contrast to various antagonistic nations (Tutsis, Tanzanians, etc.). Their refugee status was crucial to their understanding of the past (escape from massacre in their true national homeland), the present (temporary guests in Tanzania) and the future (centred upon a victorious return to the national homeland). In contrast, town refugees, who had fled Burundi in the same 1972 wave, were scattered all over the town and did not see themselves as a distinct group with a collective identity. Through chameleonic strategies of invisibility, partial assimilation and movement, they focused largely on socioeconomic security and opportunity. Although partly born out of fear, such activities came to play a central role in their proactive strategies. As such, they were the object of disapproval amongst camp refugees, who rejected assimilation in favour of the purity of exile. According to the mythicohistorical approach of the camp dwellers, Hutus needed to achieve purity as a refugee nation through hardship, resisting any hybridisation, in order to recapture the homeland when the time was ripe. Not surprisingly, differences between camp and town refugees were also great with regard to return, with the latter largely ignoring the topic but actually incorporating it in practice while the camp was rife with detailed horror stories documenting the impossibility of return.

In *Purity and Exile* and in a series of related articles (1992, 1994, 1995b), Malkki constructs a critical reading of what she calls a 'national cosmology': the modern, globally dominant representations of nationality and territoriality that underlie the very categories of 'refugees'. In particular, she warns of a 'sedentarist' bias (1995b: 208), a tendency to conceive of people's movements as inherently violent in a world of 'rooted' populations, naturally attached to territories. Singling out Liisa Malkki as a prominent exponent of what he terms 'post-modernist anti-sedentarist thinkers', Gaim Kibreab replied with a sustained polemic (1999). In Kibreab's view, anti-sedentarists stand for an empirically and politically flawed approach to forced migration. He argues that, by ignoring existing patterns of identification with place and the desire to return to locality of origin, anti-sedentarists engage in politically dangerous forms of wishful thinking, mistakenly concluding that identities are nowadays increasingly detached from territory in a global move towards a-national, deterritorialised citizenship (ibid.: 385).

Kibreab makes a number of important points on the structural constraints that shape refugee experiences, and his work provides a call to arms for social scientists not to lose sight of the oppressive nature of current migration regimes. However, some of the misunderstandings present in this debate are indicative of the problems that commonly beset the emergence of constructive discussion in the study of displacement and emplacement. Kibreab's argument assumes that a commitment to anti-sedentarism necessarily adheres to the larger project of the 'deterritorialisation of identity' (1999: 387). Moreover, it presumes that denying a necessary, essential link between territory and identity, and opposing the naturalisation of such links, implies the negation of any link at all. In contrast, we reassert the value of a critical analysis of unmarked, normative sedentarism, which we would define as the assumption that all human beings, understood collectively as cultural groups, 'belong' to a certain place on earth and derive a primordial identity from that belonging. Questioning sedentarist discourses and demonstrating their role in processes of oppression and marginalisation does not entail neglecting the impact of other dimensions in these processes. Instead of ingrained sedentarist modes of representation, Kibreab argues, it is the selfish and hostile attitudes of host governments towards refugees that are to blame for the latter's predicaments (ibid.: 388ff.). We would argue that not only can these two factors coexist perfectly well, but that they actually reinforce one another. If we were to follow their strict separation, any critical investigation of emplacement and displacement would risk being rejected as part of an exercise under a presumably postmodern manifesto (which is usually seen as the mechanical product of the position of metropolitan privilege of those accused of promoting it). To be fair, such criticisms may be called for with regard to a subfield of the scholarly interest in mobility – a body of work shaped by what could be called a 'placeless' paradigm, including often largely theoretical pieces on movement and belonging with a strong emphasis on detachment from place and shifting positioning. Many studies in this vein contain a programmatic element – they are not so much descriptions *of* as calls *for* new forms of subjectivity, particularly in response to various forms of cultural fundamentalism.[3]

In *Struggles for Home*, we approach the key concepts of both sedentarist and placeless paradigms – including territorialisation and deterritorialisation, and emplacement and displacement – as empirical issues to be investigated rather than as philosophical assessments about what characterises our age. We do not take for granted the territorial rooting of identification, but this stance cannot and should not be equated with the blanket argument that 'identities are deterritorialised'. This would be to conflate the empirical with the analytical. We explore the ways in which practices of identification are related (or not related) to territory, rather than simply assuming that they are related everywhere in the same way. The contributions gathered here are based on ethnographic work with women and men who have been subjected to practices of territorialisation brought about by counterinsurgency, border creation, 'ethnic cleansing' and economic restructuring. As a result, rather than propagating a free-floating placeless paradigm, we emphasise the need to critically investigate the unequal, differential and contested processes by which persons come to be (dis)associated – and (dis)associate themselves – with or from place.

We also aim to avoid a further problematic dimension of most sedentarist thinking, namely, the idea that if people display a strong attachment to territory, this can and even must be understood as an issue of (ethno-)nationality (Jansen 2005; Newbury 2005). In work on migrants and refugees, there is a strong presumption of authenticity attributed to this link between nationality, 'homeland' territory and a desire to return. While it is usually not spelled out why this should be the case (which only goes to show that the presumption follows the dominant 'national order of things'; Malkki 1995a), it is simply presumed that the refugees' 'real identity', if they were 'allowed to be themselves' (Kibreab 1999: 397), is their belonging to an (ethno-)national category territorialised in relation to the 'homeland and the past' (ibid.). If the contingency of such belonging, its possible temporal instability and its structural context are ignored, we end up with a reified, essentialised notion of belonging – a primordial identity that is lived in links with the 'homeland' and a yearning to return home. Even though such essentialising is becoming increasingly unacceptable in anthropology, its underlying assumptions retain some of their strength because *other* ways of relating to territoriality are often assessed in a position relative to this one.[4] Paradoxically, rather than questioning essentialised conceptions of place and identification, many studies of migration thus reinstate them by seeing movement as a move away from home and reflecting a preoccupation with rooting – sometimes more so than in studies of 'homebodies'. Clearly, there are good reasons for this interest, particularly in instances of movement towards the involuntary pole of the continuum. However, this should not divert attention from the instabilities that may characterise people's attachment to territory in the first place, as well as the transformations both the people and the places go through. Ignoring the mutually constitutive relationship of home and movement, deterritorialisation is too often simply seen as detachment from an unaffected territory that presumably remains an original, authentic, centred locality.

The contributors to *Struggles for Home* ethnographically refine such arguments. Peter Loizos's study of Cypriot home making examines the response to the promise of 'return' in the UN (United Nations) Plan for Cyprus nearly thirty years after the forced relocation of people into homogenous 'Greek' and 'Turkish' territories. In a culturally informed analysis of the maintenance of bonds between generations, and of their implications for movement, Loizos explains the Greek Cypriot 'no' to reunification. Distancing themselves from their previous village in its present appearance (repopulated and rebuilt by Turkish people) and weary of the conditions offered by the UN, he found people struggling with the abandonment of the very dream of return itself. Here, as in the case of Bosnia-Herzegovina analysed by Stef Jansen, 'ethnic cleansing' brought to the fore some of the dangers of sedentarist naturalisations of the links between people and place; both contexts thus illustrate how war is often perceived to mark the beginning of migration, as that which 'uproots'. However, in a chapter on movement through the Angolan–Zambian borderland Michael Barrett stresses that forced movements of war can often only be understood as part of a longer history of mobility. Furthermore, he argues that such mobility occurs in what he calls 'path space' – as opposed to 'geographical space' – stretching over vast areas and interconnecting people in webs of economic and social relationships. In a similar vein, turning the focus towards the everyday practices of reinventing or maintaining home, Sharika Thiranagama stresses the need to understand social relationships as constitutive of places. Her story about a Tamil woman in Sri Lanka revolves around movement and relationships to people over more than twenty years. Home emerges here through political and social histories of inclusion and exclusion and is thus not only about place but also about the people through whom we 'feel-at-home'. Yet such processes take different shapes for different groups of people. In her study of agricultural migrant workers in Andalucia, Swanie Potot shows how Moroccan migrants increasingly wished to make their home in Spain – claiming rights and entitlements in the face of racist violence. In response, Spanish entrepreneurs turned to Rumanian workers, who had, at least at that time, no such aspirations, as they were active in multilayered, flexible migration networks.

Violence

Defamiliarising the everyday language of place and belonging in both social science and migration regimes has become an ever more attractive option to anthropologists, particularly since the so-called postmodern turn of the 1980s (see Marcus and Fischer 1986). If sedentarism with its accompanying myths of 'roots' and 'return' is now exposed as a discourse to be analysed rather than a truth to be told about identities and cultures, so should conventional understandings of the role of violence in and for movement be defamiliarised. Empirical investigations of local perceptions of violence are central to this project, as they often challenge officially accepted notions of legitimacy, responsibility and means of prevention.

Current anthropological approaches to violence tend to leave the role of place rather underanalysed: it is remarkably often reduced to the 'decor' where the violence 'takes place', and seldom viewed in conjunction with phenomena constitutive of both displacement and emplacement. In contrast, the contributions gathered here investigate the relationship between violence, displacement and emplacement by conceiving of them as practices that (re)constitute conceptions, embodiments and inhabitations of space. Nationalist violence, for example, may have as its very objective the irreversible restructuring of people's notions of belonging in both territorial and social terms.[5] Studying violence in relation to place elucidates tensions between the processes that make people mobile and those that keep them in place, thus calling into question any strict boundaries between 'forced' and 'voluntary' migration. There is an inherent contradiction in the notion of 'forced' migration, which implies a lack of agency, whereas migration most certainly carries with it associations of choice and resolve (Turton 2003: 1, 6ff.). Based on the debate on sedentarism above, we believe that this contradictory potential can be fruitfully deployed in anthropological analysis. The chapters in this book show that an emphasis on pragmatism within structural limitations contributes to the increasing recognition within the study of human mobility of the inability of bureaucratically imposed categories to 'capture' actual movement. These categories are not innocent. Analyses of the regimes of interpretation that constitute them and their real effects have shown, for example, that the commonality of 'refugee-ness' does not lie in a uniform experience of forced movement but rather in a forced engagement with the interplay of structural factors such as state border regimes, legal frameworks regulating the relation between people and place, and humanitarian aid interventions.[6] As a result, to grasp the experiential realities of the women and men involved, we need to develop a comprehensive approach that treats persons who move (even if their movement is overwhelmingly involuntary) as '"ordinary people", or "purposive actors", embedded in particular social, political, and historical situations' (Turton 2003: 9), and accordingly, not as 'representatives' of 'types' of displacement.

Our critical take on both bureaucratic and social scientific forms of categorising people on the move thus extends to similar attempts at categorising the violence that affects them. Such categorisations do their share in identifying victims and locating responsibility and purpose but they rely on problematic assumptions about how different types of violence interrelate and about how, ultimately, violence (of one type) can be brought to an end. We now give some examples of how anthropologists have recently dealt with this issue, before we discuss how similar acts of typologising on behalf of states influence the movement of people.

Making explicit use of conventional categorisations, Nancy Scheper-Hughes and Philippe Bourgois work on the premise that violence begets violence (2004; see also Moser and McIlwaine 2006). They write: 'Repressive political regimes resting on terror/fear/torture are often mimetically reproduced by the same revolutionary militants determined to overthrow them ... Structural violence – the violence of poverty, hunger, social exclusion and humiliation – inevitably translates into intimate and domestic violence ...' (ibid.: 1). Regardless of how commonsensical this particular kind of mimesis appears, in this book we subject the 'inevitability' of the vicious circles of violence to critical scrutiny mainly because alleged differences between types and their interrelationships are often at odds with experiences on the ground. For example, the violence produced by state repression might include revolutionary counterstrikes, but also forced movement and some of the most extreme forms of poverty existing today. At the same time, repression may in fact 'pacify' whereas structural violence, which according to Scheper-Hughes and Bourgois necessarily translates into domestic violence, might very well be a factor in inspiring revolutionary mobilisation. Our point is that the compartmentalisation of broader structures of power into its different manifestations, as different types of violence, threatens to obscure more than it reveals. This problem, we believe, is exemplified in some of the work of John Borneman (2002), who also, if less explicitly, assumes mimetic practices of the parties to a violent political conflict. He calls for breaking the vicious circle by making warring parties 'depart' from acts of violence, and to 'render them no longer opposed'. But what if a more significant opposition resides elsewhere; not between the 'sides' locked in violent conflict?

Contributing their share to the typologising quest of our times, liberal states today produce a specific discourse on the morality of different, reified forms of violence (categorising problems to be able to administer them away). With 'globalisation' structuring movements of people and capital on an unprecedented scale, a particular kind of violence, labelled political, has been identified as a key threat to the liberal project of individual rights and responsibilities. From the perspective of the state, *political* violence exists in two forms: insurrectionary or terrorist (illegitimate), on the one hand, and overt state violence (legitimate), on the other. Both, however, cause bodily harm beyond the control of the individual (and thus liberally sovereign) victim. Their condemnation is therefore sanctioned by international jurisprudence such as humanitarian law, and political practices are accordingly deemed illegitimate – even by many of those they claim to represent – if they involve such violence. As a corollary, the suppression of political violence becomes a goal in itself, even if it heightens the impact of other forms or 'types'. Consequently, contemporary efforts to conceal the performance of state violence in non-transparent prison cells (Wacquant 2001, 2002) or to conceal the accountability for state violence by outsourcing it to non-transparent firms or militias (Löfving 2004) speak to the contestations of this particular monopoly of the state.

We would argue that it is possible to trace the desire for reified 'types' of violence and for the contested assessment of their legitimacy in the current era to the paradoxes of power within the liberal project itself and to the response of affluent 'northern' states to the (imagined or real) threats posed by 'southern' people on the move (Sassen 1999, 2005). The violence that justifies flight in the eyes of the liberal state equals 'political violence' (particularly state-performed, because states are generally endowed with the responsibility to protect their citizens from insurrectionary violence within their own borders). In contrast, those seeking refuge from a violence that in a previous paradigm was labelled 'structural', such as poverty,[7] are deemed fortune-seeking, and therefore politically illegitimate, 'economic migrants'. This, in turn, forces many people on the move to rewrite their stories in tune with a general narrative in which their suffering and subsequent migration must inevitably be the result of a violence acknowledged as 'political'. Hence, 'politics' increasingly figures as a discursive device to legitimise movement and to 'emplace' through bureaucratic means, and less as a term denoting collective organising for social change. This indicates that discontent with one's predicament in a particular societal system leads ever more people to abandon it rather than to engage in collective mobilisation to change it (Löfving 2005; cf. Hirschman 1970). Democratisation in the context of liberal globalisation (or global liberalisation) thus increasingly provides the very incentive for migration from poverty-ridden regions. But non-violent conditions for such migration remain few and far between, due to a continuing, if selectively reinforced, territorial definition of citizenship.

Let us take this opportunity to emphasise the risks associated with studying home making amongst moving people of all kinds within a conceptual framework that does not draw hard lines between 'forced' (i.e., violent) and 'non-forced' (i.e., non-violent) migration. If, instead, we conceive of relative positions on a continuum denoting one's relationship to territory and capacity for decision making with regard to mobility, this could be a dangerous game at the expense of the persons in question. The current geopolitical moment is characterised by strong hostility towards certain forms of movement, particularly those from poorer to richer contexts, and this attitude is reflected in ever-stricter border restrictions in the latter. In this exercise, northern migration regimes rely on a distinction between 'deserving' and 'undeserving' victimhood, judged largely in the place of destination. It judges not only incoming migrants at its borders, but also the ones illegitimately within, who are threatened with removal (Peutz 2006; Sassen 1999, 2005). It could be argued that, in such a context, we all have a duty to save the claims to legitimacy of those who have been or might be able to get through, glossing over the complexities and contradictions produced by the current migration regime they are experiencing. Instead, we argue that anthropological analysis should not accept, not even temporarily, the naturalised categories of that regime and the consequences of those categories, nor the moral judgements about the context of origin that such a regime entails. Not strictly separating out 'forced' migration from movement in general, we should also be aware that this analytical choice may contradict the insistence of many of our research subjects on the moral distinction between themselves and others.

We argue that the contextual relevance of such understandings should be investigated within the actually lived experiences of the women and men in question. In the texts gathered in *Struggles for Home*, we aim to highlight the ways in which contested concepts of violence and place function in tandem; how they interrelate in contemporary discourses on belonging, personhood and citizenship; and what different meanings are ascribed to them by people on the move and people who stay put, by state bureaucrats and nationalist agitators, by political activists and those 'tired of politics', and by scholars and other storytellers.

We also wish to take on the lessons of decades of feminist scholarship, which has, not least through analyses of domestic abuse, consistently pointed out the inadequacy of the universalising dichotomy of the safety of staying put 'at home' and the violence of movement (Ahmed et al. 2003). Many anthropological studies of gender and movement centre on the question of the emancipatory versus the repressive function of migration for women.[8] Patricia Pessar, for example, argues that migrating Dominican women attain a new, improved status vis-à-vis their husbands through wage labour in the USA (Pessar 2003).[9] While such observations challenge the alleged role of conjugality and household social harmony as core elements in sedentarist discourse, a later study on the migration of Peruvian domestic workers into Chile notes that employers there prefer unorganised Peruvians to more assertive Chilean housemaids and, thus, that 'the role of the "servile" woman in the household persists when women are transnationally mobile' (Hill Maher and Staab 2005: 71; cf. Gill 1994). Transnational circuits of labour might thus in fact simultaneously reproduce gender hierarchies, not only among migrants, but also in host societies. Patriarchal norms host the hegemonic capacity to define women's labour as 'cheap', which makes a gendered labour force essential to the accumulation of global capital (Mills 2003; Sassen 1998; Wright 2001). So rather than limiting the notion of violence to one type (in this case domestic), or presupposing a mimetic relationship within or between types, we opt for a more structural approach to violence, one that is attentive to changing oppressive social and economic contexts, but also to the transforming subjectivities through and by which both men and women experience and manage movement.

In a conventional account, the contributions to this book would have stressed not only the forced nature of past movement, but also the analytical privilege of that force *in the past*. However, we show that violence is not merely a property of memory. Violence lives on, beyond memory, affecting moving people and their home-making efforts in ways that cannot be explained with recourse to the mere history of war itself. For example, in Sharika Thiranagama's account, people reject repeatedly having to go through the painstaking task of reordering their lives and their world in the aftermath of recurrent violence. Memories are thus themselves regarded as violent (see Jansen 2002), and home is imagined as a place free of violence, both remembered and anticipated. Such a place, however, is not, as in sedentarist discourse, self-evidently located 'in the past' nor conceived of as 'where we come from'. This is shown clearly in Toby Kelly's analysis of experiences of confinement of Palestinians forcibly emplaced in ever smaller pieces of territory, cut off from many resources of both remembrance and anticipation. In contrast, the Rumanian workers in Swanie Potot's study are, at least in the current conjuncture, able to strategically displace themselves with regard to localised economic opportunities. As she further shows, in El Ejido this has been at the expense of other migrant labourers, originally from Morocco, precisely at the moment when those workers' claims to legitimate emplacement were increasingly met with racist violence.

Stef Jansen argues that the foreign intervention in Bosnia-Herzegovina has privileged safety through individual property over other concerns. This has rendered invisible its policies of what could be called 'forced transition', of which refugee return was in fact merely one dimension. The memory of war among returnees thus 'took place' in contexts of shifting insecurities, vulnerabilities and expectations, and those contexts were characterised by postwar reconstruction as well as post-socialist transformation. Staffan Löfving's work exposes how the liberalisation of politics during the Guatemalan peace process of the 1990s was accom-panied by a liberalisation of the economy, altering the balance between them to the detriment of the political sphere. While liberal democratisa-tion brought a move away from the organised (insurrectionary and state) violence of the twentieth century, people's capacities to politically transform their societies waned in the new, market-governed context. Peace in its contemporary guise in both Bosnia-Herzegovina and Guatemala is characterised by this suppression of some types of violence (military, political, to an extent criminal) and the persistence and even rise of other types (especially through exploitation, inequality and marginalisation). This paradox leads us to suggest that the conventional categorisation of violence mystifies power relations that prevail *through* war and peace. We therefore work with a broader notion of violence as a function of power both during and after war (cf. Binford 2002; Richards 2005).

Home Making

In order to explain our take on home making, let us start with an elucida-tion of a concept that is frequently used in passing in anthropological literature: emplacement. Usually this term is deployed in opposition to displacement, but it is defined in divergent ways. In the phenomeno-logical approach of Feld and Basso, emplacement is 'the way in which people encounter places, and invest them with significance' (1996: 8). Similarly, for Jacka, it denotes 'a process in which people re-embed social relations that have been "distanciated" and "disembedded" ... by the disruptions, dislocations, and deterritorializations of capitalism' and 'a means through which people create their own version of modernity' (Jacka 2005: 645). In such approaches, the power to emplace stands out as a capacity of the subject (see also Shaw 2007). Others see processes of emplacement as the historical negotiation between citizens and the state (e.g., Wernke 2007), while still others deploy it to understand people on the move as objects of power. Cobb, for example, defines emplacement as 'how people are drawn to, and into, places' (Cobb 2005: 564, see also Grant 2005; Siu 2007).

In *Struggles for Home*, we conceptualise emplacement on the crossroads of these approaches. We see it as the point where subjects' capacities to put themselves and others into place articulate with the power relations that unequally distribute this capacity. We thus pay special attention to the location of the power to emplace. Such a focus can reveal violence where it is obscured or mystified and provide an antidote to postmodern manifestoes of placelessness, as well as to notions that any place is, ultimately, good if it is one's own, and that people are happily 'emplaced' if no signs to the contrary are found. One important corollary of such a focus on emplacement as power ('to put in place' but also to 'invest places with significance' for oneself and for others) is that it makes the distinction between moving people and non-moving people less important than that between capacities and incapacities to work, live, rest and aspire in the place you happen to be located. Moving people and non-moving people may very well share such predicaments. In that way, Toby Kelly's chapter in this book exemplifies the powerlessness associated with statelessness, not among migrants but in a group of West Bank Palestinians whose physical movement is 'confined' to some square kilometres: they are effectively isolated and denied access to work and education. Security measures, emerging as a central ingredient in the new paradigm of violence, confine movement, but, like migration, they may set people apart from their social and economic relationships, or their livelihoods (see Stepputat in this volume). Developing this point, Staffan Löfving argues that emplacement may be considered another modality of the same process that produces displacement (see also Jacka 2005). The law figures in paradoxical ways in this equation. For the son of the peasant woman in Guatemala, whose story served as one of the entries to this introduction, taking control of one's emplacement requires an economic and social life outside the law, in the informal economy. And in Western Europe and the USA, new citizenship entails a right to social benefits, but it is also often a road leading to perpetual unemployment. Emplacement as controlled by others (being registered as a citizen by the new state) is thus legal, whereas people's own 'investments of significance' occur outside the spheres of the licit economy (see Duschinski 2007).

In *Struggles for Home*, we thus treat emplacement and displacement as twin processes, focusing on home in order to analyse the 'power to emplace oneself'. Let us now relate this back to sedentarism. The problem of the sedentarist bias, we argue, is not only that people are presumed to be naturally rooted, and that movement is therefore somehow inherently violent, but also that they are seen as *forever* rooted. Taking seriously the experiences of persons who move and of those who (sometimes, have to) stay put, and studying them as social agents, implies that we uncover the linkages between the changes in polities and social contexts through which they are moving with transformations in their individual and social life trajectories. Such intersecting transformations inform the chapters of this book, not least in terms of intergenerational household strategies of emplacement and movement that people deploy in their dealings with large-scale change. This generational dimension, it is shown, is strongly articulated with gender, resulting in structurally unequal experiences of belonging.

According to sedentarist logic, human beings are seen not only as being collectively rooted in a particular place, but also as deriving their meaningfulness, or their 'culture', from this very rootedness. As a result, people on the involuntary pole of the movement continuum in particular become a deeply problematic phenomenon, and their anticipated return reestablishes the 'natural' way of the world. Reflecting this mode of thought, the desire to return is often seen as a direct function of the depth of national belonging, charting an uneasy halfway course between a contextual notion of home and its designation as the territory previously inhabited (e.g., Kibreab 1999: 404ff.). This view is related to a common theme in migration studies: the 'myth of return'. In his eponymous 1979 book, Muhammad Anwar argued that most of his Pakistani informants thought of their residence in Britain as a temporary stage in expectation of return to Pakistan once it was economically viable to do so. In most cases, this proved to be a myth, which was nevertheless reinforced through remittances, investments, visits and kin obligations to Pakistan and resulted in a new form of British–Pakistani sociality. Particularly in later periods, because of family reunion, settlement in Britain was de facto permanent, even though Anwar's informants remained 'home-oriented'. The critical relevance of this 'myth of return' does not depend on whether people actually do go back, but on whether they cherish this 'homeland orientation', and on how it affects their lives. However, even among those leaning towards the pole of involuntary movement, the prevalence of such a professed desire to 'go home', rather than being 'invariably powerful' (Kibreab 1999: 404), varies tremendously according to individual and collective experiences as well as social, political and economic contexts.[10]

We wish to take part in ethnographic critiques of the presumed universality of a desire to return, and go beyond them, in at least two ways. First, we aim to transcend the dominant identificational–cultural focus, adding an eye for transformations in the socio-economic and political structure of the place that was left behind. Second, we believe that, even if many people on the move do express very strong nostalgia, this is not always and necessarily best understood as desire for return (see Hage 1997; Jansen 1998). As Zetter (1999) has suggested, a more accurate and useful notion might be that of a 'myth of home'. Home itself, then, needs to be problematised, and particularly the self-evidence with which it is territorialised. If we fail to do so, as we indicated above, home is all too easily represented unwittingly as a timeless entity in an unchanging context of origin, something that is particularly inappropriate if we take into account that that context is often one of dramatic transformation, such as war or socioeconomic restructuring. There is, then, an important temporal dimension to experiences of home.

Particularly in studies of people whose movement is to be understood on the 'forced'/'involuntary' pole of the continuum, this temporality often takes the form of discontinuity and, more precisely, loss. As Peter Loizos's chapter in this book shows, this includes loss of capital and entitlement, as well as dramatic disconnections from persons, objects, and environments invested with emotional attachments – often experienced as a loss of home (see also Loizos 1981, 1999). However, the home that has been lost has not simply been left behind in another place. Rather, we would argue, it has also been left behind in another time and is therefore often experienced as a previous home, irrevocably lost both spatially and temporally. Prefacing her study of Asia Minor refugees in Greece, Renée Hirschon (1998[1989]) points out the painful irony of employing the term 'repatriates' to refer to her informants, who moved from the newly emerging state of Turkey to neighbouring Greece as part of the 1920s population exchange agreed on between the two governments. 'How can you be "repatriated",' she asks rhetorically, 'to a place you do not come from, that is not your home?' (ibid.: xvii). Hirschon's point has only gained in significance in recent times, when the experience of 'being out of place' in one's presumed 'ethnic' mother-state has become evident among, for example, Serbs from surrounding post-Yugoslav areas in Serbia, Bosnian Croats in Croatia, British Zimbabweans in the UK, Eastern European *Volksdeutsche* in Germany, and Central Asian Russians in Russia. However, the argument can be taken further by problematising the seemingly straightforward relation between home and place. In addition to the question of 'how you can be "repatriated" to a place you do not come from, that is not your home,' we would ask to what extent home can simply be understood as the place you come from. Hirschon's own study (as well as Peter Loizos's chapter in this book) provides strong ethnographic evidence that home is made and remade on an everyday basis through strategies of cultural continuity, which they understand as ways of overcoming alienation as well as social disintegration.

This reliance on cultural capacities through which home is continuously recreated has been developed further by Ghassan Hage in his studies of Lebanese immigrants in Australia (1997), but Hage shifts the focus from tradition to the social realm of security, familiarity, community, and what he calls a 'sense of possibility'. Here, security denotes a set of rules that a person masters, familiarity 'a space where one possesses a maximal spatial knowledge' (ibid.: 102), and community 'a space where one possesses a maximal communicative power' (ibid.: 103). 'Sense of possibility', finally, challenges the passive notion of home as mere social and physical shelter and attaches to it the opportunities for change, improvement and the unexpected – that is, room for dreaming and imagining. This home is an ideal, and people everywhere live, at best, in what Hage calls its 'approximation'. In this model, expressions of nostalgia by people on the move become themselves a means by which a new home is built – they are strategies to approximate the ideal home in the new context, or, in Hage's words, 'a desire to promote the feeling of being there *here*' (ibid.: 108; see Turton 2005: 267). This approach corresponds with existentialist writings about the nomadic Warlpiri of Central Australia, where home is a metaphor for people's continuous negotiation between familiarity and estrangement (Jackson 1995), but it places that home more firmly in a context of social transformation.

In this book, Swanie Potot and Michael Barrett provide ethnographic case studies of people who engage, with varying degrees of success and with different requirements of stability, with the places through which they move. Their analyses show that this has diverging implications for people's struggles for home, depending on transformative developments in those places. Sharika Thiranagama contributes ethnography of expectation, aspiration, and desire to complicate seemingly nostalgic dimensions of home making. When talking of loss and displacement, her informants always recounted these through attempts to imagine future homes. However, Thiranagama's analysis does not stop at the level of imagination. She explores the desire of people not just to 're-inhabit' the world (cf. Das et al. 2002) but for the world to change for them, embracing transformation by striving to be able to condition change on local or even personal control. Sharing Thiranagama's concern for the 'what' (and not just the 'where') of home making, Löfving discusses an attempted scaling up of home from the domestic to the societal in the revolutionary project in Guatemala. He narrates a history of home among the displaced Mayan rebels from recruitment in 'private kitchens' through the state-performed 'domicide' to the contested reconstruction of the postwar nation and the ways, in peace, in which a public–private divide was discursively and politically reestablished. Both Löfving and Jansen also discuss the economic strategies to establish persistent alliances (perceived as secure or stable) against a still-changing socioeconomic environment during and after the accomplishment of 'return'. While Löfving shows how neoliberal interventions in local community formations result in the social atomisation of home, Jansen explores the unequal processes in which localised home making comes to be seen as more or less feasible by certain groups of people. Elaborating on physical, but also on social and existential dimensions of *Sicherheit* (see Bauman 1999), Jansen's comparative tale of two households' return reveals how positioning in the life course and in what he calls 'social relations-in-process' account for the differences in people's ability to successfully remake home.

Struggles for Home seeks to reconceptualise the significance of place for people on the move by positioning the often violent and always transformative tension between fixity and change at the centre of the analysis. Holding to account both cosmopolitan ideologies arguing against roots (for those who can afford to be rootless) *and* their sedentarist opponents (anxious to put everyone in their place), we investigate the importance of violence-in-residence in relation to violence-in-movement. We consider home in terms of a struggle to create possibility, to engage in what Turton's (1996) Northeast African Mursi informants called a 'search for cool ground' – a concern to find or establish secure places that may serve as bases for developing a future.

Acknowledgements

We would like to thank the anonymous reviewers, as well as Peter Loizos, Liisa Malkki, Fiona Ross, Finn Stepputat and David Turton and for their constructive comments on previous drafts of this introduction. Thanks also to the masterful language editor Anne Cleaves for her work on the entire volume. An earlier, shorter version of our argument here was pre-published in *Focaal: European Journal of Anthropology* 49 (2007).

Notes

1. For an overview of the anthropology of mobility, see Brettell (2000). See also, e.g., Colson (2003), Hein (1993), Vincent and Refslund-Sørensen (2001), and Malkki (1995b) on refugees and internally displaced persons; Gmelch (1980) and Kearney (1986) on migration and 'development'; Al-Ali and Koser (2002), Glick-Schiller, Basch and Blanc-Szanton (1992, 1995), Kearney (1995), Kivisto (2001), and Povrzanović-Frykman (2001) on migrancy, refuge and trans-nationalism. Edited anthropological volumes on belonging and locality include Lovell (1998) and Low and Lawrence-Zúñiga (2003). For more detailed discussions of mobility and home, see Ahmed et al. (2003) and Rapport and Dawson (1998).

2. In response, a number of anthropologists have developed a critical approach to prevailing notions of people's territorial fixity (see e.g. Clifford 1992; Clifford and Marcus 1986; Gupta and Ferguson 1997a, 1997b, 1997c; Olwig and Hastrup 1997; Rapport and Dawson 1998). This in turn is now provoking the counterargument that the role of movement for culture has indeed been acknowledged and studied ever since Malinowski (see Hage 2005; Loizos in this volume).

3. The results often take the form of literary-theoretical manifestoes, such as Chambers's treatise on 'migrancy' (1994) or Minh-ha's definition of our time as 'the age of exile' (1994), which itself recalls Berger's earlier dictum that global movement is the quintessential experience of our times (1984).

Sociologists (Bauman 1996, 1999; Hall 1990; Melucci 1989), anthropologists (Hannerz 1996; Rapport 1997), cultural critics (Bhabha 1994; Naficy 1999) and philosophers (Braidotti 1994; Deleuze and Guattari 1986) call for various liberating forms of 'nomadic thought', by strategically combining notions of marginality, interstitiality, non-rootedness and displacement into theoretical and political positioning (for a critique, see, e.g., Kaplan 1996).

4. For a critique, see Gupta and Ferguson (1997a: 7; 1997b: 354) and Warner (1994).
5. Jansen (2005). See also Daniel (1996); Feldman (1991); Malkki (1995a); Richards (2005); Stepputat (1994, 1999).
6. E.g., Allen (1996); Barrett (2004); Malkki (1995b); Soguk (1999); Stepputat (1994).
7. See Farmer (2005) for a recent revival of the analytical viability of 'structural violence'.
8. See e.g., Hirsch (2002); James (1999); Mills (1997, 2003); Wright (1995).
9. See also Nyberg Sørensen (1993: 109); Lawson (1998); Weinstein Bever (2002).
10. See Allen (1996); Al-Rasheed (1994); Long and Oxfeld (2004); Markowitz and Stefansson (2004); Newbury (2005).

References

Ahmed, Sara, Claudia Castañeda, Anne-Marie Fortier and Mimi Scheller (eds.). 2003. *Uprootings/Regroundings: Questions of Home and Migration*. Oxford: Berg.

Al-Ali, Nadia, and Khalid Koser (eds.). 2002. *New Approaches to Migration: Transnational Communities and the Transformation of Home*. London: Routledge.

Allen, Tim (ed.). 1996. *In Search of Cool Ground: War, Flight, and Homecoming in Northeast Africa*. Oxford: James Currey.

Al-Rasheed, Madawi. 1994. 'The Myth of Return: Iraqi Arab and Assyrian Refugees in London'. *Journal of Refugee Studies* 7(2/3): 199–219.

Anwar, Muhammad. 1979. *The Myth of Return: Pakistanis in Britain*. London: Heinemann.

Barrett, Michael. 2004. *Paths to Adulthood: Freedom, Belonging, and Temporalities in Mbunda Biographies from Western Zambia*. Uppsala: Acta Universitatis Upsaliensis.

Bauman, Zygmunt. 1996. 'From Pilgrim to Tourist – Or a Short History of Identity', in *Questions of Cultural Identity*, ed. Stuart Hall and Paul duGay, pp.18–36. London: Sage.

———. 1999. *In Search of Politics*. Cambridge: Polity.

Berger, John. 1984. *And Our Faces, My Heart, Brief as Photos*. London: Writers and Readers.

Binford, Leigh. 2002. 'Violence in El Salvador: A Rejoinder to Philippe Bourgois', *Ethnography* 3(2): 201–19.

Bhabha, Homi K. 1994. *The Location of Culture*. London: Routledge.

Borneman, John 2002. 'Reconciliation after Ethnic Cleansing: Listening, Retribution, Affiliation', *Public Culture* 14(2): 281–304.

Braidotti, Rosi. 1994. *Nomadic Subjects: Embodiment and Sexual Difference in Contemporary Feminist Theory*. New York: Columbia University Press.

Brettell, Caroline B. 2000. 'Theorizing Migration in Anthropology: The Social Construction of Networks, Identities, Communities, and Globalscapes', in

Migration Theory: Talking across Disciplines, ed. Caroline B. Brettell and James F. Hollifield, pp. 97–135. London: Routledge.

Chambers, Iain. 1994. *Migrancy, Culture, Identity*. London: Routledge.

Clifford, James. 1992. 'Travelling Cultures', in *Cultural Studies*, ed. Lawrence Grossberg, Cary Nelson and Paula Treichler, pp. 9–116. London: Routledge.

Clifford, James and George Marcus (eds.). 1986. *Writing Culture: The Poetics and Politics of Ethnography*. Berkeley: University of California Press.

Cobb, Charles R. 2005. 'Archaeology and the "Savage Slot": Displacement and Emplacement in the Premodern World', *American Anthropologist* 19(4): 563–74.

Colson, Elizabeth. 2003. 'Forced Migration and the Anthropological Response', *Journal of Refugee Studies* 16(1): 1–18.

Daniel, E. Valentine. 1996. *Charred Lullabies: Chapters in an Anthropography of Violence*. Princeton: Princeton University Press.

Das, Veena, Arthur Kleinman, Margaret Lock, Mamphela Ramphele and Pamela Reynolds (eds.). 2002. *Remaking a World: Violence, Social Suffering, and Recovery*. Berkeley: University of California Press.

Deleuze, Gilles and Félix Guattari. 1986. *Nomadology: The War Machine*. New York: Semiotext(e).

Duschinski, Haley. 2007. '"India displacing Indians for the Sake of India": Kashmiri Hindu Migrant Vendors and the Secular State', *PoLAR: Political and Legal Anthropology Review* 30(1): 90–108.

Farmer, Paul. 2005. *Pathologies of Power: Health, Human Rights, and the New War on the Poor*. Berkeley: University of California Press.

Feld, Steven and Keith H. Basso (eds). 1996. *Senses of Place*. Santa Fe: School of American Research Press.

Feldman, Allen. 1991. *Formations of Violence: The Narrative of the Body and Political Terror in Northern Ireland*. Chicago: Chicago University Press.

Gill, Lesley. 1994. *Precarious Dependencies: Gender, Class and Domestic Service*. New York: Columbia University Press.

Gilroy, Paul. 2000. *Against Race: Imagining Political Culture beyond the Color Line*. Cambridge, MA: Belknap Press of Harvard University Press.

Glick-Schiller, Nina, Linda Basch and Cristina Blanc-Szanton (eds.). 1992. *Towards a Transnational Perspective on Migration*. New York: New York Academy of Sciences.

———. 1995. 'From Immigrant to Transmigrant: Theorizing Transnational Migration', *Anthropological Quarterly* 68(1): 48–63.

Gmelch, George. 1980. 'Return Migration', *Annual Review of Anthropology* 9: 135–59.

Grant, Bruce 2005. 'The Good Russian Prisoner: Naturalizing Violence in the Caucasus Mountains', *Cultural Anthropology* 20(1): 39–67.

Gupta, Akhil, and James Ferguson. 1997a. 'Culture, Power, Place: Ethnography at the End of an Era', in *Culture, Power, Place*, ed. Akhil Gupta and James Ferguson, pp. 1–29. Durham: Duke University Press.

———. 1997b. 'Beyond "Culture": Space, Identity, and the Politics of Difference', in *Culture, Power, Place*, ed. Akhil Gupta and James Ferguson, pp. 33–51. Durham: Duke University Press.

———. 1997c. 'Discipline and Practice: "The Field" as Site, Method, and Location in Anthropology', in *Anthropological Locations*, ed. Akhil Gupta and James Ferguson, pp. 1–46. Berkeley: University of California Press.

Hage, Ghassan. 1997. 'At Home in the Entrails of the West: Multiculturalism, "Ethnic Food", and Migrant Home-building', in *Home/World: Space,*

Community, and Marginality in Sydney's West, ed. Helen Grace, Ghassan Hage, Leslie Johnson, Julie Langsworth, and Michael Symonds, pp. 99–153. Annandale: Pluto Press.

———. 2005. 'A Not So Multi-sited Ethnography of a Not So Imagined Community', Anthropological Theory 5(4): 463–75.

Hall, Stuart. 1990. 'Cultural Identity and Diaspora', in Identity: Community, Culture, Difference, ed. Jonathan Rutherford, pp. 222–37. London: Lawrence and Wishart.

Hannerz, Ulf. 1996. Transnational Connections: Culture, People, Places. London: Routledge.

Hein, Jeremy. 1993. 'Refugees, Immigrants, and the State', Annual Review of Sociology 19: 43–59.

Hill Maher, Kirsten and Silke Staab. 2005. 'The Dilemmas of Working Women's Empowerment in Santiago, Chile', International Feminist Journal of Politics 7(1): 71–88.

Hirsch, Jennifer S. 2002. '"Que, pues, con el pinche NAFTA?": Gender, Power and Migration between Western Mexico and Atlanta', Urban Anthropology and Studies of Cultural Systems and World Economic Development 31(3/4): 351–87.

Hirschman, Albert O. 1970. Exit, Voice, and Loyalty: Responses to Decline in Firms, Organizations, and States. Cambridge, MA: Harvard University Press.

Hirschon, Renée. 1998 [1989] Heirs of the Greek Catastrophe: The Social Life of Asia Minor Refugees in Piraeus. Oxford: Berghahn Books.

Jacka, Jerry K. 2005. 'Emplacement and Millennial Expectations in and Era of Development and Globalization: Heaven and the Appeal of Christianity for the Ipili', American Anthropologist 107(4): 643–53.

Jackson, Michael. 1995. At Home in the World. Durham: Duke University Press.

James, Deborah. 1999. 'Bagagešu (those of my home): Women Migrants, Ethnicity, and Performance in South Africa', American Ethnologist 26(1): 69–89.

Jansen, Stef. 1998. 'Homeless at Home: Narrations of Post-Yugoslav Identities', in Migrants of Identity, ed. Nigel Rapport and Andrew Dawson, pp. 85–109. Oxford: Berg.

———. 2002. 'The Violence of Memories: Local Narratives of the Past after Ethnic Cleansing in Croatia', Rethinking History 6(1): 77–93.

———. 2005. 'National Numbers in Context: Maps and Stats in Representations of the Post-Yugoslav Wars', Identities: Global Studies in Culture and Power 12(1): 45–68.

Kaplan, Caren. 1996. Questions of Travel: Postmodern Discourses of Displacement. Durham: Duke University Press.

Kearney, Michael. 1986. 'From the Invisible Hand to Visible Feet: Anthropological Studies of Migration and Development', Annual Review of Anthropology 15: 331–61.

———. 1995. 'The Local and the Global: The Anthropology of Globalization and Transnationalism', Annual Review of Anthropology 24: 547–65.

Kibreab, Gaim. 1999. 'Revisiting the Debate on People, Place, Identity, and Displacement', Journal of Refugee Studies 12(4): 384–410.

Kivisto, Peter. 2001. 'Theorizing Transnational Immigration: A Critical Review of Current Efforts', Ethnic and Racial Studies 24(4): 549–77.

Lawson Victoria A. 1998. 'Hierarchical Households and Gendered Migration in Latin America: Feminist Extensions to Migration Research', Progress in Human Geography 22(1): 39–53.

Löfving, Staffan. 2004. 'Paramilitaries of the Empire: Guatemala, Colombia, and Israel', *Social Analysis* 48(1): 156–60.

———. 2005. 'Outline to a Critique of Liberal Peace: Guatemala', in *El Caribe Centroamericano*, ed. Jussi Pakkasvirta, pp. 167–95. Helsinki: Renvall Institute.

Loizos, Peter. 1981. *The Heart Grown Bitter: A Chronicle of Cypriot War Refugees.* Cambridge: Cambridge University Press.

———. 1999. 'Ottoman Half-lives: Long-term Perspectives on Particular Forced Migration', *Journal of Refugee Studies* 12(3): 237–63.

Long, Lynellyn D. and Ellen Oxfeld (eds.). 2004. *Coming Home? Refugees, Migrants, and Those Who Stayed Behind.* Philadelphia: Pennsylvania University Press.

Lovell, Nadia. 1998. 'Introduction: Belonging in Need of Emplacement?', in *Locality and Belonging*, ed. Nadia Lovell, pp. 1–24. London: Routledge.

Low, Setha M. and Denise Lawrence-Zúñiga. 2003. 'Locating Culture', in *The Anthropology of Space and Place: Locating Culture*, ed. Setha M. Low and Denise Lawrence-Zúñiga, pp. 1–47. London: Blackwell.

Malkki, Liisa. 1992. 'National Geographic: The Rooting of Peoples and the Territorialization of National Identity among Scholars and Refugees', *Cultural Anthropology* 7(1): 24–45.

———. 1994. 'Citizens of Humanity: Internationalisms and the Imagined Community of Nations', *Diaspora* 3(1): 41–67.

———. 1995a. *Purity and Exile: Violence, Memory, and National Cosmology amongst Hutu Refugees in Tanzania.* Chicago: Chicago University Press.

———. 1995b. 'Refugees and Exile: From Refugee Studies to the National Order of Things', *Annual Review of Anthropology* 24: 495–523.

Marcus, George, and Michael M. J. Fischer. 1986. *Anthropology as Cultural Critique: An Experimental Moment in the Social Sciences.* Chicago: Chicago University Press.

Markowitz, Fran and Anders Stefansson (eds.). 2004. *Homecomings: Unsettling Paths of Return.* Lanham, MD: Lexington Books.

Melucci, Alberto. 1989. *Nomads of the Present: Social Movements and Individual Needs.* London: Hutchinson Radius.

Mills, Mary Beth. 1997. 'Contesting the Margins of Modernity: Women, Migration, and Consumption in Thailand', *American Ethnologist* 24(1): 37–61.

———. 2003. 'Gender and Inequality in the Global Labor Force', *Annual Review of Anthropology* 32: 41–62.

Minh-ha, Trinh T. 1994. 'Other than Myself/My Other Self', in *Travelers' Tales: Narratives of Home and Displacement*, ed. George Robertson, Melinda Mash, Lisa Tickner, Jon Bird, Barry Curtis and Tim Putnam, pp. 9–26. London: Routledge.

Moser, Caroline O.N. and Cathy McIlwaine, 2006. 'Latin American Urban Violence as a Development Concern: Towards a Framework for Violence Reduction', *World Development* 34(1): 89–112.

Naficy, Hamid (ed.). 1999. *Home, Exile, Homeland: Film, Media, and the Politics of Place.* London: Routledge.

Newbury, David. 2005. 'Returning Refugees: Four Historical Patterns of "Coming Home" to Rwanda', *Comparative Studies of Society and History* 20: 252–85.

Nyberg Sørensen, Ninna. 1994. 'Roots, Routes and Transnational Attractions: Dominican Migration, Gender and Cultural Change', *European Journal of Development Research* 6(2): 104–19.

Olwig, Karen Fog and Kirsten Hastrup (eds.). 1997. *Siting Culture: The Shifting Anthropological Subject*. London: Routledge.

Pessar, Patricia R. 2003. 'Transnational Migration: Bringing Gender In', *International Migration Review* 37(3): 812–46.

Peutz, Nathalie 2006. 'Embarking on an Anthropology of Removal', *Current Anthropology* 47(2): 217–41.

Povrzanović-Frykman, Maja (ed.). 2001. *Beyond Integration: Challenges of Belonging in Diaspora and Exile*. Lund: Nordic Academic Press.

Rapport, Nigel. 1997. *The Transcendent Individual: Towards a Literary and Liberal Anthropology*. London: Routledge.

Rapport, Nigel and Andrew Dawson (eds.). 1998. *Migrants of Identity: Perceptions of 'Home' in a World of Movement*. Oxford: Berg.

Richards, Paul (ed.). 2005. *No Peace No War: An Anthropology of Contemporary Armed Conflicts*. Oxford and Athens: James Currey and Ohio University Press.

Sassen, Saskia. 1998. *Globalization and Its Discontents: Essays on the New Mobility of People and Money*. New York: New Press.

———. 1999. *Guests and Aliens*. New York: New Press.

———. 2005. 'Regulating Immigration in a Global Age: A New Policy Landscape', *parallax* 11(1): 35–45.

Scheper-Hughes, Nancy and Philippe Bourgois. 2004. 'Introduction: Making Sense of Violence', in *Violence in War and Peace: An Anthology*, ed. Nancy Scheper-Hughes and Philippe Bourgois, pp. 1–31. Malden and Oxford: Blackwell Publishing.

Shaw, Rosalind. 2007. 'Displacing Violence: Making Pentecostal Memory in Postwar Sierra Leone', *Cultural Anthropology* 22(1): 66–93.

Siu, Helen F. 2007. 'Grounding Displacement: Uncivil Urban Spaces in Postreform South China', *American Ethnologist* 34(2): 329–50.

Soguk, Nevzat. 1999. *States and Strangers: Refugees and Displacements of Statecraft*. Minneapolis: Minnesota University Press.

Stepputat, Finn. 1994. 'Repatriation and the Politics of Space: The Case of the Mayan Diaspora', *Journal of Refugee Studies* 7(2/3): 175–85.

———. 1999. 'Politics of Displacement in Guatemala', *Journal of Historical Sociology* 12(1): 54–80.

Turton, David. 1996. 'Migrants and Refugees: A Mursi Case Study', in *In Search of Cool Ground*, ed. Tim Allen, pp. 96–110. Oxford: James Curry.

———. 2003. 'Refugees, Forced Resettlers, and "Other Forced Migrants": Towards a Unitary Study of Forced Migration', New Issues in Refugee Research Working Paper No. 94. Geneva: UNHCR.

———. 2005. 'The Meaning of Place in a World of Movement: Lessons from Long-term Field Research in Southern Ethiopia', *Journal of Refugee Studies* 18(3): 258–80.

Vincent, Marc and Birgitte Refslund-Sørensen (eds.). 2001. *Caught between Borders: Response Strategies of the Internally Displaced*. London: Pluto Press.

Wacquant, Loïc. 2001. 'The Penalization of Poverty and the Rise of Neo-liberalism', *European Journal on Criminal Policy and Research* 9: 401–12.

———. 2002. 'The Curious Eclipse of Prison Ethnography in the Age of Mass Incarceration', *Ethnography* 3(4): 371–97.

Warner, Daniel. 1994. 'Voluntary Repatriation and the Meaning of Return to Home: A Critique of Liberal Mathematics', *Journal of Refugee Studies* 7(2–3): 160–74.

Weinstein Bever S. 2002. 'Migration and the Transformation of Gender Roles and Hierarchies in Yucatán', *Urban Anthropology* 31(2): 199–230.

Wernke, Steven A. 2007. 'Negotiating Community and Landscape in the Peruvian Andes: a Transconquest View', *American Anthropologist* 109(1): 130–52.

Wright, Caroline. 1995. 'Gender Awareness in Migration Theory: Synthesising Actor and Structure in Southern Africa', *Development and Change* 26: 771–91.

Wright, Melissa W. 2001. 'Desire and the Prosthetics of Supervision: a Case of Maquiladora Flexibility', *Cultural Anthropology* 16: 354–73.

Zetter, Roger. 1999. 'Reconceptualizing the Myth of Return: Continuity and Transition amongst the Greek-Cypriot Refugees of 1974', *Journal of Refugee Studies* 12(1): 1–22.

1

RETURNING TO PALESTINE
Confinement and Displacement under Israeli Occupation
Tobias Kelly

Subhi was bored.[1] During the summer of 2001, he had not been able to leave the West Bank Palestinian village where he had been living for the last six months, and his world had shrunk to the few square kilometres between the river that ran past the village to the west and the hills that rose to the east. In a vain attempt to ease his boredom, he would often stroll along the dried-out riverbed but come to a stop after a few hundred metres as he neared the crossroads and a potential Israeli checkpoint. He would then turn around and walk back to the other edge of the village, before retracing his steps all over again. Whereas before the start of the second *intifada* in September 2000 Subhi had made regular trips to Ramallah, Jerusalem and Tel Aviv for work, to visit friends, or go shopping, over the last few months he had seen nothing but the grey buildings and olive trees of his village.

Subhi was born in the mid-1960s in a village that I have called Bayt Hajjar, which stands east of the 1949 Armistice Line between the Hashemite Kingdom of Jordan and Israel.[2] In 1967, when the Israeli army invaded the West Bank, Subhi's family was forced to flee along with many other people from the surrounding villages, and ended up in one of the refugee camps outside the Jordanian capital of Amman. Then, in the mid-1990s, the governments of Jordan and Israel signed a peace treaty making it possible for Jordanian citizens to enter Israel and the West Bank relatively easily. With a three-month tourist visa in his Jordanian passport, Subhi returned to the West Bank for the first time in over twenty-five years. He quickly found a job on a building site in Israel and, overstaying his visa, decided to settle in his native Bayt Hajjar. Soon he was renting a small apartment on the edge of the village and married one of his distant cousins. However, in late September 2000 clashes broke out between Israeli soldiers and Palestinian demonstrators, as frustrations over the failures of the Oslo Peace Process spilled over into the start of the second intifada. The roads around Bayt Hajjar became increasingly full of Israeli military patrols and checkpoints, and as a result Subhi was often too afraid to leave the village. He was worried that the Israeli soldiers would find out that he had overstayed his tourist visa and deport him back to Jordan.

Life in exile (*ghurba*) across the Middle East and beyond has been a defining feature of Palestinian experience, and the Palestinian national movement has made the collective 'right of return' (*haq al-'awda*) a central aspect of its political demands (Bisharat 1997; Masalha 2005; Sayigh 1984). However, whilst Subhi had 'returned' to the West Bank, his initial displacement was now combined with an experience of confinement. Although as a child he had fled Bayt Hajjar, he was now stuck there, unable to move for fear of arrest. By focusing on the lives of Palestinians such as Subhi, this chapter explores the ways in which experiences of displacement are formed in the tensions between the processes that make people mobile and those that keep them in place (Shamir 2005). As such, displacement is never simply a physical movement across space, but also involves transformations in the political, social and economic practices through which people are related to place. In this process, movement and fixity are not opposed conditions, but can coexist simultaneously. For many Palestinians, the ad hoc interventions of the region's states have meant that their presence in any place is always contingent, yet they also face severe restrictions on moving elsewhere. This has produced a situation where displacement and return, absence and presence, movement and confinement are entwined with one another. People such as Subhi are caught in the often violent spaces in between, unable to feel secure in any given place, but too afraid to move on, as their sense of 'being at home' or in 'exile' is constantly made and unmade.

The specific focus here is on the experiences of the residents of a group of villages in the Latrun area of the West Bank. From the summer of 2000 to the spring of 2002, I conducted ethnographic fieldwork in one of the villages on the eastern fringe of this area. This chapter therefore describes a period before the building of the wall across the West Bank, which has served to intensify the processes discussed below.

The Regulation of Movement and Confinement

The twin processes of displacement and confinement run through modern citizenship regimes (Appadurai 1996; Hannerz 1996). Mobility and flow exist alongside rootedness and territory, sometimes in the same spaces and amongst the same people. However, these processes are not equally distributed. A small minority find it relatively easy to travel, whilst most people are stuck in place, unable to move despite great need. For many people migration is necessary for economic and political survival, yet there are increasing restrictions on the movement of many categories of person (Friedman 1997). In this context, Ronen Shamir has urged an examination of the processes of closure, entrapment and containment, which make mobility a scarce resource (2005; see also Torpey 1997; Bauman 2002: 83).

Whilst experiences of displacement cannot be forced into neat analytical boxes (Turton 2003), there are common experiences created through bureaucratic and administrative processes by which movement is regulated (Verstraete 2003). Legal practices in particular play a significant role in attempting to define the places where people do and do not belong, and where they can and cannot move to. Work permits, visas, passports and border patrols create 'legal' and 'illegal' migration, and legal treaties define who is a refugee, who is a migrant and who is an 'illegal' alien. Critical approaches to refugee and migration law have quite rightly highlighted the ways in which the rigid determinism and naturalisations of legal categories distort the complex processes through which people are forced to move or stay still (Chimni 1998; Harney 1999). However, sensitivity to the arbitrary determinism of law should not blind us to how the particularities of legal status play a central role in shaping many people's experiences of place. Legal status is not a neutral framework that describes experiences of displacement or return, but is instead involved in their very production.

Crucially, the attempts of legal regimes to keep people in or out of place can never be guaranteed to be successful. Rather than being coherent, the movement of people is regulated through the various ad hoc and often contradictory interventions of states (De Genova 2002). Not only are international and national legal boundaries problematically enforced, but also the categories of person who are allowed to cross through these boundaries are indeterminate. As Calavita argues, for example, in her work on immigration laws in the late nineteenth-century USA, anti-Chinese racism clashed with the economic desire to trade with China (2000). The result was a contradictory system of law that tried to open the way for the immigration of Chinese merchants but prevent the entry of Chinese 'coolies'. The inherent problems of making this distinction created opportunities for Chinese labourers to pass as merchants, undermining the attempts to police US borders. The 'incompleteness' of the practices that attempt to relate people to place means that they simultaneously act as a source of constraint and can open up spaces for movement. While legal practices can block flows of people, they may also produces spaces for movement in unpredictable ways.

The instability of attempts to relate persons to place means that the presence of many people, even as they try to gain a more secure foothold, is often contingent and fragile. The distinction between 'legitimate' and 'illegitimate' presence is not given once and for all but is constantly shifting and people can feel 'out of place' without having moved anywhere. As De Genova argues, for example, the selective enforcement of immigration laws means that Mexican migrants are often present on

US territory only as constantly deportable aliens, whose presence is always dependent on the actions of those who act in the name of the US state (2002, 2005). Such tensions can mean that displaced persons are often caught between the legal categories of absence and presence (Coutin 2005), never completely secure in any given place, but never completely able to move on.

Rather than the processes of movement and containment, exile and return being seen in opposition, they should both be understood in the wider context of the instabilities in the processes through which people are related to place. This means that limiting anthropological analysis to an unmasking of the naturalisations of immigration law is only a necessary first step (see Jansen and Löfving in this volume). The contingency of legal status is often all too obvious to many displaced people, as they try to negotiate the boundaries of the state. In order to take our understandings of the relationship between experiences of displacement and return a step further, we need to undertake an empirical exploration of the ways in which the arbitrariness of migration regimes produces particular tensions between movement and containment, and, in doing so, unequal distributions of relative security and insecurity.

The Boundaries of Citizenship

The regulations of movement take place within the context of specific local struggles over the boundaries and meanings of citizenship. Class, race and gender interact to create historically particular configurations of relative mobility and constraint (see, for example, Carapico and Würth 2000). For West Bank Palestinians their inclusion and exclusion from the protections of citizenship has taken place within a context where legal rights have been predominantly distributed according to ethnonational principles. However, the boundaries of the Israeli state are fundamentally fragmented and contradictory, producing an unstable, ethnically based 'mobility regime' (Shamir 2005).

Since the Israeli occupation of the West Bank in 1967, there have been intense debates over its implications for the boundaries of the Israeli state (Kimmerling 1983; Rabinowitz 2003). The Israeli right has argued that the West Bank should be treated as 'liberated' Israeli territory, while sections of the Zionist left have urged a return of the Israeli military to its 1967 borders. In the context of these wider debates, hundreds of thousands of Israeli citizens have settled in the West Bank.[3] At the same time, there has been pressure from various sections of the Israeli military, as well as some sectors of Israeli capital, to incorporate the Palestinian population of the West Bank into the Israeli economy (Bornstein 2002). Not only would dependence on the Israeli economy make the cost of Palestinian resistance to the Israeli occupation that much higher, but also Palestinians could provide a source of readily available, cheap, semi-skilled and unskilled labour for the Israeli economy. These territorial and economic claims to the West Bank have also had to face the local Palestinian residents in the area. Although parts of the Israeli state have been keen to integrate the Palestinian residents into the Israeli economy, full annexation of the West Bank would also mean the legal incorporation of the Palestinian population into the political institutions of the Israeli State, therefore potentially undermining the Jewish majority in Israel.

In the face of these tensions between claims to territory and populations, the territorial boundaries of the Israeli state in the West Bank have not been defined. This means that while the West Bank may not have been formally annexed, there has also been a refusal on the part of successive Israeli governments to recognise the 1949 Armistice Line between Israel and Jordan as an international frontier. The Israeli population of the West Bank has been integrated into the 'protective orbit' of the Israeli state, while Palestinian residents of the area have effectively been treated by the Israeli state as 'foreign non-residents'. In this context, legal status has been produced and given meaning at the intersection of tensions between Israeli territorial claims to the West Bank, the desire to maintain Israel as a Jewish state, and perceived security fears. As a result, the legal status of the Palestinian residents of the West Bank has been contingent and constantly shifting.

The History of Displacement from Latrun

The Latrun area of the West Bank sits in the centre of historical Palestine, at the point where the hills that rise from the Jordan valley come down to meet the plain of Israel. The region is made up of several villages, built around the Abbey of Latrun. Bayt Hajjar stands on the area's eastern fringes. The area was the scene of several fierce battles during the war of 1948, as it overlooked the strategically important Tel Aviv–Jerusalem road (Morris 1999). When the Jordanian–Israeli Armistice was signed in 1949, the area remained under Jordanian control and stuck out like a thumb into the centre of Israel. The new Armistice Line lay just a few kilometres to the west and south of Latrun, and due to a dispute over the exact position of the opposing forces on the date the Armistice was signed, much of the area was declared no man's land.

The creation of the Armistice Line would have profound implications for the residents of the region. Although the villages of Latrun were not occupied by the Israeli army, Palestinians from the villages to the south and west passed through the area as they were forced to flee. Under Israeli law, those Palestinians who had fled the territory that was declared part of the new State of Israel were categorised as 'absentees' and denied Israeli citizenship, residence or entry, irrespective of the location of their former residence (Davis 1997: 55–59). Those who tried to return to their homes found that they were unable to do so, as a newly militarised border had been created behind them through the middle of what had been Mandate Palestine.[4] The residents of the villages in the Latrun were eventually granted Jordanian citizenship when the West Bank was annexed to the Hashemite Kingdom of Jordan in 1950.

However, the creation of the Armistice Line meant that many of the villagers of Latrun were separated from their families and their land. The Line ran straight through their social and economic relationships. Subhi's mother, for example, who was from one of the villagers to the west of Latrun, was cut off from the rest of her family, as she had followed her husband to live in Bayt Hajjar. Much of the farmland belonging to the villagers was also lost, either to Israeli-controlled territory or to no man's land. Subhi remembers that his mother tried several times to make visits to her family on the other side but found the way blocked by Israeli soldiers, and several people trying to make the trip were shot dead. In the late 1950s there was a series of raids by villagers from the Latrun area into Israel, and by Israeli troops into the West Bank, that left scores of people dead. During one famous incident that Subhi often told me about, the local civil defence force apparently repulsed a raid by Israeli soldiers. One woman was killed, and her son, who later grew up to be a teacher in the village's school, still displays the scar that he received as the result of a bullet wound. As they were cut off from much of their land, and due to the recurring violence, many people migrated either to the Jordanian capital of Amman or further afield to the Gulf or to South America, in order to find work.

During the first few hours of the 1967 war between Israel, Jordan, Egypt and Syria, troops from the Israeli army took control of Latrun. One of Subhi's distant cousins served in the Jordanian army as a cook, and Subhi would often tell me with great amusement how that man had woken up on the morning of the invasion to find that the other Jordanian soldiers had fled, leaving him surrounded by Israeli troops. On the second night of the invasion, Israeli military jeeps drove through the Latrun villages of Yallu, Imwas and Bayt Nuba, and ordered the residents to leave their homes. Over the next few hours all twelve thousand villagers packed up the few belongings they could carry and began to walk east. These people were joined by the residents of other neighbouring villagers, fearful that their villages would be next.

In the days after the war, the Israeli military announced on the radio that people across the West Bank should return to their homes. However, the former residents of Yallu, Imwas and Bayt Nuba were forbidden to do so, and the area was declared a closed military zone. Those who tried to return were met by Israeli army checkpoints, and several people were shot at by Israeli patrols. From the nearby hills, they could see that all the buildings in Imwas, Bayt Nuba and Yallu had been blown up by Israeli military engineers, and all traces of the villages completely destroyed. Unable to return home, some of these people sought shelter in nearby villages. As not all of the land of Bayt Nuba had been declared a closed military zone, a few of its former residents rented homes in Bayt Hajjar, while farming what remained of their land.[5] Others from the destroyed villages, as well as from places such as Bayt Hajjar, Subhi's family among them, had fled all the way across the Jordan River to Amman.[6] These people, as well as the villagers who had migrated to Amman in previous years, were now cut off from Latrun by the newly militarised Cease Fire Line along the Jordan valley.[7]

Immediately after the 1967 occupation, the Israeli military conducted a census, which was then used to create a new population registry for the West Bank. Some of Subhi's aunts and uncles had stayed in their homes in Bayt Hajjar as the Israeli tanks rolled by. Determined not to be forced out of their homes, as many Palestinians were in 1948, they decided to remain in their homes, despite the destruction slightly down the road. Subhi often told me that he wished his immediate family had shown such *sumud* (steadfastness) and remained in the West Bank. Subhi's family members who remained were included on the new census and were issued with West Bank identity cards and given West Bank residency rights. However, these residency rights were contingent and could be taken away by the Israeli military if the holders were deemed to have moved their 'centre of life' away from the West Bank or if they were declared a perceived 'security threat'.[8] One of Subhi's cousins went to study medicine in Hungary, on a scholarship from the Palestinian Communist Party, and was prevented from returning after an Israeli official at the border post between the West Bank and Jordan told him that he had been out of the area for too long and was no longer considered a 'resident'. Those, like Subhi's immediate family, who were absent from the West Bank during this census were not put on the population registry at all and were therefore forced to remain on the East Bank of the Jordan.

Importantly, after 1967 the West Bank was not formally annexed to the Israeli state, and the Hashemite Kingdom of Jordan still claimed it as Jordanian territory. As a result, those Palestinians who were resident in the West Bank, such as Subhi's aunts and uncles, also had residency rights in Jordan. Even if Subhi could not make the trip to the West Bank, his cousins could come and visit him. However, in 1988 the Jordanian government, partly as a result of its recognition of the Palestine Liberation Organisation's (PLO's) declaration of independence that year, renounced its claim to the West Bank. West Bank Palestinians, such as those who lived in Bayt Hajjar, stopped being considered Jordanian citizens and lost their residency rights in Jordan. Although they were issued Jordanian passports as travel documents, these were issued for two-year periods, making them easily distinguishable from the passports held by Jordanian citizens.

Rosemary Sayigh has argued that many of the Palestinians who fled the violence of the 1948 war had no sense that they were crossing legal frontiers (1988: 12). This was also the case in the Latrun area in 1967. When they crossed the Jordan River, the people who fled from Latrun did not cross an international border, but one was effectively created behind them in the form of the 1967 Cease Fire Line. Even those who stayed in the West Bank were prevented from returning to their villages due to the creation by the Israeli military of a closed military zone around their former homes. Although initially the villagers of Latrun fled because of fear of violence, legal processes had tried to regularise their displacement. Armistice lines, military orders, international agreements and citizenship legislation created legal boundaries and shifted the ways in which the villagers related to place. Subhi's family went from being Jordanian citizens, resident on Jordanian territory, to being defined as non-residents, denied West Bank identity cards and therefore unable to pass through the newly established border posts over the Jordan River. The Palestinian population who had been resident in the West Bank were divided in two by the 1967 occupation. Those who had stayed in the West Bank during the 1967 war became stateless persons with contingent residency rights in the West Bank, while those who were on the East Bank of the Jordan River immediately after 1967 remained Jordanian citizens but had no de facto right of entry or residency in the West Bank. It was these new forms of legal status created by the Israeli occupation that had profoundly disrupted the social and economic relationships of the people of Latrun. While they had initially fled their homes temporarily, it was the legal processes that forced them to remain out of place.

The Israeli Occupation and 'Return'

After 1967, the vast majority of those displaced from Latrun in 1967 continued to live outside the West Bank. In the 1990s, however, some of the villagers, Subhi among them, were able to 'return' to the area around their villages. The next section of this chapter will examine how and under what conditions they were able to do so.

Through the 1960s and 1970s the area around the 1949 Armistice Line became increasingly incorporated into the Israeli economy, as many Palestinians went to work in Israel. At the same time, the Israeli government began to build new settlements across the West Bank. In 1970, a religious *moshav*, or collective farm, known as Mevo Horon was established directly over the site of the village of Bayt Nuba. In the mid-1970s, with the help of the Canadian Jewish National Fund, a public park was founded on the land of the village of Imwas, and many of its olive and fruit trees were incorporated into the new forests planted in the area. The land that had previously belonged to the residents of Yallu was incorporated into surrounding Israeli cattle farms.

Those former residents of Yallu, Bayt Nuba and Imwas who had remained in the West Bank joined the other Palestinians in the area who went to work in the Israeli economy. Usually they found work within the 1948 borders of Israel, but often they were employed in the newly built

Israeli settlements in the West Bank. One family, originally from Bayt Nuba, but who now lived in the same building as Subhi and I, worked along with about ten other Palestinians in the settlement of Mevo Horon. The eldest brother had started work milking cows in the early 1980s and had eventually recruited his brothers and brothers-in-law. In total five members of the same family worked in the *moshav*. Some of the family looked after the cattle while others took care of the turkey sheds. When I asked one of the brothers what he felt about working directly above the site of his family's destroyed home, he just shrugged his shoulders. 'What can we do?' he said, 'I need to feed my family.' He told me that they never talked about 'politics' with the *moshav* residents but just got on with their jobs. These jobs had the advantage of not requiring the work permits that were needed to go to work in Israel, as the area around the moshav was not legally incorporated into Israel. While the work paid the relatively high wages of the Israeli economy, it was just a few kilometres' walk across the fields from where they were currently living in the West Bank.

In the mid-1990s the Israeli state signed peace agreements in quick succession with the PLO and the Hashemite Kingdom of Jordan. As a result, by the mid-1990s the issuing of identity cards and the maintenance of the West Bank population registry, and thereby Palestinian residency rights in the West Bank, had been taken over by the Palestinian National Authority (PNA). However, although the population registry was maintained by the PNA, the Israeli government retained the power to vet and veto any new entries. The Israeli state also still controlled all points of entry to the West Bank as well as maintaining numerous checkpoints across the region. This meant, in practice, that Israeli officials maintained the ability to grant or take away residency rights. At the same time, although no formal arrangements were made for the return of those displaced by the 1967 war, the Oslo Peace Agreements created several new routes for some to 'return' to the West Bank. First, it became possible for people with Jordanian passports to enter the West Bank and Israel on tourist visas. Second, the Oslo Agreements stipulated that several thousand Palestinians who had previously been denied access to the West Bank were allowed to 'return' as nominated employees of the PNA. Villagers of Latrun were amongst both sets of people.

Most of the people who 'returned' did so using Jordanian passports and tourist visas. Subhi is a typical example, and I estimated that there were several dozen men, and perhaps up to fifty women, who had 'returned' to the Latrun area in this manner. Attracted by the relative prosperity in the West Bank, they either married local Palestinians or simply overstayed their visas. Those who married people with West Bank identity cards, often relatives who had remained in the West Bank in 1967, then applied for residency status under family reunification programs. Although this process could take years, and often was not successful at all, these people would remain in the West Bank on their Jordanian passport. It was even said that Israeli soldiers at checkpoints gave people who had Jordanian passports less attention than those who held Palestinian identity cards.

A close friend of Subhi's, a man called Obeida, offers an example of the people who 'returned' as PNA employees. Obeida was born in Yallu in 1965, and his family fled during the 1967 war, first to Ramallah and eventually to Amman. While in Jordan, his father became active in the *Fatah* movement, and in September 1970, when the PLO had clashed with the Jordanian army, his family left once again, this time to Syria. Partly because of his father's contacts in the PLO, Obeida eventually won a scholarship in the early 1980s to study law in Yemen. In the late 1980s Obeida returned to Jordan, where tension between the PLO and the Jordanian state had cooled considerably, and set up his own legal practice. Throughout his time in Yemen, Syria and Jordan, Obeida remained active in the PLO. With the creation of the PNA in 1994, he returned to the West Bank with his father, wife and children, and rented a flat in Bayt Hajjar. Obeida chose Bayt Hajjar, he told me, because he still had family who lived nearby. Furthermore, rent in the village was much cheaper than it would have been in Ramallah, to which he would commute everyday. Initially Obeida worked as a judge in the PNA military court, before being transferred to the civilian police to work as a lawyer in their enforcement division. Those people like Obeida who had come to the West Bank were popularly referred to as the *a'idun* (returnees) and dominated many of the powerful and highly paid jobs in the PNA.

If legal practices had been used to regularise the displacement of the people from the destroyed villages of Latrun, these same processes were simultaneously used by some people to 'return' (Calavita 2000: 27). Whereas in Obeida's case his 'return' was facilitated by the international legal agreement between the PLO and the Israeli state, Subhi was able to come back to the West Bank because of the seemingly more mundane processes of tourist visas and family reunification programs. The issuing of tourist visas opened up ways for people to 'return' to the West Bank, even if they were not legally classified as being a 'resident'. However, these people 'returned' to the West Bank under legal conditions very different from those under which they had left. During the second intifada, these changed legal conditions were to have profound effects on their lives, and their legal presence would become increasingly questioned.

Fear and the Uncertainties of 'Return'

After the start of the second intifada in late September 2000, the roads around Latrun became covered with Israeli checkpoints. In early 2001, a high fence was built around the settlement of Mevo Horon, which, as well as being the place of employment of several former residents of Bayt Nuba, was also a favoured route used by Palestinians to bypass the checkpoints and try to get to work in Israel. At the same time, the permanent checkpoint that was used to control movement across the Armistice Line was moved several kilometres further east and now stood between Mevo Horon and the rest of the West Bank. This caused major problems for the Palestinians who worked in the settlement. Although Mevo Horon had not been legally annexed into Israel, the Palestinians who worked there had to pass through this permanent checkpoint in order to get to work. As it was the last checkpoint before Israel, the soldiers usually asked the workers for their Israeli work permits. However, as the settlement was not 'legally' inside Israel, the workers could not apply for one. This left them in something of a catch-22 situation. Sometimes an informal agreement was made between the settlers of Mevo Horon and the soldiers, whereby the settlers would come and pick up the workers at the checkpoint and then escort them back at the end of the day. However, this agreement was completely contingent on the soldiers, and as the soldiers were routinely rotated, it failed to work more often than it did work. Sometimes the soldiers on the checkpoint in the morning would let the workers through, but when the workers tried to return in the afternoon, they were detained for being in Israel 'illegally'. Some of the workers decided that in order to go to work they would risk jumping the fence that surrounded the settlement. However, while the settlers did not seem to mind this and in many respects encouraged it, the Israeli soldiers patrolling the area often reacted violently. Several people were shot at while attempting to climb the fence and, as a result, many of the people who worked in the settlement were too afraid to go to work at all.

The workers at Mevo Horon were not the only people who became afraid. Movement around the West Bank was severely restricted for many Palestinians. Where previously Obeida's job with the PNA had meant that he found it relatively easy to move around the West Bank, this all changed during the second intifada. The Israeli military accused the PNA security forces of being involved in attacks on Israeli soldiers and civilians. As a result, the Israeli air force bombed several Palestinian police stations, including the office where Obeida worked, and detained hundreds if not thousands of Palestinian security officials. In May 2001, another member of the PNA police force, who lived next door to Obeida, was detained at an Israeli military checkpoint. He only returned to the village four months later, much quieter and thinner. Obeida was therefore increasingly apprehensive when moving around the West Bank, in case the Israeli soldiers who patrolled the roads discovered that he worked for the PNA. Often he would only travel once he had checked with the bus and taxi drivers that there were no checkpoints on the roads he intended to use that day. Obeida even began to talk about returning with his family to Jordan if he could find a suitable job.

Subhi was increasingly scared that the increase in checkpoints would mean his being discovered for having overstayed his tourist visa, that he would be deported back to Jordan, separating him from his young family. As a result, he remained in the village and hardly moved, too afraid to go to work. By the time I left the West Bank in the spring of 2002, he was becoming increasingly frustrated. Not only did he not have a job and a way of feeding his children, but he was also stuck in a small two-bedroom flat, with his wife's family constantly coming by. Like many of the men in the village he used to wander aimlessly around the village, sitting in the front of shops for a cup of tea, or watching the news from various Arab satellite TV channels. The various satellite news channels being broadcast out of Qatar, Lebanon or Dubai were often their only way of connecting with the events happening in Ramallah, just a few miles away over the hills. They would talk longingly about the trips they had previously made with families and friends to the beaches and restaurants of Israel, and how this compared to the current boredom of their everyday lives. They would also often ask me, and each other, how long the *wada'a* (situation) would go on for, and how soon they might be able to return to work. Obeida used to get very angry with Subhi every time he suggested that sitting at home was now *'adi* (normal). Obeida was adamant that his enforced confinement to the village was just a temporary interruption.

Although Subhi, Obeida and the workers of Mevo Horon had physically 'returned', they had done so under deeply ambiguous legal conditions, meaning that their legal right to be present was always in question. The legal practices that regulated their displacement and confinement were often indeterminate. It was unclear whether they were legally entitled to be in the places where they found themselves, marking their encounters with Israeli soldiers with considerable fear. Obeida, Subhi and many others were often uncertain whether their visas, identity cards or permits would enable them to move freely around the West Bank. Given broader political transformations, including the Oslo Peace Process and the second intifada, the meanings and implications of their legal status were constantly shifting. The fact that the 'returnees' had come back to the West Bank through legal processes, rather than operating outside them, meant that they were still subject to the force of legal categorisation, turning their original displacement into an experience of confinement. Crucially, this confinement did not operate merely through determinate legal boundaries but through anxiety created out of the indeterminacy of their legal status.

Concluding Remarks

A demand for a return from exile has been a central feature of Palestinian collective life. However, Subhi, Obeida and the other former residents of Latrun had not returned to the West Bank simply because of some abstract longing for home, but because of a mixture of economic need, kinship connections and regional political developments. Yet, the place to which they came back had been the object of intense economic, social and political transformation. Despite their return to the West Bank, many of them found that they were no longer entirely 'at home'. Although Subhi and Obeida had 'returned', they did so under political and legal conditions very different from those under which they had left. The displacement of the villagers of Latrun was not simply a physical movement across space; it was also a transformation in the ways in which they were related to place (Malkki 1995: 496). As such, displacement does not necessarily require movement, but can also involve feelings of insecurity whilst staying still, as people find political and economic conditions changing around them.

For the former residents of Latrun, displacement and constraint were entwined within one another, as the lack of a secure legal status that would have attached them to a place meant that they were unable to move. Although the 'returnees' of Latrun represent but a tiny fraction of all displaced Palestinians, their experiences are illustrative of a wider Palestinian experience of tensions between absence and presence, movement and restriction. Without secure citizenship their presence in any given place has been contingent, dependent on changing political and economic conditions. After 1948, thousands of Palestinians who had remained in what became Israel, but who had fled their homes, were defined by the seemingly rather tautological category of 'present absentees' and prevented from returning to their property, which was requisitioned by the state (Davis 1997: 48). The Israeli anthropologist Smadar Lavie has described the Palestinian citizens of Israel as being 'refugees in their own land' (1996: 61). Palestinians in the Arab world face a similarly precarious situation, although in a very different political context. Palestinian refugees in Lebanon, for example, have no clear legal status and are often treated under the same laws that define the status of foreigners in general, and thereby prevented from working in many jobs or having access to public services (Sayigh 1988: 17). In this process, displacement and return should not be seen as opposed conditions, but as being simultaneously made and unmade in everyday life. Any problematisation of notions of home and return of course raises the risk of undermining the political struggles of the people of the region (Hanafi 2005). However, it also forces us to ask what a meaningful return might look like for the Palestinian diaspora. The experiences of the former residents of Latrun suggest that we look beyond narrowly spatial definitions to explore the economic, political and legal conditions that enable people to feel 'at home'.

While the history of Zionist colonialism, Palestinian statelessness and economic instability across the Middle East is very particular, many people across the world face similar tensions between presence and movement (Coutin 2005; De Genova 2002, 2005). It has been famously suggested that 'modernity' is marked by a desire to categorise, classify and fix people in place (Bauman 1993). The attempt to map out distinct territories, mark borders and assign categories of people to one side or the other is arguably a central part of this process. In practice, such classifications only produce further uncertainties, as many people, refugees among them, are unable quite to fit into the boxes assigned to them. However, it is not a question of either being in or out, absent or present, classified or unclassifiable, but often of being both simultaneously. The displaced are neither entirely in nor entirely out of place, but caught uncomfortably in between. Ambivalence about location and presence is the ever-present twin of the search for order. Crucially, not all people experience these tensions in the same way. There is a political economy to uncertainty. In particular, the ability to move or to stay in place, and feel secure in doing so, is a major source of inequality (Shamir 2005). Transnational movements of capital and military power have forced many people to move in order to find work or security, yet the same people also face serious problems when they attempt to cross borders. At the same time, others are free to move almost at will, or able to find safety 'at home' without a problem. The particular roles of class, gender and race in these processes depends on distinct local struggles over the implications and meanings of citizenship. The task, then, is to explore the historical contexts that determine which displacements are made temporary or permanent, which movements are made 'legal' or 'illegal', and which presences are deemed legitimate or not. Only by doing so can we understand how the historically shifting relationships between constraint and movement mean that some people never feel secure in any given place, yet are unable to move on without fear and anxiety.

Notes

1. This chapter has previously appeared in a slightly different format as 'Returning Home? Law, Violence, and Displacement among West Bank Palestinians', *Political and Legal Anthropology Review* 2004, 27(2). The research for this essay was made possible by an Economic and Social Research Council (ESRC) Ph.D. studentship and an ESRC post-doctoral fellowship held at the London School of Economics. I would also like to thanks the participants of the 'Doing Violence to Place' panel at the EASA 2004 conference, and Stef Jansen and Staffan Löfving in particular for their helpful comments. The fieldwork for this chapter was carried out between August 2000 and February 2002 in the Ramallah region of the West Bank. Where appropriate, identifying names have been changed.
2. The name of Bayt Hajjar, as well as the names of the people in this chapter, has been changed. The names of the destroyed villages of Latrun have been kept because of their historical notoriety.
3. The existence of the settlements has also been condemned by Palestinians, and many others, as illegal under international law (PLO: 2004).
4. In addition, those who could not return to their homes in Israeli-controlled territory, or were separated from their means of livelihood, were put under

the care of the United Nations Relief and Works Agency for Palestine Refugees in the Near East (UNRWA). Importantly, the 1951 UN Refugee Convention explicitly excluded from its protection those people who were deemed to be receiving help from a specifically created UN refugee organisation (Article 1d). As Palestinian refugees were nominally under the care of UNRWA, they were therefore usually excluded from the protection of the Convention.

5. By the late 1990s they numbered about three hundred people.
6. According to some estimates, about 200,000 people, or one-fifth of the West Bank's population, fled to the East Bank of the Jordan during the 1967 war, with the highest concentration being from border villages such as those in the Latrun area (Dodd and Barakat 1968: 5).
7. In the short term the displaced of 1967 were put under the care of UNRWA (Dale 1974: 585). However, in the long run they were not given the status of UNRWA registered refugees. In part this was because the issue of whether they had crossed an international frontier was highly contentious. In July 1967 the Israeli government announced that it was prepared to hear applications from those displaced by the 1967 war to return to the West Bank, through a process organised by the International Red Cross (Dodd and Barakat 1968: 57). Over 170,000 people applied, and 14,000 were allowed to return to the West Bank before the process was suspended, never to be continued, in August of that year.
8. According to some estimates, over 150,000 Palestinians have lost their residency rights since 1967 (Dodd and Barakat 1968).

References

Appadurai, Arjun. 1996. *Modernity at Large: Cultural Dimensions of Globalization.* Minneapolis: University of Minnesota Press.

Bauman. Zygmunt. 1993. *Modernity and Ambivalence.* Cambridge: Polity Press.

———. 2002. *Society Under Siege.* Cambridge: Polity Press.

Bisharat, George. 1997. 'Exile to Compatriot: Transformations in the Social Identity of Palestinian Refugees in the West Bank', in *Culture, Power, Place: Explorations in Critical Anthropology*, ed. Akhil Gupta and James Ferguson, pp. 203–33. Durham: Duke University Press.

Bornstein, Avram S. 2002. *Crossing the Green Line Between the West Bank and Israel.* Philadelphia: University of Pennsylvania Press.

Calavita, Kitty. 2000. 'The Paradoxes of Race, Class, Identity, and "Passing": Enforcing the Chinese Exclusion Acts, 1882–1910′, *Law and Social Inquiry* 25(1): 63–94.

Carapico, Sheila and Anna Würth. 2000. 'Passports and Passages: Test of Yemeni Women's Citizenship Rights', in *Gender and Citizenship in the Middle East*, ed. Suad Joseph pp. 61–91. Syracuse, NY: Syracuse University Press.

Chimni, B.S. 1998. 'The Geopolitics of Refugee Studies: A View from the South', *Journal of Refugee Studies* 11(4): 350–74.

Coutin, Susan. 2005. 'Being En Route', *American Anthropologist* 107(1): 195–206.

Dale, William. 1974. 'UNWRA: A Subsidiary Organ of the United Nations', *International and Comparative Law Quarterly* 23(3): 576–609.

Davis, Uri. 1997. *Citizenship and the State: A Comparative Study of Citizenship Legislation in Israel, Jordan, Palestine, Syria and Lebanon*. Cambridge: Ithaca Press.

De Genova, Nicholas. 2002. 'Migrant "Illegality" and Deportability in Everyday Life', *Annual Review of Anthropology* 31: 419–47.

———. 2005. *Working the Boundaries: Race, Space and 'Illegality' in Mexican*. Chicago and Durham, NC: Duke University Press.

Dodd, Peter and Halim Barakat. 1968. *River Without Bridges: A Study of the Exodus of the 1967 Palestinian Arab Refugees*. Beirut: Institute for Palestine Studies.

Friedman, Jonathan. 1997. 'Global Crises, the Struggle for Cultural Identity and Intellectual Porkbarreling: Cosmopolitans Versus Locals, Ethnics and Nationals in an Era of De-hegemonisation', in *Debating Cultural Hybridity: Multi-Cultural Identities and the Politics of Anti-Racism*, ed. Pnina Werbner and Tariq Modood, pp. 70–89. London: Zed Books.

Hanafi, Sari. 2005. 'Rethinking the Palestinians Abroad as a Diaspora: The Relationship between the Diaspora and the Palestinian Territories', in *Homelands and Diasporas: Holy Lands and Other Places*, ed. André Levy and Alex Weingrod, pp. 97–122. Stanford: Stanford University Press.

Hannerz, Ulf. 1996. *Transnational Connections: Culture, People, Places*. London: Routledge.

Harney, Colin. 1999. 'Talking about Refugee Law', *Journal of Refugee Studies* 12(2): 101–34.

Kimmerling, Baruch. 1983. *Zionism and Territory: The Socioterritorial Dimensions of Zionist Politics*. Berkeley: University of California Institute of International Relations.

Lavie, Smadar. 1996. 'Blowups in the Borderzones: Third World Israeli Authors' Gropings for Home', in *Displacement, Diasporas and Geographies of Identity*, ed. Smadar Lavie and Ted Swedenburg, pp. 55–96. Durham: Duke University Press.

Malkki, Liisa. 1995. 'Refuges and Exile: From Refugee Studies to the National Order of Things', *Annual Review of Anthropology* 24: 495–523.

Masalha, Nur (ed.). 2005. *Catastrophe Remembered: Palestine, Israel and the Internal Refugees*. London: Zed Books.

Morris, Benny. 1999. *Righteous Victims: A History of the Zionist-Arab Conflict, 1881–1999*. New York: Alfred Knopf.

PLO. 2004. 'Settlements, Permanent Status Issues'. Retrieved 13 July 2004 from http://nad-plo.org.

Rabinowitz, Dan. 2003. 'Borders and Their Discontents: Israel's Green Line, Arabness and Unilateral Separation', *European Studies: A Journal of European Culture, History and Politics* 19: 217–31.

Sayigh, Rosemary. 1984. *Palestinians; From Peasants to Revolutionaries*. London: Zed Books.

———. 1988. 'Palestinians in Lebanon: Status Ambiguity, Insecurity and Flux', *Race and Class* 30(1): 13–32.

Shamir, Ronen. 2005. 'Without Borders? Notes on Globalization as a Mobility Regime', *Sociological Theory* 23(2): 197–217.

Shiblak, Abbas. 1995. 'Residency Status and Civil Rights of Palestinian Refugees in Arab Countries', *Journal of Palestine Studies* 25(3): 36–45.

Torpey, John. 1997. 'Coming and Going: On the State Monopolization of the Legitimate 'Means of Movement', *Sociological Theory* 16(3): 239–59.

Turton, David. 2003. 'Refugees, Forced Resettlers and "Other Forced Migrants": Towards a Unitary Study of Forced Migration', *New Issues in Refugee Research Working Paper* No. 94. Geneva: UNHCR.

Verstraete, Ginette. 2003. 'Technological Frontiers and the Politics of Mobility in the European Union,' in *Uprootings/Regroundings: Questions of Home and Migration*, ed. Sara Ahmed, Claudia Castañeda, Anne-Marie Fortier and Mimi Sheller, pp. 225–50. Oxford: Berg.

2

TROUBLED LOCATIONS

Return, the Life Course and Transformations
of Home in Bosnia-Herzegovina

Stef Jansen

NIJEDNA KUĆA KÔ SVOJA, NIJEDNA RIJEKA KÔ DRINA
(Not one house is like one's own, not one river is like the Drina)
— *Banner at 2001 meetings of displaced persons in Tuzla*

Cool Ground: Return and Social Projects of Home

Five years after the end of the 1992–95 military violence in Bosnia-Herzegovina, hundreds of thousands of survivors of 'ethnic cleansing' signed up for return. But most could not fail to notice the dramatic transformations their prewar place of residence had undergone over the past decade. In 2001, people's memories of the two villages at the heart of this chapter[1] – Bistrica, in a shaded valley, and Izgled, perched on a hill range overlooking the Drina – evoked almost archetypically bucolic landscapes. Meanwhile, however, they had actually become unrecognizable. Buildings had been destroyed, forested areas had been decimated for firewood, and fields and orchards were now overgrown and believed to be mined. In Izgled, the banner's proclamation that no river is quite like the Drina had been perversely reinforced by the river's wartime significance: it had become the interstate border with Serbia, and many returnees remembered the corpses that had floated in it.

Such a context of 'ethnic cleansing' provides a particularly challenging site to investigate the role of violence in place making, and especially to assess the value of sedentarism, which I define here as a discourse, prevalent in refugee studies and policies, that naturalises the link between people and place (see the introduction to this volume). On the one hand, the very logic of 'ethnic cleansing' contains a stark reminder of the danger of positing such essentialised links rooting persons into territory. On the other hand, the rootless fantasies proposed by some as an anti-sedentarist antidote sound cruelly naive to those violently expelled from 'their' places. Wishing to avoid the pitfalls of both fixing sedentarist and free-floating anti-sedentarist paradigms, some scholars argue for a middle ground that factors in transformations of places and persons as well as continued attachment to a culturally defined home locality (Markowitz and Stefansson 2004; Stefansson 2004a, 2004b). Working with Bosnian repatriates in Sarajevo, Stefansson draws attention to their pragmatic attempts to reestablish 'a sense of normal life, which in its turn is defined by three key issues: creating sustainable livelihoods, finding a place of relational identification [and] developing a site of cultural attachment' (2004b: 174). He argues that, despite radical wartime transformations, for some Bosnians it may be tempting to go home – indeed, his findings, like my own, demonstrate that it may be. More precisely, they demonstrate not only that it may or may not be *tempting* but also, I anti-sedentaristically reiterate, that it may or may not be *home*.

This text channels legitimate criticisms of anti-sedentarism and sedentarism towards a call for a culturally sensitive political economy of displacement and emplacement – investigating the conditions in which certain (re)makings of home come to be seen as more feasible than others. My starting point is that embodied attachment to place should not be taken for granted and that it is all the more problematic when combined with an exoticist approach to non-Western Others, somehow locating them closer to nature. Rather, embodied attachment to place should itself be analysed as a possible dimension in the making of home. Zetter has shown how Cypriot refugees mythologised the home from which they had been expelled and hoped that return would bring about its restoration, but he warns that home includes a 'living organism of relationships and traditions stretching back into the past' (1999: 12). Likewise, Jackson has stressed the transgenerational, collective aspect of home making among Warlpiri in Australia, adding that a 'sense of home is grounded less in a place *per se* than in the activity that goes on in a place' (1995: 148). Importantly, these relationships and activities take shape in particular political and socioeconomic contexts. Constructions of home, part of individual and collective life trajectories, make certain places into 'idioms' for power relations through which people position themselves and others (Gardner 1995: 272).

Among refugees, the prevalence of a 'home-orientation' – often referred to as 'myth of return' – varies according to their previous political and socioeconomic positioning (Al-Rasheed 1994). Moreover, return movements are not only affected by but are also thoroughly implicated in ongoing transformations of both returnees and societal structures (Gmelch 1980; Long and Oxfeld 2004). A useful approach to these issues is proposed by Turton (1996), who found Mursi refugees in Ethiopia to be 'in search of cool ground' – trying to find or establish a place characterised by relative security to start a project towards a better future. Bosnians too,

I discovered, were more preoccupied with finding such 'cool ground' than with return per se. More precisely, return to the place where home had been located would only be feasible for them if it promised such 'cool ground'. A possible return home was thus conceptualised as a social project to construct a 'sense of possibility' (Hage 1997), a basis from which individual and collective lives could be (re)launched.

This chapter aims to provide building blocks for an analysis of displacement and emplacement, conceptualising home making as a dynamic social process in which relationships to places and persons are produced. This, I argue, allows us to address the importance of place in home through an emphasis on personhood and transformative social relations, rather than on assumptions of sedentarist memory. Such an approach sheds a light on differential attitudes towards return among displaced Bosnians and embeds them in social relations, drawing attention to factors such as gender, class, education and life stage. Elsewhere, in an individual case study, I have deployed this approach to analyse why a Bosnian Serbian man preferred to remain in the Serbian-controlled town where he had found shelter (Jansen 2003). Instead of returning to his prewar place of residence, now in Bosniac-controlled territory, this displaced person wished to live with 'his own people' in what to me was an 'ethnically cleansed area', but to him was 'liberated national territory'. In this chapter, I bring the same approach to bear on return movements in Bosnia-Herzegovina, arguing that it allows us to critically analyse a variety of phenomena, from attempts at (il)legal emigration to proclamations – such as the one in the banner opening this chapter – that seem to underscore sedentarist interpretations. Slogans of that kind abounded in Bosnian displaced persons' (DP) associations. Their emphasis on embodied attachment to a particular (usually rural) landscape was articulated both with competing nationalist discourses that territorialised home as a national homeland and with the return policies of the foreign intervention agencies (FIAs),[2] which focused on physical safety in localised bricks-and-mortar private property. In this chapter I analyse the predicament of returnees in northeast Bosnia-Herzegovina in order to subvert such reductionist conceptualisations of home. Paying particular attention to people's stage in the life course, I trace dynamics of home making in relation to differential insertions of personhood into the socioeconomic and political context of Bosnia-Herzegovina. In particular, I explain how the twin emphasis of the FIAs on safety and property sidelined other dimensions of 'intimations of homeliness' (Bauman 1999; Hage 1997), and how this oversight was conveniently congruent with their 'reforms' policies. In this way, I argue, rather than a reinstatement of a previous situation, return was experienced by many Bosnians as one dimension of a process of societal transformation.

Degrees of Minority Return in Bosnia-Herzegovina

Let us now turn to two households in northeast Bosnia-Herzegovina. While the pseudonyms (like the real names) of the Savićes and the Mehmetovićes make them recognizable as having Serbian and Bosniac backgrounds, respectively, they shared appearance, language, and a host of other characteristics associated with rural life in this region. There had been little intermarriage here and a complex history of conflict and shifting alliances during the Second World War (Duijzings 2002), but in the Yugoslav state, villagers had shared schooling, health care, markets and public services on the municipal, republican and federal levels. In the 1990s, both households suffered wartime 'ethnic cleansing' and later became 'minority returnees' – bucking the dominant trend, they returned to prewar places of residence in municipalities now under political control of national Others. Nationality was clearly a factor in their predicaments, but we shall focus here on other factors that are often overlooked (see Jansen 2005a, 2005b).

The 1995 Dayton Agreement had put an end to the post-Yugoslav wars by recognising Bosnia-Herzegovina as a sovereign state consisting of two nationally homogenised Entities that were produced by the military violence: *Republika Srpska* (RS) and the Federation of Bosnia-Herzegovina ('the Federation'), the latter itself effectively divided between Croatian- and Bosniac-dominated territories. The Mehmetovićes's village, Izgled, was now part of RS territory while the Savićes's village, Bistrica, had been incorporated into the Bosniac-dominated part of the Federation. Much of the former front line had been consolidated as an Inter-Entity Boundary Line (IEBL), and it is this line that the Savićes and the Mehmetovićes crossed five years later in a mirror movement as minority returnees. In a sedentarist interpretation, their return had thus drawn a definite line under their displacement: these people were *back home*, living proof that homecomings were possible. Or were they?

Joka and Živko Savić, Bistrica, 2001

Both infirm due to advanced age (around seventy years old), Joka and Živko Savić were registered Serbian minority returnees in Bistrica, on the Federation side of the IEBL. In Yugoslav times, Bistrica had been almost homogenously Serbian-populated, cuddling up to a Bosniac-inhabited village. Like many elderly Serbs, the Savićes reminisced about harmonious and reciprocal coexistence. Bistrica had been located at a convenient distance from the towns of Tuzla and Zvornik, both 'mixed' regional centers. Joka and Živko had both worked in socially owned industries nearby and retired on the eve of Yugoslavia's disintegration. Their plan had been to spend their days in the family house, with a garden they had always kept for their own use.

In 1992, Bistrica fell under control of the armed forces of RS, inheritors of the Yugoslav People's Army. Partly due to Bistrica's proximity to a front line, most women and children, including Joka, had sought shelter in nearby towns that had by then been 'cleansed' of non-Serbian inhabitants and of most symbols of their presence. The Savićes' daughter had moved in with her sister-in-law in Serbia and still lived there, while her husband spent most of the 1990s in Switzerland. Živko had stayed on, and their two sons had been mobilised to fight elsewhere. However, within months, an offensive by the Bosniac-dominated Army of Bosnia-Herzegovina saw the RS Army withdraw from Bistrica, and all remaining Serbian inhabitants followed suit. The Savićes and their youngest son's household occupied a Bosniac-owned flat in Zvornik, now in RS. Virtually all houses in Bistrica were looted and severely damaged, and the Army of Bosnia-Herzegovina established a base nearby. The village was subsequently inhabited by Bosniac expellees from the Zvornik area, some of them repatriated refugees.

In the immediate postwar years, Serbian nationalist authorities strongly opposed return of both expelled Bosniacs and of their 'own' DPs, but by 2000 some Serbian prewar inhabitants of Bistrica applied for foreign assistance to reconstruct their abandoned houses on the far hillside of the village. Initially, these minority returnees were fearful both of their new Bosniac neighbours and of Serbian anti-return militants, but soon neighbourly relations in Bistrica became established, based on the stated agreement that no one wished to live in a stranger's house (*u tuđoj kući*) but that circumstances forced some to temporarily do so.

Mirsad Mehmetović, Izgled, 2001

Registered Bosniac minority returnees in RS, Mirsad Mehmetović and his wife Enisa, both about thirty, lived with their two daughters and Mirsad's mother in Izgled.[3] Prewar Izgled had been a Bosniac-inhabited set of kin-based clusters of houses, near the regional center, Zvornik. Since the 1970s, scores of Izgled men had become migrant construction workers. Mirsad's father had commuted weekly to Beograd, the Yugoslav and Serbian capital, located a few hours away. Others had worked in contractual labour for Beograd firms in non-aligned and socialist states and in Germany, investing salaries in houses and durables. Women did unpaid housework and engaged in small-scale agriculture, and some younger ones were employed nearby.

Serbian (para)military formations attacked Izgled in 1992 and hastily organised local Bosniac units were unable to respond. All able-bodied men, including Enisa's father and brother as well as Mirsad's father, had been taken away. Almost every household was directly affected by these mass disappearances. All other villagers were deported to what had now become Bosniac-controlled territory. Izgled had then been looted, torched and mined. Many survivors became DPs around the town of Tuzla, where, like the Mehmetovićes, they occupied houses owned by Serbs who had fled in the other direction. Many men who had escaped in time and numerous underage boys had joined the Bosniac-controlled Army of Bosnia-Herzegovina during the war. Mirsad, who had already fought in Croatia during his military service in the Yugoslav People's Army in 1991, had also signed up. The nearby front line had remained stable during the war and had later been transformed into the IEBL.

The Dayton Agreement assigned the remnants of Izgled to RS, on a narrow strip of territory between the IEBL, separating it from the Federation, and the Drina, now the state border with Serbia (Federal Republic of Yugoslavia). The area had long been considered extremely unsafe, but with the support of the main Bosniac political parties, DPs in Tuzla had planned collective return. In the late 1990s, many who had found refuge in third states had been repatriated and moved once again into internal displacement in the Tuzla area. By 2000, following a familiar pattern, DPs from Izgled had secured foreign funding and organised clean-up visits and overnight stays in tents. Foreign organisations had also improved a dirt track and restored electricity and water supply. A partly reconstructed house then served as overnight accommodation for all. After early incidents with Serbian DPs housed nearby, by 2001 foreign protection had been scaled down and there was a reasonable working relationship with local RS police patrols.

Neither village had a post office, café or shop, even though one Izgled family did retail some basic foodstuffs and household goods. No employment opportunities existed locally and, due to discrimination, minority returnees were also last in line in the unlikely case that jobs did crop up nearby. Farming, previously a sideline, had now become central to survival, supplemented by tiny and delayed pensions, humanitarian aid and remittances. Agricultural activities fell mainly to women, with the men crowding the building sites. Still, while some foreign assistance was available for agriculture, most returnees lacked the resources to work the overgrown land and were afraid of landmines.

Joka and Živko Savić, Bistrica, 2001

The Savićes were one of two elderly couples who had returned permanently to Bistrica. Electricity and water had recently become available, and a dirt track had been patched up slightly, but most recipients of reconstruction assistance only spent some weekends or holidays there, tentatively working on their houses. Some never visited, whereas others came regularly, including a man who had spent the war years in Germany and had recently bought a house in Serbia. In the spring of 2001, this man appeared almost daily, working to repair his wife's parental house, and driving back a considerable distance every evening. Most other prewar inhabitants remained displaced in

RS, while still others now resided in Western Europe. Most people had relatives abroad and, with the exception of the elderly Serbian returnees, virtually every household explored possibilities of emigration.

All households retained the accommodation in RS they had occupied during displacement, even though they received reconstruction assistance on the basis of the whole household returning. The Savićes' application had actually included themselves *and* their oldest son's household, thus paving the way for a larger structure. Their house-in-reconstruction had initially been used as overnight shelter for all villagers reconstructing their houses, but unlike most, Joka and Živko had rebuilt it to the point where it was minimally inhabitable – a feat which, they told me, had featured as an item on a German TV report. However, both of their sons lived with their households in Zvornik, the elder in a house purchased before the war and the other in Bosniac-owned accommodation. The latter had also signed up for reconstruction and return, but, like many others, had not completed the work to make his house habitable by postwar Bosnian standards. He said this was because the deterioration of the road made commuting to his informal Zvornik job more difficult than before.

Mirsad Mehmetović, Izgled, 2001

Dozens of houses were being built and rebuilt where a much larger Izgled had existed. In reciprocal efforts, returnees made one section of their house habitable, collecting the means to reconstruct other parts at a later stage. For these reasons, Izgled occupied a place of pride among foreign donor organisations in this 'difficult' region, and during spring and summer weekends it was buzzing with activity. However, only a few villagers, mainly elderly people such as Mirsad's mother, had actually moved into their houses as their first and only residence. Although reconstruction assistance usually included an explicit conditionality clause of actual return, most, like Enisa and Mirsad, maintained a working-week presence in the Tuzla area and failed to vacate Serbian-owned accommodation there. Foreign humanitarian aid was crucial in enticing people to engage in reconstruction, and this aid featured prominently in the complaints of villagers about the favouritism and false promises of 'the foreigners', who, for their part, rightly suspected that a portion of building materials was illicitly traded. They also belatedly discovered that the beneficiaries of several reconstructed houses had emigrated to the West, with more attempting to do so.

The Mehmetovićes had considered two houses in the village theirs: Mirsad's parental house and a villa across the track belonging to his uncle, who had been a *Gastarbeiter* in Germany for thirty years. Mirsad said the latter now wanted to gain German citizenship and then return for his retirement. For the time being, only the foundations of his villa were distinguishable. The Mehmetovićes spend the nights in the partly reconstructed parental house, while building a new one for Mirsad and Enisa's household (they had got married while displaced in the Tuzla area). Those Izgled adults who could – particularly men – hung on to (in)formal employment in the Federation. Mirsad still worked for the army near Tuzla on monthly contracts. His salary was a matter of resentment among some other villagers, who wildly overestimated the actual amount. Mirsad simply counted himself lucky to have a job at all.

Associated with different sides in the conflict, the Savićes and the Mehmetovićes had engaged in mirror movements across the IEBL, and as registered minority returnees whose actual return was a matter of degree, they were faced with similar concerns in postwar Bosnia-Herzegovina. But how did they evaluate their return?

Joka and Živko Savić, Bistrica, 2001

Despite their dire living conditions, Joka and Živko Savić compared their current situation favourably to the 'awful' years of displacement in Zvornik. All they wished for, they said, was that their children and grandchildren would visit more regularly. No city life could tempt them, they stated, and they had been 'the first ones on the list' to apply for return and to actually move back to Bistrica. When describing that day, Živko exclaimed, 'I was so happy to return home [na svoje]. This is mine! This is where I belong!' Joka joined in: 'Oh, son, you should have seen how happy we were when we returned. All the time in Zvornik I wanted to come back here. This is where I spent my life, this is where I want to be. We lost a lot, we had a house and we had everything in and around it, but when I think about it, I was lucky ... I thank God that [my sons] are alive! I look at other mothers, they lost one or two or even five children in the war! What a fate! We lost a lot, but on TV I see those people in tents, and I think: I can't complain. People who have been hit by earthquakes and floods – they need help as well! So I don't think we have it that bad ... Now nothing matters anymore. Now I can die and thank God.'

Mirsad Mehmetović, Izgled, 2001

Although he was rebuilding a house in Izgled, Mirsad Mehmetović did not see a long-term future in Bosnia-Herzegovina and launched consecutive attempts to secure (il)legal entry into Western states. Almost all households in Izgled had relatives scattered around the world as refugees. Some villagers had recently been admitted to the US, and this had intensified activity on the emigration front. Hoping to secure a US visa for his family, Mirsad was following the then common trajectory, involving a fictional claim of refuge in Croatia. When stopped at the border post on his third trip to Croatia, he put the usual DEM 30 in his passport in order not to have it stamped (crucial to this strategy). 'It was some new, young guy,' Mirsad sniffed. 'He went by the book and I was done for bribing. I got a year's worth of prohibited entry into Croatia. But I am telling you, I would leave tomorrow if I could. I wouldn't stay here. What's here for me? What can I do here? I would go anywhere. Just give me a visa, for whichever country, and I would go straight away ... Nobody wants to stay here anyway. Everybody wants to go abroad. Only old people perhaps, because they have already lived [their lives]. When they know that their children are okay, they want to return home [na svoje] ...'

The difference in evaluation of remaking home could hardly be starker: whereas Joka and Živko Savić expressed great joy about returning to their prewar place of residence, Mirsad Mehmetović desperately wanted to leave his. A range of sociological factors are at play in such experiences – for example, gender, urban/rural and class differences – but in the remainder of this text I focus on one of them: people's stage in the life course and the corresponding insertion of their personhood in the changing political and socio-economic Bosnian context (see Bougarel 2005). In this way, I hope to highlight the value of conceptualising home as the 'cool ground' that is projected in social engagements with place, whether through return or not.

Political Economies of Displacement and Emplacement

The Dayton Agreement stipulated the right of all the displaced to 'freely return to their homes of origin' and this was key to the Western-led intervention, due to the lack of funds for compensation, pragmatic anti-asylum concerns in refugee-receiving states, a moral argument against 'ethnic cleansing', and a wider sedentarist understanding of human belonging (Jansen 2005b, 2007). Ample resources were invested in return, and by January 2001 just under one-third of the almost 2.5 million displaced Bosnians were registered as returnees.[4] However, two-thirds of all DP returns and more than 90 percent of all refugee repatriations had taken place within or to the Federation. Most refugees had been deported in 'assisted or organised repatriation' policies by host governments, and a majority of them 'relocated' into internal displacement in areas dominated by political forces of their own nationality (Black 2002: 131; Phuong 2000: 174). These people could only be counted as having 'returned home' if 'home' were to mean their being within the borders of a sovereign state that hardly functioned as such. By 2001, about a quarter of all returnees were 'minority returnees', and it was an important stated FIA objective to increase this figure. After a peak return season in 2003, it is now widely considered that a point of saturation has been reached with just over a million registered returnees (Philpott 2005).

The return issue was also central to the strategies of local nationalist parties (Ito 2001), sometimes amounting to campaigns of 'ethnic engineering' elaborating on wartime 'ethnic cleansing'. In the 1990s, Serbian and Croatian nationalists in particular had demographically 'secured' certain areas through strategic 'implantation' of their own nationals, thus consolidating the division of Bosnia-Herzegovina. Using promises and threats, they now discouraged these same people – such as the Savićes' sons – from returning across the IEBL. Refusing to evict 'their' DPs from occupied Bosniac-owned accommodation, they assured themselves of electoral support and foot soldiers for 'spontaneous' violence. In addition, although local authorities were officially responsible for implementing minority return, they obstructed the return of Bosniacs through intimidation, direct or proxy violence, and non-intervention, except to 'harmless' places and in insignificant numbers – and even then mainly in order to satisfy foreign demands. In partial contrast, the main Bosniac nationalist parties favoured a unitary Bosnia-Herzegovina, even if in a rather inconsistent manner. While no national group constituted an absolute majority in Bosnia-Herzegovina, Bosniacs were the most numerous and the most likely to express loyalty to Bosnia-Herzegovina as a state. Providing only lukewarm cooperation for the return of non-Bosniacs to the territory under their control, Bosniac nationalist politicians were quick to capitalise on people's right to vote in their prewar place of residence and became actively involved in Bosniac DP associations known as 'communes in exile'. Hence, Bosniac minority return movements into RS also allowed interventions in the national-demographic puzzle and, in 2000–01 northeast Bosnia-Herzegovina saw substantial volumes of minority return in targeted villages just across the IEBL. Organised return to the Izgled area, for example, was seen by some Serbs as an attempt to cut RS territory in two at this narrow strip between the Federation and the Serbian border.

In any case, Bosniac minority returnees thus often reinhabited the remnants of remote hamlets, accorded little strategic importance by Serbian local authorities. Like Izgled, these places had lain abandoned for years and did not involve competition over housing since there was none left. Violent incidents still occurred, but return to towns such as Zvornik was much more controversial and dangerous, because accommodation there would require the eviction of Serbs displaced from the Federation. Return to Izgled illustrates how, through movement en bloc, Bosniac minority returnees thus constituted local majorities in villages that formed part of a RS municipality. This pattern was replicated, to a lesser extent, by Serbs in a few places in the Federation, but in 2000–01 Serbian minority returnees in the Federation were concentrated in urban zones. Still, urban returns were proportionally smaller in scale and, given the exchange value of city accommodation, often constituted mere repossessions with intention to sell (see Jansen 2007).

With FIAs and local nationalist forces making return into a key object of struggle, it is not surprising that we do not find the kind of random return movements we would expect if individual decisions of homesickness were the main determinant of return. In fact, a large majority of displaced Bosnians did *not* return to their prewar place of residence. Reluctance was particularly great among those who had found refuge abroad, mainly Bosniacs from what is now RS. Interest was greater among DPs,[5] but many, even among those who had signed up for return, also considered exchange or sale of their property. Almost no one who had not owned accommodation in their prewar place of residence wished to return, and many others simply justified their interest by saying they 'had nowhere else to go' (UNHCR 2003). In explaining such patterns, existing studies point to the above conflict between the return policies of the FIAs and local nationalist politicians (e.g., Albert 1997; D'Onofrio 2004; Fischel de Andrade and Delaney 2001), but another significant dimension of the predicament of displaced Bosnians is conspicuous in its absence. It is this dimension that I address now.

My research made me increasingly aware that Bosnians experienced a combination of forced migration and what I would call 'forced transition' – a transformation from Yugoslav socialist workers' self-management, via a predatory war economy to some form of neoliberal capitalism. This transformation, if mentioned at all, is usually referred to with the neutral-sounding term 'reforms'. Elsewhere (Jansen 2006b) I have explored in more detail how the FIA focus on national coexistence and the restitution of property obscured and *therefore* reinforced foreign-imposed 'transition' policies. Let me summarise the argument here: While many local and foreign observers called for *more* 'reforms' in Bosnia-Herzegovina, the particular shape of the intervention served to depoliticise not only displacement and return, but also society as a whole. In other post-socialist contexts, cuts in public services and reductions in other forms of state intervention usually followed from conditional multilateral assistance policies. In Bosnia-Herzegovina, such policies were imposed directly by the Dayton protectorate and, anyway, most of the job had been done already: many socioeconomic institutions that had not been destroyed during the war had collapsed due to the disintegration of the Yugoslav market and infrastructural decay. Those that survived were now endangered by 'transition' – they were unprofitable in capitalist terms – and many of those that might contain a promise in a capitalist future fell prey to nationalist elites through crooked privatisation processes (Papić 2001; Schierup 1999).

In line with the dominant Western representations of Bosnia-Herzegovina, these overwhelming changes are all too often neglected in work on displacement, except in general references to poverty and unemployment, and to the disadvantageous legacy of socialism (e.g., Stefansson 2004b: 176). But 'transition' itself, however incomplete it was according to its advocates, had powerful effects for the displaced (cf.

Phillips 2004: 151). This was particularly clear from the experiences of minority returnees: considerable foreign funds were invested in property restitution, reconstruction and safety, but much less was done with regard to people's livelihoods upon return. For the vast majority of Bosnians, no attractive or even feasible economic opportunities resulted from the FIA-enforced 'reforms', which instead brought humanitarian aid and the promotion of self-employment through micro-credit schemes and donations of seeds, animals, and so on. These programs were usually run through non-governmental organisations, which was partly a response to obstruction by local nationalist politicians but which was also congruent with the neoliberal onslaught on any sense of entitlement to a public sector.

The cases of Bistrica and Izgled indicate that such experiences of 'transition' came to be articulated with another underestimated factor in Bosnian transformations of home: an increased preference for urban residence.[6] War-related displacement had strengthened earlier migration into the cities (Allcock 2002; Bougarel 1996; Jansen 2005c; Lukić and Nikitović 2004), and this process, in turn, was reinforced by the self-initiated wartime occupation of city flats on the part of majority-identified (hence by no means 'ethnically cleansed') people from surrounding villages. Although the original background to rural habitats in Bosnia-Herzegovina had been a kinship-based pattern of ownership of agricultural land, villagers in Izgled and Bistrica had *not* lived primarily off agriculture before the war. Rather, while they had also worked the land (particularly women), their insertion into the Yugoslav developmentalist modernisation process had been shaped largely through labour market participation by most men and, to a lesser extent, women (see Lockwood 1973). With the war, extended Bosnian families had been scattered across the globe, and the socialist program of disclosure of the countryside had been abandoned: transport and communications had deteriorated, and previous employment in socially owned workplaces had all but disappeared.

Unsicherheit, Location and the Life Course

If the issue of return was part and parcel of competing political strategies in Bosnia-Herzegovina, this does not imply that returnees were powerless pawns in the hands of local and foreign authorities. Put simply, most DPs understood the FIA safety-cum-property policies for what they were, and they made provisions in case they were evicted from occupied accommodation by signing up for return programs. With reconstruction assistance targeted at cross-IEBL minority return, most of the Izgled population fell into this category. While the Savićes reflected this pattern in Bistrica, we saw how it was much less common among Serbian DPs in 2001. Later, many Serbs actually lamented having 'missed the boat', often couching their frustration in the wider stereotype of Bosniacs as shrewd instrumentalists and 'pets' of the FIAs (Jansen 2003). In any case, I found that, rather than blindly serving as guinea pigs in the making of Dayton Bosnia-Herzegovina, returnees had usually weighed, to the best of their knowledge, the risks and opportunities of returning versus staying put. The recent experience of 'ethnic cleansing', the subsequent losses, and the generalised precariousness of Bosnia-Herzegovina made people wary about subjecting their loved ones and themselves to the risks associated with full-time minority return. So, aware that the FIAs also tended to bet on several horses at once, notably by encouraging return and coexistence *and* consolidating wartime territorial conquests in two Entities, Bosnian DPs hedged their bets. Next I explain how they went about making the return process theirs.

DP households assessed concerns of security and opportunity in relation to varying degrees of fear, homesickness, political pressure, financial assistance, local and transnational networks, and so on. As we saw, actual minority return was a matter of degree, with systematic age-related differences. By January 2001, 80 per cent of minority returnees belonged to social categories that were considered 'non-threatening' by the dominant forces in the majority group (United States Committee on Refugees 2001: 6). There was a gender imbalance, with men of 'military age' underrepresented due to wartime disappearance (especially among Bosniacs in northeast Bosnia-Herzegovina) but also due to fear of revenge and perhaps reluctance to face responsibility. However, the above figure mainly indicates a predominance of elderly people, and the smallest commitment to return was consistently found among young, upwardly mobile parents (Lukić and Nikitović 2004: 102; UNHCR 2003). In addition to safety concerns, FIAs tended to explain this within a sedentarist paradigm in reified culturalist portrayals of elderly, rural Bosnians desperate to return to their land. Likewise, the Savićes and Mirsad Mehmetović indicated that elderly persons were dying to return and returning to die, but they related this pattern more specifically to intra-household relations and generational dynamics conditioning insertions into political-economic structures. I now take their lead to interpret differential decision making about whether to return or not, and to what 'degree', in terms of people's positioning in the life course and in social relations-in-process in the peculiar Bosnian context.

Following Freud, Zygmunt Bauman (1999: 17) uses the German term *Unsicherheit* to encompass all three of the following dimensions: insecurity (what one has learned and achieved may not remain valid and valuable), uncertainty (what one knows may not be a sufficient basis to make decisions) and unsafety (one may be subject to physical harm). He points out that under neoliberalism, the state is increasingly reluctant to even pretend that it deals with the first two and effectively privatises them, thus reducing all anxieties of Unsicherheit to safety issues only. I found an amplified version of this in Bosnia-Herzegovina. There was still widespread fear of living in an area under political and police control of national Others, and many local authorities purposively maintained this fear. But, as in Bistrica and Izgled, foreign protection had made most return sites relatively safe, and potential returnees were well informed about this.[7] Hence FIA return policies did take responsibility for safety, but due to their focus on restitution of property they rendered security and certainty private concerns, beyond the realm of what politics could or should engage with. Once Bosnian society was successfully 'reformed', these private concerns would be regulated by 'the market'.

However, home is more than just shelter from physical harm (see Hage 1997: 102ff.), and anxieties about coexistence and minority status, as well as about livelihood in postwar Bosnia-Herzegovina, led most households to be careful about the 'degree of' their return. Return patterns thus reflected a new political-economic geography, as the IEBL had recon-figured maps in both practical and imaginative terms and reallocated places to a new type of marginality. This became an integral part of everyday considerations among displaced Bosnians, and, compared to their prewar lives, returnees often shifted what could be called their *Sicherheits* horizon following the Entity logic of Dayton Bosnia-Herzegovina. Hence, in contrast to a prewar Zvornik orientation, Izgled returnees now relied entirely on the Tuzla area for health services, education, administration, economic activity, and so on. A foreign donor had reconstructed a school in a nearby village, but obstruction by the RS authorities and by the returnees themselves had ruled out its use for the foreseeable future.[8] In Bistrica there were no returnee children, but life was now almost exclusively oriented towards Zvornik as opposed to Tuzla. Most returnees in both places still carried documents of the other Entity and many retained an occupied property there, effectively straddling the IEBL. This often involved collective household strategies whereby elderly, retired family members returned to settle permanently in their prewar village, whereas the younger ones engaged at most in part-time return. When confronted by employees of foreign agencies or anyone perceived as such, people tended either to deny this situation or explain it as temporary. However, it seemed that few had any intentions of disambiguating the process voluntarily.[9]

Such household strategies constituted an insurance policy against excessive Unsicherheit, crucial for those still bearing the scars of war-related displacement and facing the precariousness of postwar Bosnia-Herzegovina. On the one hand, signing up for return and hence qualifying for reconstruction assistance was an opportunity to repossess property and to make actual return possible. On the other hand, keeping one foot in the other Entity limited exposure to the risks associated with minority return, and it allowed the maintenance of networks and engage-ments built during displacement. In practice, strategies often simulta-neously included conflicting strands: seeking to retain occupied property in the area of displacement, obtaining reconstruction assistance for return to a certain degree, and seeking emigration to a Western state.[10] In Bosnia (and in Serbia, Croatia and Kosovo) I have as often been approached by DPs for help with assistance for reconstruction and return as I have been for help with their visa application, or, if that had failed, buying my passport. Crucially for my argument here, these were often the same people.

If dreams and acts of return were strongly intertwined with intra-family relationships and generational phases, these in turn should be understood in relation to socioeconomic conditions in Bosnia-Herzegovina. The combination of war and 'transition' has brought down living standards dramatically, and minority returnees were doubly hit by towering unemployment due to discrimination on the shrunken labour market.[11] But their situation was extremely contradictory. On the one hand, many returnees resented being thrown back into a peasant existence of attempted self-sufficiency and de facto dependency on aid. On the other hand, the enforcement of 'reforms', justified with a promise of 'entry into Europe', encouraged those unwillingly re-peasantified Bosnians to simultaneously increase other – this time capitalist – expecta-tions of modernisation (see Chase 2002; Ferguson 1999).[12] Faced with this contradiction, the vast majority of displaced Bosnians I got to know over the years, wherever they were, considered the Bosnian home they once had to be irrevocably lost. Rather than longing to return to the locality where that home – usually captured in terms such as 'a normal life' – had been experienced, they relied on a mixture of resignation and mourning. Many nostalgically recalled a typically Bosnian way of life, hinged upon a sociality in the context of the relative Sicherheit of the socialist Yugoslav federation. Regardless of their feelings on socialism and nationalism, most concurred that their previous lives had been much better than their current ones (of course, disagreement existed as to who was to blame for that). But the point was that that 'normal life' was gone, and few had illusions of time travel to a past home. Moreover, they themselves had changed, as ongoing societal transformations interacted with changes in the life trajectories of particular individuals in particular households (see Jackson 1995: 126). Positioning in the life course and in social relations-in-process are therefore crucial considerations in understanding why Joka and Živko Savić celebrated their return home with unambiguous joy, whereas Mirsad Mehmetović did not see a future in Izgled.

The case of the Savićes (and of mother Mehmetović) indicates that for some elderly persons minority return constituted a feasible option. While it would be exaggerating to call this a 'homecoming to the future' (Stefansson 2004a), their trajectory was not entirely out of tune with their prewar expectations. Certainly, Joka and Živko had thought their retirement would be much more comfortable, but city life, remember, could not tempt them. While their circumstances were infinitely more miserable than they could have foreseen, to a degree they did have the planned quiet life of retirement, tending the garden around the family house. They had returned full-time to a reconstructed house in Bistrica, supported by three children who had households of their own and who were, to their relief, alive and doing fine given the circumstances. Their daughter lived in Serbia and their sons, who had received assistance too, remained in Zvornik: one in his own property and the other in an occupied Bosniac-owned flat. The elderly couple had no schooling concerns, and when in need of health care, they called on their sons. The Savićes had retired before the war and were not dependent on the labour market. Of course, with the average pension standing at less than US$90 in the Federation and less than US$60 in RS, this was hardly a position of economic comfort (*Oslobođenje*, 30 October 2000: 4). Still, their return simultaneously allowed the couple to spend their remaining years 'at home' and the wider household to repossess property with minimal Unsicherheit for all involved. To a sufficient degree, return to Bistrica allowed them to live as the persons they imagined and were expected to be – it allowed a socially embedded emplacement of that personhood.

Others, like the Savićes' children and Mirsad Mehmetović, found themselves in another stage of their life course and faced different predicaments in terms of the emplacement of their personhood. Mirsad, Enisa and their daughters retained occupied Serbian-owned accommodation in the Tuzla area, visiting Izgled on weekends and holidays. Only Mirsad's mother lived in Izgled permanently. Even regardless of safety considerations, if 'returning home' meant eking out a life through subsistence farming, few adults with children and younger people in general considered this a feasible option. The few who, like Mirsad, were employed in nearby towns, were endangered by contractual precariousness and, given the location of such jobs across the IEBL, often had even less reason to commit to permanent return to areas without any livelihood opportunities (see Green 2005; Holt 1996; Jansen 2002, 2006a). In the initial phases of minority return this problem was rendered less prominent by the need for reconstruction labour: most men (whose numbers, I recall, had been decimated in Izgled) were engaged in building houses, while women, who were involved in the former in less visible ways, also ran the households and engaged in small-scale agriculture for household consumption. But what would these people do afterwards? This question was strongly gendered as, in the absence of their fathers, young men like Mirsad were confronted with a particularly sharp discrepancy between the lack of opportunity in the precarious Bosnian economy and even greater expectations to be breadwinners than had already existed previously in these patriarchal households. Mirsad Mehmetović had been a young man living with his parents in 1990, and ten years later he had lost his father and had become a married father of two. The experience of war and displacement had brought the loss of loved ones and livelihoods, as well as new responsibilities to construct 'cool ground' from which to build a future for his household. Having been expelled almost a decade earlier, Mirsad believed emigration could be a way to reduce his household's exposure to Unsicherheit and to start fulfilling their reformu-lated expectations of 'modernisation'. He mentioned that perhaps he would retire to Izgled, but it was clear that, at least for now, the place did not afford him the 'sense of possibility' to construct his envisaged and expected personhood as a young father, as it resisted a socially embedded emplacement of this personhood.

Conclusion

In this chapter I have analysed the workings of people's stage in the life course in the emplacement of home in early postwar Bosnia-Herzegovina, through the prism of personhood and the tensions between opportunities and expectations in particular local contexts. While elderly displaced Bosnians were more likely to yearn for and to actually remake home in their prewar place of residence, many others, especially younger ones with children, straddled official categories as they focused on the practicalities of having to make home for their households. What is 'cool ground' for the former may not be 'cool ground' for the latter, because home is not simply a shelter from unsafety, but also a base where insecurity and uncertainty can be reduced and confronted (Bauman 1999: 17; Hage 1997: 102ff.). After the war, most people in Bosnia-Herzegovina felt they were worse off than they had been before and, perhaps even more important, worse off than they had ever imagined they would be. Some, of course, hailed what they considered to be the 'liberation' of their nation (Jansen 2003) but, given the precariousness that pervaded postwar Bosnia-Herzegovina, this was rarely considered as sufficient reason for celebration or for so much as a generally positive outlook. Still, in their own ways, competing nationalist discourses did provide sources of some sense of security and certainty to many people. FIA return policies, on their part, represented an interweaving of the sedentarism of the nationalisms they were meant to oppose with a mantra of 'reforms'. Their neoliberal reluctance to even engage with wider concerns of Sicherheit, reducing home merely to safety and property, failed to appeal as an alternative for most Bosnians. With little to compensate for the massive changes in their lives, many felt forced to start all over again, if not for themselves, then at least for their children. Now, if this was what was required, and if they themselves, the society in which they lived, and the particular locality where home had once been grounded had been radically transformed, it is no surprise that many considered starting over again in a different place altogether. In fact, many of the refugees who had returned to Bosnia-Herzegovina in the glow of early postwar enthusiasm had soon focused their energy on regaining access to a foreign state. Hence, particularly people who had invested heavily in starting new households, with great responsibilities to others, saw return not as a restorative but as a transformative process on the societal, household and individual level. If they had to start over again anyway, they reasoned, they might as well *also* look for 'cool ground' in a place without the handicap of a postwar Bosnia-Herzegovina location. Thus, while the desire for a 'normal life' might entice some to return, the more common scenario involved 'searching for better places, where the possibilities of leading a normal life were deemed to be more realistic' (Stefansson 2004b: 182).

My study has highlighted the complex social nature of the building of such 'cool ground'. Clearly, the patterns I exposed contained a dimension of economic strategising for material benefits, but an eye for the dynamics of life trajectories and the transgenerational social webs in which they exist refutes reductionist interpretations. My analysis of the role of the life course highlights forms of personhood (channelled through relations of kinship and gender) that may or may not be successfully articulated in place-making projects and that condition people's insertion into a societal context. A dynamic political economy of home as an affective construct that can only be approximated thus casts light on why many Bosnians combined various strategies in their search for 'cool ground'. They were confronted with multilayered, prolonged precariousness caused by war and by 'transition'. As in other, not war-affected, neoliberalising contexts of intensifying Unsicherheit, their search for 'cool ground' often included more reactive elements of risk avoidance and of protecting some vestiges of worth, than of proactive instrumentalism. Hence, the experiences of displaced Bosnians are best understood through an approach that retains the significance of place in home, but infuses it with the dynamics of developing social relations and political–economic transformation. People's imaginings and acts of return were inextricably linked to a 'sense of possibility', and the perceived potential of a location for the emplacement of their personhood conditioned effective coping with Unsicherheit and, more positively, the creation of a social base for recognition, and, ultimately, for hope. Rather than reducing home retrospectively to a remembered site of *be*longing, we should also analyse it prospectively as a socially constituted object of longing.

Acknowledgements

I thank the people of Bistrica and Izgled for their hospitality. Also thanks to Staffan Löfving, to anonymous reviewers, and to other colleagues who provided constructive criticism when I presented this work at the Sarajevo *Centar za ljudska prava* (Bosnia-Herzegovina), at the Max Planck Institute for Social Anthropology (Germany), at the University of Maynooth (Ireland), at the Universities of Manchester and Leeds, and at UCL (UK).

Notes

1. I carried out long-term ethnographic research among displaced Bosnians in northeast Bosnia-Herzegovina, Serbia, Australia and The Netherlands (2000–01) in a project developed with Andy Dawson and financially supported by the Toyota Foundation, the Leverhulme Trust and the University of Hull. Pseudonyms are used for persons and villages. All translations are mine. Following local use, I refer to 'Internally Displaced Persons' as DPs and 'Bosnian' is short for the non-national term 'Bosnian-Herzegovinian'. An earlier version of this text appeared in *Focaal: Journal of European Anthropology* no. 49 (2007).

2. I use the term 'foreign intervention agencies' to refer to Western-led intergovernmental structures and to major so-called non-governmental organisations, most of which are dependent on the same governments to all intents and purposes. The use of this blanket term reflects representations among Bosnians and foreign personnel alike. The latter preferred the even more problematic term 'international community', as did the mainstream media. Except in contexts controlled by precisely those FIAs, most Bosnians tended to refer to *stranci* (the foreigners), sometimes specifying the state in question.

3. While I spent many afternoons with Joka Savić, gender segregation was strong in rural Bosniac-inhabited places like Izgled. Except for interactions with elderly women, such as the owner of the house-in-reconstruction containing the bare concrete room where I stayed, I mostly socialised with Izgled men, helping on the building sites during the day and talking and playing football in the evening. Younger women were often present too but retained a distance from an unmarried foreign man such as myself. I thus refer to Mirsad Mehmetović's story on an individual basis, but relate it to his role as husband and father.

4. All figures, unless otherwise indicated, are UNHCR (United Nations High Commissioner for Refugees) statistics (see www.unhcr.ba).

5. In a 1997 survey, 22.5 per cent of Serbs said they wished to return, as compared to 80 percent of Bosniac respondents (UNHCR/Commission for Real Property Claims 1997). With many returned already, a 2003 poll among Bosniac DPs in Tuzla found that 55 per cent stated a wish to return to RS (UNHCR 2003). Note that the interviewers were usually perceived as exercising control over the allocation of assistance, thus limiting respondents' likelihood to exclude return entirely.

6. A UNHCR/Commission for Real Property Claims survey (1997) found that 84 per cent of all DP respondents reluctant to return said they wished to live in a town. Studies of return migration outside of Bosnia-Herzegovina have also highlighted urban relocation; even returnees to rural areas rarely engage in agriculture (Gmelch 1980).

7. E.g., through daytime return visits, contacts with other returnees and/or former neighbours, DP associations, media reports. Some ignored this information if it contradicted nationalist representations (Jansen 2003).

8. In 2001, 85 per cent of Bosniac returnee children in RS went to school in the Federation (United States Committee on Refugees 2001: 6).

9. In 1999 an estimated 60 per cent of all reconstructed houses were inhabited (Cox 1999: 232). However, in contrast to a militant hard core (see Jansen 2003), many DPs privately expressed not only resignation at the prospect of eviction

from occupied accommodation, but also agreement with the principle. They did not want to live 'in a stranger's house', but they saw no alternative.

10. An estimated 250,000 people left Bosnia-Herzegovina in the first five postwar years. In a 2001 poll, well over half of respondents aged eighteen to fifty stated they would emigrate if they could (UNDP 2004: 54).

11. A 2000 survey among returnees to RS found that only 5 per cent were employed (UNHCR 2000a). Particularly vulnerable were widows and single mothers, elderly and disabled persons (UNHCR 2000b).

12. I substitute 'modernisation' for Ferguson's 'modernity' in order to describe the transformative dynamics involved. Ironically, a common channel for successfully engaging with those expectations was through contacts, experience and funding in FIA jobs.

References

Albert, Sophie. 1997. 'The Return of Refugees to Bosnia-Herzegovina: Peacebuilding with People', *International Peacekeeping* 4(3): 1–23.

Allcock, John B. 2002. 'Rural-Urban Differences and the Break-up of Yugoslavia', *Balkanologie* 6(1–2): 101–34.

Al-Rasheed, Madawi. 1994. 'The Myth of Return: Iraqi Arab and Assyrian Refugees in London', *Journal of Refugee Studies* 7(2–3): 199–219.

Bauman, Zygmunt. 1999. *In Search of Politics*. Cambridge: Polity.

Black, Richard. 2002. 'Conceptions of 'Home' and the Political Geography of Refugee Repatriation: Between Assumption and Contested Reality in Bosnia-Herzegovina', *Applied Geography* 22(2): 123–38.

Bougarel, Xavier. 1996. *Bosnie: Anatomie d'un conflit*. Paris: La Découverte.

———. 2005. 'Dayton: Dix Ans Après: la Leurre des Bilans', *Critique Internationale* 29: 9–24.

Chase, Jacquelyn. 2002. 'Privatization and Private Lives: Gender, Reproduction, and Neo-liberal Reforms in a Brazilian Company Town', in *The Spaces of Neoliberalism: Land, Place, and Family in Latin America*, ed. Jacquelyn Chase, pp. 119–40. Bloomfield, CT: Kumarian Press.

Cox, Marcus. 1999. 'The Dayton Agreement in Bosnia-Herzegovina: A Study of Implementation Strategies', *British Yearbook of International Law* 70: 201–43.

D'Onofrio, Lisa. 2004. 'Welcome Home? Minority Return in South-East Republika Srpska'. *Sussex Migration Working Paper* No. 19, University of Sussex. http://www.sussex.ac.uk/migration/1-3-3.html.

Duijzings, Ger. 2002. *Geschiedenis en herinnering in Oost-Bosnië: De achtergronden van de val van Srebrenica*. Amsterdam: Boom/NIOD.

Ferguson, James. 1999. *Expectations of Modernity: Myths and Meanings of Urban Life on the Zambian Copperbelt*. Berkeley: California University Press.

Fischel de Andrade, José H. and Nicole B. Delaney. 2001. 'Field Report: Minority Return to South-Eastern Bosnia, a Review of the 2000 Return Season', *Journal of Refugee Studies* 14(3): 315–30.

Gardner, Katy. 1995. *Global Migrants, Local Lives: Travel and Transformation in Rural Bangladesh*. Oxford: Clarendon.

Gmelch, George. 1980. 'Return Migration', *Annual Review of Anthropology* 9: 135–59.

Green, Sarah. 2005. *Notes from the Balkans: Locating Marginality and Ambiguity on the Greek-Albanian Border*. Princeton: Princeton University Press.

Hage, Ghassan. 1997. 'At Home in the Entrails of the West: Multiculturalism, "Ethnic Food", and Migrant Home-building', in *Home/world: Space, Community, and Marginality in Sydney's West*, ed. Helen Grace, Ghassan Hage, Leslie Johnson, Julie Langsworth, and Michael Symonds, pp. 99–153. Annandale: Pluto Press.

Holt, Julius. 1996. 'Looking Beyond the Towns: Facts and Conjectures about Rural Returnees in the Ogaden and "Somaliland"', in *In Search of Cool Ground: War, Flight and Homecoming in Northeast Africa*, ed. Tim Allen, pp. 143–52. Oxford: James Currey.

Ito, Ayaki. 2001. 'Politicisation of Minority Return in Bosnia-Herzegovina – the First Five Years Examined', *International Journal of Refugee Law* 13(1–2): 98–122.

Jackson, Michael. 1995. *At Home in the World*. Durham: Duke University Press.

Jansen, Stef. 2002. 'The Violence of Memories: Local Narratives of the Past after Ethnic Cleansing in Croatia', *Rethinking History* 6(1): 77–93.

———. 2003. 'Why Do They Hate Us? Everyday Serbian Nationalist Knowledge of Muslim Hatred', *Journal of Mediterranean Studies* 13(2): 215–37.

———. 2005a. *Antinacionalizam: Etnografija Otpora u Zagrebu i Beogradu*. Beograd: XX Vek.

———. 2005b. 'National Numbers in Context: Maps and Stats in Representations of the Post-Yugoslav Wars', *Identities* 12(1): 45–68.

———. 2005c. 'Who's Afraid of White Socks? Towards a Critical Understanding of Post-Yugoslav Urban Self-perceptions', *Ethnologia Balkanica* 9: 151–67.

———. 2006a. 'The (Dis)comfort of Conformism: Post-war Nationalism and Coping with Powerlessness in Croatian Villages', in *Warfare and Society*, ed. Ton Otto, Henrik Thrane and Helle Vandkilde, pp. 433–46. Aarhus: Aarhus University Press.

———. 2006b. 'The Privatisation of Home and Hope: Return, Reforms, and the Foreign Intervention in Bosnia-Herzegovina', *Dialectical Anthropology* 30(3–4): 177–99.

———. 2007. 'Remembering with a Difference: Clashing Memories of Bosnian Conflict in Everyday Life', in *The New Bosnian Mosaic*, ed. Xavier Bougarel, Elissa Helms and Ger Duijzings, pp. 193–208. London: Ashgate.

Lockwood, William. 1973. 'The Peasant-Worker in Yugoslavia', *Studies in European Society* 1: 91–110.

Long, Lynellyn D. and Ellen Oxfeld (eds.). 2004. *Coming Home? Refugees, Migrants, and Those Who Stayed Behind*. Philadelphia: Pennsylvania University Press.

Lukić, Vesna and Vladimir Nikitović. 2004. 'Refugees from Bosnia and Herzegovina in Serbia: A Study of Refugee Selectivity', *International Migration* 42(4): 85–110.

Markowitz, Fran and Anders Stefansson (eds.). 2004. *Homecomings: Unsettling Paths of Return*. Lanham, MD: Lexington Books.

Papić, Žarko (ed.). 2001. *Policies of International Support to South-east European Countries: Lessons (not) Learnt from Bosnia-Herzegovina*. Sarajevo: Open Society Institute.

Phillips, James. 2004. 'Repatriation and Social Class in Nicaragua', in *Coming Home? Refugees, Migrants and Those Who Stayed Behind*, ed. Lynellyn D. Long and Ellen Oxfeld, pp. 150–69. Philadelphia: Pennsylvania University Press.

Philpott, Charles. 2005. 'Though the Dog Is Dead, the Pig Must Be Killed: Finishing with Property Restitution to BiH's IDPs and Refugees', *Journal of Refugee Studies* 18(1): 1–24.

Phuong, Caroline. 2000. '"Freely to Return": Reversing Ethnic Cleansing in Bosnia-Herzegovina', *Journal of Refugee Studies* 13(2): 165–83.

Schierup, Carl-Ulrik (ed.). 1999. *Scramble for the Balkans: Nationalism, Globalism and the Political Economy of Reconstruction*. Basingstoke: Macmillan.

Stefansson, Anders. 2004a. 'Homecomings to the Future: From Diasporic Mythographies to Social Projects of Return', in *Homecomings: Unsettling Paths of Return*, ed. Fran Markowitz and Anders Stefansson, pp. 2–20. Lanham, MD: Lexington Books.

———. 2004b. 'Refugee Return to Sarajevo and Their Challenge to Contemporary Narratives of Mobility', in *Coming Home? Refugees, Migrants and Those Who Stayed Behind*, ed. Lynellyn D. Long and Ellen Oxfeld, pp. 170–86. Philadelphia: Pennsylvania University Press.

Turton, David. 1996. 'Migrants and Refugees: a Mursi Case Study', in *In Search of Cool Ground: War, Flight and Homecoming in Northeast Africa*, ed. Tim Allen, pp. 1–22. Oxford: James Currey.

UNDP. 2004. *Early Warning, Quarterly Report (January–March 2004)*. Sarajevo: UNDP.

UNHCR. 2000a. *Returnee Monitoring Study: Minority Returnees to Republika Srpska*. Sarajevo: UNHCR.

———. 2000b. *Daunting Prospects. Minority Women – Obstacles to Their Return and Integration*. Sarajevo: UNHCR.

———. 2003. *Survey on DPs in Tuzla Canton from the Podrinje Area, RS*. Tuzla: UNHCR.

UNHCR/Commission for Real Property Claims. 1997. *Return, Relocation and Property Rights*. Sarajevo: UNHCR/CRPC.

United States Committee on Refugees. 2001. *Country Report BiH*. Washington: USCR.

Zetter, Roger. 1999. 'Reconceptualizing the Myth of Return: Continuity and Transition amongst the Greek-Cypriot Refugees of 1974', *Journal of Refugee Studies* 12(1): 1–22.

3

THE LOSS OF HOME

From Passion to Pragmatism in Cyprus

Peter Loizos

In 1974, following twenty years of intermittent political conflict in Cyprus, there was a military confrontation between the Greek Cypriots and Turkey, which ended with the Greek Cypriots being driven out of 36 per cent of the island, Turkey remaining as an occupying power speaking for the Turkish Cypriot minority. Many Greek and Turkish Cypriots in the island suffered losses and became displaced. In effect, within a few months of the ceasefire of August 1974, the island, an ethnic patchwork until 1963, and then a territory violently disputed between the two main groups in many different sites, was violently divided into two nearly homogeneous ethnic zones: a zone occupied by Turkey in the north with Turkish Cypriots within it, and a Greek Cypriot zone in the south. The main focus here is on how the Greek Cypriots of Argaki – a mixed village near Morphou in the northeast of the island – dealt with loss of village, houses and land, and the diverse and shifting meanings of 'home' during their thirty-year exile. The key argument involves their changing perceptions of their priorities and their reactions to a UN-brokered peace plan. At the start of their 'protracted exile' (Zetter 1994) the Greek Cypriot refugees were understandably obsessed with the loss of their homes, and they were clear and certain that they wished to return to them 'on their knees if need be'. By the time nearly thirty years had elapsed, a majority of them voted to reject a political settlement that would have allowed half the displaced people to return over a period of years to their original homes. They believed that a 'better' UN plan would then become possible.

The kinds of time factors involved in their changing perceptions were several. First, there was what we may call their personal 'experiential time' – the amount of time each person had passed in the community from which they had been displaced, and the kinds of social, emotional and economic local commitments that lived time had involved. The suggestion is that experiential time influenced individual perceptions of the desirability of 'return'. In Greek Cypriot culture, both men and women typically experience four main statuses, which are linked to biological and social maturation: childhood, youth, marriage with dependent children, and old age, when children have reached independence. These life stages are more discriminating than the standard label for refugees as first or second 'generation'. They are a refinement of the postfunctionalist attempt to generalise a 'developmental cycle' for the family, household or domestic group. As refugees grew older, they became less oriented to the homes they had lost, and more oriented to where their children and grandchildren were now living. Secondly, there was the time of 'protracted exile' – a durational time dating life from 1974, the year of displacement, and marking the number of years spent as refugees, living in the shadow of an unresolved 'Cyprus Problem'. During this durational time, individuals were inevitably influenced by the ways the political elite defined exile, and future policies towards it. There was a trend towards a politics of ethnic consensus antagonistic to Turkey, as the source of the displacement, and unwilling to accept a legal role for Turkey in the future of the state. Finally, there was their perception that the actual UN constitutional package on offer at the time was not the best deal they could hope for, and that a 'better deal' could be expected later.

Displacement and Localised Identity

As the editors make clear in the introduction, there have been lively debates in recent years on how far anthropologists in general, and students of refugees in particular, have been blocked in their understanding of migrants by their traditional aptitude for studying face-to-face communities with sedentary lifestyles. Since from early in the discipline anthropologists studied people who moved – hunter-gatherers, pastoralists, shifting cultivators and Gypsies – and since every trainee anthropologist learns this during apprenticeship, it seems unlikely that most practitioners are deeply insensitive to the fact that the sedentary life has never been a plausible human universal.

But some of us in our apprentice fieldwork missed possibilities for appreciating the contingent nature of the links between locality and identity (Appadurai 1995). My own 1968 study of Argaki village did not give much weight to marriage into towns or other villages, or assess the significance of migration from the village. A household survey was carried out that asked questions linked to these issues, but the responses never got the analytic attention they deserved, partly because of my restricted focus on one single village, partly because informants emphasised the village as a moral community and partly because four out of every five marriages were between two Argaki-born partners. So it was easy to lose sight of marital, labour or status-seeking migration, and thus to focus exclusively on the solidary village and to forget the implications of marginal movements. The dominant theoretical focus was on the political solidarity of the village, striving to manage the divisiveness of links to national politics (Loizos 1975).This does not materially affect the analysis of those who were displaced in 1974, except to note that some of them sought refuge with kin who had already migrated and who were not refugees in the eyes of the state, although they had also lost access to their natal communities and any property therein.

In the first fifteen months of their displacement Argaki Greeks again emphasised the lost village and their painful feelings and real-time difficulties of living without it. Both men and women were shocked to find themselves in improvised accommodation, cut off from the land that gave many of them their livelihoods, with dependent children to provide for, disaggregated and dispersed in many sites (Loizos 1981).

Although Greek refugees formed a national association, as well as a number of local associations, they did not emerge in national politics with a 'refugee party', and their votes tended to be distributed across the main four national parties that have dominated the republic for the last thirty years. These parties were consulted by the president of the day in the national council, and it is fair to say that there was a consistent line followed by the national politicians from shortly before the death of President Makarios in 1977 until recently. This line insisted on the right of all refugees to return to their homes, formally including Turkish Cypriots, and in principle accepted that a future state would be a bi-zonal and bi-communal federation (Palley 2005: 1–3).

The objects of Greek Cypriot diplomacy were to seek the international community's assistance in persuading Turkey to leave the island. This Turkey refused to do. The Cyprus problem was an ethnic conflict, a mobilised nationalist inability to share power peacefully, and two conflicting zero-sum visions of how the island should exist. Turkey now insisted that these problems had been 'solved'. It demanded that the Greek Cypriots let go of their illusions of dominance and dreams of *Enosis* (political union with Greece) and accept 'faits accomplis' – facts on the ground. It insisted that the Turkish occupation zone was now a state but could not persuade other states to recognise it, since Article 2(4) of the UN Charter prohibits the use of force by a third party for solving problems of secession.

Since 1945, several states had occupied parts of neighbouring states, or entities, and not been made to withdraw: Israel in Palestine and Syria, India in Goa, Indonesia in Irianjaya. The Argaki refugees lived the early years of displacement hearing their leaders make angry speeches condemning Turkey and insisting on the moral clarity of the Greek refugees' right of return. But many, even in 1975, sensed that return was unlikely. While hoping for a magical door to open that would restore them to what had been, for many, days of good fortune, they started to rebuild their lives and livelihoods as best they could.

Precisely because the national rhetoric presented Greeks as blameless victims of Turkey's ambitions and aggression, and because, in a very real way, the majority of Argaki people had done little or nothing to contribute directly to their fate, the loss of home became represented in daily discourse as a matter of deep injustice: Turkey had no justification for its actions, and that was that. Few raised their voices or questioned this collective 'line' for many years, and those who did, did it quietly rather than publicly.

This led to a situation where what people said in public tended to conform closely to the line taken by the national council. Listening to Greek Cypriots' talk about these issues was a little like being in a Communist country prior to 1989 – public uniformity was standard. They might say different things in private. This was particularly the case with the refugees and their rehousing. Roger Zetter (1982, 1986) has pointed to the paradox of a national claim that all the refugees were to return, supported by a public housing program for the poorer refugees that put them in specially designed housing estates that had the air of permanence and were visibly different from, and inferior to, the houses Cypriots would build for themselves, and to which the state granted them no title. Having crossed the threshold of such homes, I can say that the Argaki refugees tended to tell me apologetically, 'This is a refugee house.' In Greek the same word *to spiti* has to cover both 'house' and 'home' in English. Many visitors to refugees in Cyprus report that they have been told very forcefully, whether in English or in Greek, '*This* is not my *home* … My *home* is in Kyrenia' (Hadjiyanni 2002; Jordan 1999). The only reason such things were not said to me was because I knew where their prewar homes were, and they knew I knew.

The meaning of this insistence was intimately linked to powerful feelings of injustice and loss. But what implications do such statements have for the middle and longer term? No matter how strongly someone hopes for and believes in the likelihood of their return, how much or how little in terms of decorating and making your 'temporary' residence comfortable do you do? And for how long? What kinds of investments do you or do you not make (Zetter 1999)? At what point do you start to feel in some way that it really has become your home? Some Argaki refugees told me after twenty-five years that they had become accustomed to thinking of the place they now lived in as home. They tended to have been those who were younger – under twenty – in 1974, who had spent less of their lives working in and (as one says in Greek) 'living' Argaki.

It is clear to me that as time went by, people started to treat their lived environment more and more like home in the following quotidian senses: they decorated their dwellings and they cultivated their gardens; they got to know their neighbours, although some said they had not made good friends among them; they entered into sociable relations with local shopkeepers. Had these primary refugees (men and women from fifteen to twenty and above in 1974) been asked by outsiders – journalists, foreign politicians and diplomats – if they now regarded the places they lived in as their homes, or their proper homes, or their permanent homes, many of them would have answered, 'No, *my home* is Argaki, Morphou.' But this would have been an identification of their attachment with their place of origin and an emphasis on property rights and the injustice of being made 'homeless' in 1974, legitimate at the time it first happened, amplified by many years of national repetition of grievance, injustice and victimhood. The hurt congealed in the wounds of the mind.

So, there are public discourse answers, and rather different private discourse answers, defined by contexts and whether or not one is, for the moment, 'representing' the refugees as a whole and 'speaking for the nation', or telling someone more privately how things seem to you in an imperfect world.

It seems to have been the case that Turkish Cypriots living in the north who were allocated Greek houses in zones they believed stood a probable chance of being returned to the Greeks, tended not to invest much in the properties. Casual inspections of a few homes in Akcay (as Argaki is called in Turkish) lead me to think that this was the case. A competing explanation might have been the relative poverty of the Turks living there, and the relative lack of investment undertaken by the Turkish authorities.[1]

Factors That Mitigated Displacement

The loss of the village was a loss of easy daily sociality as well as property. The men would see hundreds of other men, many of whom were relatives, daily in Argaki's coffee shops and taverns. Card playing was a favourite male recreation, as was *tavli* (backgammon). So, the men lost the village as a series of open clubs. The women lost the companionship of neighbours, and having kinswomen and in-laws living within a mile, always a legitimate reason for a visit when work patterns permitted.

This loss looked absolute at first sight, in the sense that the village of fifteen hundred souls dispersed into twenty-five different sites in Cyprus, and a dozen or more families permanently emigrated to the USA, UK, Canada and Australia. Sets of siblings found themselves in different towns and villages. These were definite costs, and people mentioned them with feeling.

But this longer-term adjustment of the Argaki refugees to the loss of the village was – in the cold light of analysis – somewhat softened by two kinds of technological changes, fruits of rapid modernisation of market and state infrastructure. As Zetter (1992) has argued, the Greek Cypriot governments of the late 1970s and early 1980s, following the Emergency Plans of the Planning Bureau, invested in infrastructural projects because they could deploy refugee labour while making an investment in future development. This meant that a series of good motor roads soon linked the main towns of the island and the larger villages. At the same time, due to rapid economic development from the late 1970s and throughout the 1980s, motor car ownership became very widespread very quickly. This meant the pains of separation were somewhat alleviated, for a mixture of state and market reasons.

The second technology 'fix' was market led, not state led. This was the rapid diffusion of the telephone to every household. The rise of the mobile phone was not yet foreseen. Refugees rarely mention these changes themselves – they are taken for granted, part of the *habitus*, nearly invisible. But an analyst must note their consequences for managing separation.

Of course, the refugees would have preferred to have acquired cars and telephones without losing their community. They would probably have acquired such goods some years earlier had they not been displaced, and had the national economy continued on the growth trajectory of the early 1970s. That is not in question. I am simply saying – making sociology and anthropology social sciences as 'dismal' as economics – that these separations would have been worse in a premodernised society, or one where economic development moved more slowly, or went backwards, as it did in post-socialist Europe, between 1989 and 1995. There was an 'economic miracle' in Cyprus that is only now running out of fuel. It often served the refugees well (Christodoulou 1992; Strong 1999).

One other point to keep before us: back in the village the core unit for production and consumption was the nuclear family living in its own house, with or without attached parents of one partner or the other. In practice, these units experienced forced migration together. The nature of displacement for the Greek Cypriots did not permanently fragment family households. Although a breadwinner might depart for months at a time seeking income, the basic integrity of the household and nuclear or extended family was stressed and strained but not disrupted to the point of rupture. There was no increase in marital separations among Argaki refugees. This is important as a step in the next part of the argument.

Revisiting the Village

When, after twenty-nine years as refugees, there again seemed a chance that a UN initiative might allow the Argaki refugees to return to their village, many discussed the practicality of returning in thoughtful and unsentimental ways. The Argaki Greeks had taken a close interest in what had happened to their houses and orange groves. There were a few opportunities for news to travel. A Turkish Cypriot wedding video involved a drive around the village to show off the bridal pair. A copy of this video found its way into the south and was passed from family to family among Argaki Greeks, so that the current condition of the village could be appraised. Everyone hoped to see their own home. One adventurous Argaki businessman, with a British passport, took himself to the north (something most Greek Cypriots at that time were nervous of doing), hired a taxi and was driven to Argaki. His impressions were soon all around the Argaki diaspora. He was reported to have become 'dizzy' because familiar places had become so unfamiliar. Some people heard that their orange trees had dried out, or in some cases been cut down and the land put to other uses. Numbers of old mud-brick houses had collapsed, with or without local encouragement, when they became dangerous to children.

So, people were reflecting in practical terms on how exactly they would manage were they to return. Livelihood issues and respective age were important too. Briefly, those who had lived and worked in Argaki as adults, had invested in homes and fields, were most concerned with the idea of a possible return. They were more oriented to the past, the lost village and lost properties. Those who had been younger, and left the village either as children or as young unmarried adults, tended to have matured and made their livelihoods as refugees away from the village, away both physically and mentally. They were more future oriented. Those with dependants were less willing to consider a move that might leave them without a means to earn their living.

A sense of these differences can be grasped from considering a few situations in depth: Petris and Maroulla HajiChristodoulou had had three children under the age of ten when they left Argaki (Loizos 1981: 129–31). He was nearly forty, she in her early thirties. In the first two years away from Argaki, they had lived in Stroumbi village, in Paphos, where Petris had worked as a tailor, and Maroulla had found any agricultural work she could get. Later they decided to come and live in the Turkish Quarter of Paphos, near Maroulla's parents. They had found a reasonably modern formerly Turkish Cypriot house and settled in. Petris ran a coffee shop for a while, and then they started renting land and growing early vegetables for North European markets. Their children had grown up, and shown an aptitude for study. One daughter had married and opened a tourist restaurant. A son had studied engineering in Bulgaria and returned with a Bulgarian bride. They found jobs locally. Another son had studied electrical engineering and returned with ideas about how to develop the use of plastic hothouses for growing not vegetables, which many other people were doing, but flowers: there are hundreds of tourist hotels in Cyprus and they tend to want fresh flower displays on dining tables. This business flourished because the son, Christos (who had been about five in 1974, and so had lived his formative years away from Argaki) worked at it with great energy. His father and mother joined him – Petris had lost interest in the coffee shop, and the flowers were obviously more rewarding. Christos married a young woman who was happy to manage the accounts of the business.

In 2003 we had several discussions about the possibility of the latest UN peace initiative – the Annan Plan – coming into effect. Christos had used Turkish Cypriot land for the flower business. He was quite sanguine. He explained that if he were required to compensate the Turkish Cypriot owner, he could do it by bringing him into the business as a sleeping partner. His mother, however, wanted him to agree that if Argaki again became available to them, they would move back as a family. His first reaction was to emphasise the difficulties of dismantling a flourishing business, and starting it up from scratch somewhere else, and moving house. The discussion went on for some time. In the end, to keep his mother happy, he said he was sure they would find a way to return to the village. But although he may have temporarily convinced her, he was being diplomatic. He was a very effective and ambitious businessman, and to break down a successful business and transport it to another place without the supports and with new marketing logistics problems would not have made sense to him. It would have been a major step backwards.

One way to summarise what was happening, year by year, was to look at children and grandchildren. Over the course of three decades of displacement, many old people died and were buried near their displaced children. As Zetter has noted (1999), the desire to be able to visit parental graves divides those whose parents were buried in the prewar village from those whose parents have died in the new locations. But, as Colson (1971) noted, ancestral graves in a new settlement site become reasons for starting to see the new residence site as no longer 'new' but as now containing the protection of the ancestors. Greek Cypriots did not worship their ancestors, but they did revere them.

Children who were in primary school pre-displacement grew into maturity as refugees, learned to make new friends, and, without knowing they were doing it, came to regard their social world as normal, not exile, no matter how often their parents reminded them of the lost village (Constantinou 2004). Some of these children internalised the idea that the people of Argaki were an exceptional set of people. They learned to take pride in their origins, as had the children questioned by Tassoulla Hadjiyanni (2002). But although these thoughts had been derived from a *place*, the collectivity of Argaki people survived in diaspora, and were to be seen and heard from at weddings, which were sometimes high-powered and high-spirited affairs, and at funerals, inevitably sober and more reflective. *Pace* Zetter (1999), the villagers continue to celebrate weddings and funerals without residing in the village because their relations with each other were only *contingently* derived from the village. They were derived at a deeper level from the non-local bonds of marriage, consanguinity, friendship and shared memories of past proximity. I leave it to others to decide if this continuity represents preservation of a previous community identity, or the creation of a new, or renewed one. To me, the issue is more formal than substantive.

The children and grandchildren of the primary refugees, however much they sought to maintain economic rights and benefits from government, have made their lives where they are, and while they empathise with their parents, and would like them to have the closure they wished for when they sought to return, do not themselves wish to 'return' to somewhere that means less to them than where they are now. Before they were able to visit the village, these younger people expressed curiosity about it, and some said they would like to experience the rich, dense social life their parents had often mourned and commemorated in their hearing. They might comment critically on the character of social relations in the place they were currently living in, but few spoke as if they would have wished to return with their parents. They were where they were.

Crossing the Line

On 23 April 2003 the authorities in the north of Cyprus took everyone by surprise, by announcing a unilateral readiness to relax movement controls on the line that had divided the two communities since August 1974. During the previous twenty-nine years there had been all kinds of restrictions on movement. There were a few controlled crossing points, and permission had to be sought by Greek Cypriots to go to the north. Few sought permission, both because their own government discouraged them from doing so, and because many had doubts about their security in the north, as a result of the way many Greeks had been treated in Turkish hands during and after the war. Turkish Cypriots had similar reservations about visiting the south, and their regime usually discouraged individual movement. Nevertheless, as the years went by, and the war and its horrors became an ever more distant memory, Turkish labourers started to come across to seek work in the south, at first a trickle, then some hundreds, and finally several thousand. There were also visits made by bi-communal peace groups, groups of teachers, of journalists, and other professional and artisanal groups, sometimes arranged by the trade unions, sometimes by peace activists. Such visits had also been faciliated by the UN in the small strip of territory it administered, known variously as the Buffer Zone and the Dead Zone. Such short-term visits were liable to veto at short notice, particularly from the Turkish side. The Turkish leader Rauf Denktash in general wished to discourage bi-communal contacts as pointless, and to insist that as long as the Greek Cypriots diplomatically obstructed the recognition of his regime, the Turkish Republic of Northern Cyprus (TRNC), nothing should be done that could be interpreted as a gesture of goodwill towards Greek Cypriots. At times, however, he could suspend this formally hostile stance. Greek Cypriot refugee groups, and nationalist lobbyists, would also picket the Ledra Palace checkpoint and try to deter both tourists and Greek Cypriots from crossing to the north.

Thus, for the vast majority of Greek Cypriots, the north was for nearly thirty years a zone they could not or did not visit, and those few who did, did so under clouds of suspicion from their own people. For Greek Cypriot refugees, not being able to live in their villages of origin, work their lands, operate their factories and businesses was a matter both of emotional pain and severe economic disadvantage. For non-refugee Greeks, and for non-refugees in the Armenian community, being denied the right to visit over one-third of the island, parts of which were of religious significance (such as the Monastery of Apostle Andreas in Karpassia, or the Armenian monastery called Surp Magar, another place of outstanding natural beauty in the Kyrenia mountains), were deprivations they shared with the refugees, even though their lives had not usually been so seriously disrupted. When, in recent years, trips to the shrine at Apostle Andreas were permitted, it proved to be a focus of great emotion for the devout.

For some time prior to the relaxation of movement control, there had been a major build-up of political pressure in the TRNC. The first signs had been a series of demonstrations in July 2000 after most of the banks had collapsed, linked as they were to banks in Turkey that were similarly in turmoil. The demonstrations brought thousands of people into the streets in a way that had been unusual in the north, and once they started to demonstrate, they did not stop. Cyprus was entering the last stages of a process that was designed to allow the enlargement of the European Union, and the Republic of Cyprus had put in its application many years previously, had been studiously completing the chapters of formal acceptance of EU laws, and would enter Europe on 1 May 2004.

The EU's hope was that the two communities would settle their differences and enter Europe as a single federal entity. But as the countdown started, it became clear that Denktash had serious doubts about the wisdom of such a policy and started to raise major difficulties about it. He wanted the entity known as the Turkish Republic of Northern Cyprus recognised before negotiations for entering Europe could proceed.

The younger and more educated Turkish Cypriots had wearied of life in an authoritarian polity with an underperforming economy, and looked to entering Europe as the chance for a brighter future. There was also a sense that the bloodletting of the past was now a long way behind them, and that it might be possible to enter into a political arrangement with the Greek Cypriots that would work for both sides. Thus, what started out as demonstrations of exasperation over bank collapses, corruption and political cronyism, transformed into a movement for democracy, peace with the Greeks and entry into the EU. It went in for ever more confident mass demonstrations that were clearly threatening to Denktash's legitimacy and policies. As this oppositional chrysalis became an attractive butterfly, Denktash began to look increasingly like Yesterday's Man (Navaro-Yashin 2003).

The sudden announcement that crossing points would be opened found the Greek Cypriot leadership off balance. They did not know what to make of it and suspected it was some kind of Trojan horse, whose deeper meaning was obscure but from which trouble might result. That was my first reaction, too. Accordingly, they temporised. But Greek popular reactions left the Greek politicians looking confused, for in a short time many thousands of Greek Cypriots presented themselves at the Ledra Palace checkpoint seeking to visit the north, with Turkish Cypriots in large numbers wishing to come south. There were queues that required many hours' patient waiting before the Turkish and Greek police could complete their formalities and allow people in. The media coverage was both local and international, and for some days there was a great deal of excitement. People in the queues looked happy and expectant.

What did it mean? Some commentators were quick to suggest that Denktash hoped the movements would lead to unpleasant incidents that would once again provide negative evidence about Greek–Turkish relations. This did not happen. Days, weeks and months went by without serious incidents, and in this period there were many thousands of contacts between Greek and Turkish Cypriots that passed off in an unremarkable and sometimes heart-warmingly good-tempered manner.

People crossed the line for all kinds of reasons (see also Demetriou 2004; Dikomitis 2005). Mature refugees were keen to see their former homes, and in some cases to make contact with old friends from whom they had been separated by state-designed policies. Sometimes they were accompanied by children who had never seen these homes but had heard a lot about them. Non-refugees of mature years wanted to visit again parts of the island they had enjoyed before the war, like Kyrenia, Famagusta and Karpassia, and reconnect with their memories, or enjoy the pleasures of landscapes long missed in their own right. There were youngsters, refugees and non-refugees, who had grown up hearing the school-led discourse of a 'Divided Homeland' who said they wished to visit those parts of 'their fatherland' which had been artificially kept from them until now.

The deep ambivalence of the Greek Cypriot leadership to the new situation was soon apparent. Politicians started pronouncing judgementally on what should and should not be done by Greek Cypriots who went to the north. It was suggested that they should not spend the night there, that they should not spend money there, that they should not use restaurants or hotels that belonged originally to Greek Cypriots.

Ambivalence was also noticeable at the level of private individuals and within families. The first issue people had to decide about was whether or not to go. For some weeks, when people met each other in the workplace, or in the street, or spoke on the phone, the first question was, 'Have you been?' If it was a conversation between two people from the same community, i.e., from Argaki, then the question was about having been to the village itself. There were significant numbers of people who announced that they would not go because this would involve 'showing their passport to Denktash' – this was the first line of refusal. Later, after some months, those still refusing to go declared that they did not wish to go and 'be offered coffee in their own homes'. They could not accept the status of a guest or visitor to the houses they had once lived in, now occupied by a Turkish Cypriot or, even more difficult, a mainland Turkish settler. In some cases, an Argaki man or woman who had at first stated that they would not go, had to sit at home while their spouse went, and then after some time, relented, and made a visit.

There was an atmosphere of optimism in the air, particularly among the Greek and Turkish Cypriot peace activists. International television news coverage outside Cyprus gave the event a very positive spin. For some weeks it looked as if something fundamental was about to change, and change for the better. The Greek Cypriot state television service started sending news teams across the line daily, following individuals and recording their reactions. The coverage would show friendly encounters between Greeks and Turks, and do quick interviews with individuals about how they felt about the new situation and its implications. Some coverage showed Greek Cypriots visiting churches and cemeteries. Some of these had been well preserved and protected; others had been neglected and perhaps sometimes vandalised. The music on the soundtrack played over men and women looking unhappily for parental grave sites was usually very harrowing and portentous.

Other accounts of visiting and revisiting across the line show all kinds of highly emotional attempts to reengage with lost communities: a church renovated in a quiet way in one place (Dikomitis 2005), a portfolio of thoughtful photographs that show settlers from Turkey not as threatening and predatory interlopers but as quiet, unassuming people caught in the usual predicaments of making livings and making lives (Philippou, personal communication).

Many Argaki visitors agreed that the village proved smaller in reality than in their memories. They tended to complain that the village looked poor and run down. People were sad and bitter if their orchards had died or been cut down, or their houses collapsed or modified. The critical comment tended not to give the Turkish residents much benefit of the doubt. The general upshot of the comments was that the village had gone downhill, been spoiled, become Turkish, was now in Turkey – was in fact a huge disappointment. Those who felt this way said they would not wish to make a further visit. But these judgements, although made with the cultural certainty that Greek Cypriots favour, often proved unstable. Some people who said they would not visit a second time found themselves doing so. Some people who had said they would not go at all, later gave in to curiosity. The new line of defence tended to be that they had visited their former homes but had not liked what they had found. To reduce these attitudes and actions to a clear idea – people were often uncertain, ambivalent, and changeable. The direction of change went from open and positive to more closed and negative. Perhaps, as Zetter (1999) implied, some contradictions had finally been resolved, and some illusions had been dispelled. Perhaps the Argaki Greeks were finally, and clear-headedly, living in the present as present, in 'real time', painfully real time?[2]

People were aware of how warmly or coolly they had been received, and those who were courteously and sensitively received often made a point of mentioning it. One Turkish Cypriot woman had kept a package she had been given for safekeeping unopened for twenty-nine years, and returned it to its rightful owner, and there were other equally heart-warming incidents. There were, inevitably, also stories of cold receptions, of doors slammed in faces with the words, 'Go away. This is our house now.'

Christos Pelavas made a number of visits to Argaki, and on one of them an elderly Turkish Cypriot, Ali Hoja, produced a photo he had been waiting to give to the right person. It was a strange photograph, with drops of muddy rain water on it in places, but when he saw it, Christos was immensely happy to have it. It showed his mother, his father, and his father's seven brothers. He had not seen it before and he found it very moving. Now he could have it reproduced and distributed to all his five brothers and sisters, and perhaps to the larger cousinhood, all the children of the men in the photo. Christos was impressed both by the photo and what it meant, and by the fact that Ali Hoja had taken the trouble to keep it for so long. That was a sign of being '*athropos*', which in Cypriot dialect means a really decent human being.

On that visit to the village, we were sitting with a group of older Turkish Cypriots, men from Argaki, and some from Potamia, when one of them offered the following explanation for why the village had lost its Greeks, why the island had ended up divided. 'Greece and Turkey gave us weapons, and we put each other's eyes out', he said. As a rigorous explanation, it left a great deal to be desired, but as a gesture of sympathy and goodwill it could hardly have been improved upon. The lifting of movement restrictions had made such exchanges possible, even if that was not its primary intention.

Two years after the opening date, there was still a significant number of Greek Cypriots who had not made at least one visit – perhaps as many as 40 per cent – but the number was slowly declining.

Among those who had visited, the range of reactions was wide. Several people returned in a state of shock. A 35-year-old woman described her father's visit to Famagusta like this: 'When he came back, he could not speak for nearly a week. When finally he did speak, he said, "I think we should simply build a wall between us and them."' Another Famagusta man, a customs officer of mature years who did not want his name to be used, told the following story:

I knew I didn't really want to go because I felt very strongly about it all, but my daughter, who had been hearing about it all her life, wanted very much to go, and I felt I didn't want her to go alone, so I went with her. I found my way quite easily – I remembered the streets and what they looked like and I found my own street, and drove up to my house and started to put my car into the garage without thinking what I was doing. *Two Turks came out and started shouting at me and I was in Intensive Care the same night.*

Not everyone could get something positive from crossing the line and revisiting the past. But many could, and did. Thirty years' separation and a climate of entrenched antagonism at the leadership level still had not extinguished positive attitudes among particular individuals towards their former neighbours. Small human gestures – a package kept unopened, a photograph preserved, a banknote pressed into a pocket, a bottle of brandy gifted quietly, hugs, laughter, a good memory retained and remembered – were testimonies to losses that had not been willed by the people who made these gestures but who, being few in numbers and with lesser power, had been unable to stop the inertial tectonics of separation.

The Referendum of 1 May 2004

The referendum of 1 May 2004 was a drama for both Turks and Greeks, and one that obsessed everyone on the island for many months. It divided both ethnic communities deeply, and within each community it often led to heated debates within families, and within groups of friends. No attempt was made to deal with the legal niceties of the plan, which had been drafted by lawyers and would have involved the attachment of 7,000 pages of EU laws for its implementation. Most Cypriots read newspaper summaries of a few thousand words. A summary of the 'Property Regime' of the plan produced by the Peace Research Institute of Oslo and designed to clarify issues for the voters, ran to forty pages. The aim here is to convey refugee perceptions, a sense of what was at stake and the sorts of contexts that seem to have influenced people's decisions.

The Referendum of 1 May 2004 was a consultation on the Annan Plan, the most recent of numerous United Nations attempts to resolve the conflict between the two divided communities by producing what would have amounted to a peace treaty and a constitutional agreement to found a new federal state, a United States of Cyprus, bi-zonal and bi-communal (Palley 2005).

Turkey was required to release some 9 per cent of the island's territory, reducing the zone reserved for Turkish Cypriot (and Turkish settler) residence to 25 per cent. The Greek zone would thus have increased to 75 per cent, as the Buffer Zone, the 2 per cent under UN control, would be reabsorbed by the two constituent states. The plan envisioned a phased reduction of Turkish soldiers on the island over many years, and a dissolution of the Greek Cypriot National Guard.

The property issue was to be dealt with in rather complex ways. The Greek Cypriots in the returned Greek-administered zone would get their property back but would not be able to return until fresh provision had been made for the Turkish occupants. For the remainder of formerly Greek Cypriot land, there was a formula that would allow the current occupant to retain the property if he or she had spent more on it since acquisition than it had originally been worth in 1974. If this was not the case, the Greek Cypriot owner had a theoretical right to reinstatement, or compensation.

But there were to be restrictions on the number of Greek Cypriots who could return as residents in the Turkish Cypriot Constituent State. The formula would allow the oldest back first and, with the passage of time, the next oldest cohort, but with a maximum of 7 per cent Greek returnees being accepted in any given village, rising to 14 per cent after eleven years (Palley 2005: 166). For those not able to repossess and reside in their properties, there was to be compensation. Argaki Greeks would have got all their properties back, as they would have returned to a zone that would have been wholly within the Greek Cypriot Constituent State.

During the year in which the process of consulting the political decision makers was unfolding, there were five versions of the plan, with what in retrospect were thought to be some highly significant changes. In the last weeks, new points were announced in the media, but voters discussed them, as did their leaders, against a timetable that was moving ever closer to 1 May, the day when the Republic of Cyprus was due to enter the European Union. The liberal internationalists of the UN and the EU hoped that the referendum would lead to a United Cyprus, as did many Greek and Turkish Cypriots.

Why Most Greek Cypriots Voted 'No'

A referendum vote is an aggregate of thousands of individual decisions, but decisions taken in an overwhelmingly social context. It goes without saying that different sections of the population had different reasons for how they voted, and this is not the place for a detailed analysis.

In brief: Greeks voted no for many reasons, and not all for the same reasons. Some voted no because they believed in what they had learned in school: 'Cyprus is a Greek island, and must not be divided.' They saw the Annan Plan as compromising that vision of Cyprus. Many voted no because 1974 had left them with a deep fear of Turkey and a mistrust of that state's future intentions. They believed that the Annan Plan would allow Turkey to continue to dominate the island, and that it would swamp it with Turkish settlers. Others, young people not yet born in 1974, voted no because they had been deeply disturbed by seeing on television, in August 1996, the murder of a Greek Cypriot by a mob of Turkish extremists, and the shooting of his cousin, at Deryneia. These young people had also had a state education in antagonism towards Turkey, and they were the highest proportion of rejectionists. Others voted no tactically because they felt the plan could be improved and that they would have better opportunities in the future to extract concessions from Turkey and did not believe the liberal internationalists' claim that this was a 'last chance'. And many who might have voted yes, voted no because the Communist Party, AKEL, told them to do so.

Mainland Greeks had said no to Mussolini's humiliating military ultimatum in 1940 and fought a successful war against the Italians. This was their last occasion for military pride. Greek Cypriot nationalists said no to various British constitutions and took pride in their armed struggle to free the island from colony status. The year 1974 was a major blow to Greek Cypriot pride, and a painful humiliation. It was the end of twin illusions about Greece as Destiny and the power of Greece to protect them. Saying no in 2004 to Turkey, the USA, the UK and the UN while at the same time saying yes to Greek Cypriot entry to the EU had a 'fatal attraction' partly because of its historical resonances and partly because it was an act of collective self-assertion. Subsequent analysis showed that only fractionally more refugees voted yes than did the general population.

More prosaically, it could be said that Annan Plan's Version Five (the plan went through five modifications from its first public presentation until the final referendum vote) simply did not offer the Greek Cypriots enough. The two key moves that would have allowed a majority of them to support it would have been: (1) a shorter timetable for the total withdrawal of the Turkish Army; and (2) an unequivocal right of return for all refugees. Turkey probably appreciated this perfectly well, and by adding conditions at the last minute that would push the Greeks in the opposite direction, Turkey appeared to be choosing to take the short-term gain of being the party saying yes to Annan, thus climbing out of the moral quagmire that its 1974 overkill had created, without losing control of the north, a powerful bargaining chip on the issue of its own long-hoped-for entry to the EU. But it is possible that Turkey had no such intentions – we will have to wait for the diplomatic historians to unpack this issue.

The timetable for withdrawal would have been conditional on steady and peaceful progress, and the unequivocal right of return would not have been exercised by a significant proportion of the Greek refugees, as they would have been apprehensive about living in a Turkish-administered space.

A large number of Greek Cypriots were deeply apprehensive about how things might go after an agreement. The new state looked like a risky leap in the dark with a fear of either rapid escalation of political conflicts, or unpredictable economic costs that would be borne by the Greeks, as victims of 1974, where they felt that Turkey, as the 'aggressor', should have been compensating them.

With the long view, the thirty-year view, one can see that the time for a peace treaty and a fresh start was much sooner, and that the longer the antagonistic separation continued, the more people became both schooled in enmity and secure in the reduced state they rebuilt in the south of the partitioned island. The shock and humiliation of 1974 was too great for the Greek leadership to transcend.

The knife of partition remained fixed in the wound of the Greek body politic. What the Greeks were finally offered by the international system seemed to 75 per cent of them to be too little, and too late. The other 25 per cent certainly had their doubts, but they were prepared to gamble on times having changed and the practicality of a fresh start.

Conclusion: The Loss of Home – From Passion to Pragmatism

It is possible to distinguish several phases in Argaki Greek Cypriot feelings and thoughts about 'home', and to distinguish different sets of people whose age and obligations at the time of displacement also shaped perceptions. Much of my recent research has been on a cohort (a term with less ambiguity than the fuzzy 'generation') who were adults with dependent children in 1974, that is, they were typically aged twenty-five to fifty. They had 'lived' the village, grown up in it and invested labour in property there. They found the overnight loss of this property painful and temporarily disorienting, and all declared for many years that they would return to Argaki if the opportunity arose. After they had been refugees for fifteen or twenty years, had created new livelihoods, and become used to the places they were now living in, they could be heard to express thoughts about return having to be something they would have to think about and weigh up. Later still, in years twenty-five to thirty of their exile, they could refer to the difficulties that would arise because their children and grandchildren were well established in the south. And once they got a chance to see the village as it was in 2003, their perceptions of return seem to have shifted dramatically. They came to see the village as decisively 'spoiled' and the dream of return as now chimerical. The best anyone could suggest was that if their properties became available to them again they could use them at weekends or for a summer holiday.

For people who had been young children before 1974, the pull of the village was much less powerful. They spoke of not giving up their 'human rights' to the property their parents owned there, and they accepted the parental view of Argaki people as an especially good sort of people. They tended to share parental disappointment with the actual village when they visited it. They saw their parents as primary victims of an injustice but tended to say that they themselves had been less affected by the dislocation. These generalities do not account for every individual perception. But since a majority of Greek Cypriots and a majority of all the Greek refugees voted against the plan that would have allowed many of the refugees to return, even though a substantial minority would have wanted the opportunity to do so, we can see the divisions even though we cannot break them down as far as we would like to. In my view these differences were driven, first, by political ideas – mistrust of Turkey, for example – rather than the sociological variables of class and education. Secondly, refugees from regions that would have remained in Turkish Cypriot control would have been more likely to vote against the plan, and those from Morphou and Famagusta (towns in the 9 per cent of territory that would be transferred to Greek Cypriot control) to vote for it. But at the end of the process, if my argument about Greek Cypriots' orientation to children and grandchildren, to the present and the future, is correct, the simplest answer is that the Annan Plan came 'too late' for refugees. The simplest answer is not, of course, the whole answer, as this chapter has tried to make clear. A political agreement needed to have come in the first ten years of exile, before the older refugees had remade their livelihoods, and before their children had developed school peer groups and grown up in particular neighbourhoods. The plan was 'too little' for all Greek Cypriots in terms of meeting security fears, fears of failing to cooperate successfully with the Turkish Cypriots, and the desire to remain in control of their own smaller state and their own lives, rather than take fresh risks.

Notes

1. For further material on the Turkish Cypriots and their specific responses to the political upheavals of the period under discussion, the reader may consult Bryant 2004; King and Ladbury (1982); Navaro-Yashin (2003); Oberling (1982); Patrick (1976); Scott (1995).
2. For it has been suggested by Volkan and Itzkowitz (2000) that the Greeks as a people have shown themselves incapable of accepting the reality of losses of territory, and that they continue to dwell psychologically in the past rather than the present. 'Real time' is an expression used by media editors to distinguish between events being broadcast as they happen, in an uncut, unedited form, and recordings of past events that have been edited. 'Real time' is a continuous unedited present.

References

Appadurai, Arjun. 1995. 'The production of locality', in *Counterworks: Managing the Diversity of Knowledge*, ed. Richard Fardon, pp. 204–25. London: Routledge.

Bryant, Rebecca. 2004. *Imagining the Modern: The Cultures of Nationalism in Cyprus*. London and New York: I.B. Tauris.

Christodoulou, Demetrios. 1992. *Inside the Cyprus Miracle: the Labours of an Embattled Mini-Economy*. Minnesota: University of Minnesota Press.

Colson, Elizabeth. 1971. *The Social Consequences of Resettlement: The Impact of the Kariba Resettlement upon the Gwembe Tonga*. Manchester: Manchester University Press.

Constantinou, Costas. 2004. 'The Differential Embodiment of Home: an Ethnographic Study on Constructing and Reconstructing Identities among Refugees in Tahtakallas'. Master's Thesis in Sociology, Intercollege, Nicosia.

Demetriou, Olga. 2004. To Cross or Not to Cross? Subjectivisation and the Absent State in Cyprus. Paper presented at the International Studies Association Annual Conference, Montreal, Canada.

Dikomitis, Lisa. 2005. 'Three Readings of a Border: Greek Cypriots Crossing the Green Line in Cyprus', *Anthropology Today* 21(5): 7–12.

Fosshagen, Kjetil. 1999. '"We Don't Exist": Negotiations of History and Identity in a Turkish Cypriot Town'. Thesis submitted for the Cand. Polit degree, Department of Social Anthropology. University of Bergen.

Hadjiyanni, Tassoulla. 2002. *The Making of a Refugee: Children Adopting Refugee Identity in Cyprus*. New York: Praeger.

Jordan, Andrew. 1999. 'A Cypriot Tragedy and a New Identity: Analysing Refugee Assistance Programmes and Their Impact on Cultural Relationships in post-1974 Cyprus'. Thesis submitted for the Master's Degree in the Department of Anthropology, University of Durham.

King, Russell and Sarah Ladbury. 1982. 'The Cultural Construction of Political Reality. Greek and Turkish Cyprus since 1974', *Anthropological Quarterly* 55: 1–16.

———. 1988. 'Settlement Renaming in Turkish Cyprus', *Geography* 73: 363–67.

Loizos, Peter. 1975. *The Greek Gift: Politics in a Cypriot Village*. Oxford: Blackwell.

———. 1981. *The Heart Grown Bitter: a Chronicle of Cypriot War Refugees*. Cambridge: Cambridge University Press.

———. 2000. 'Are Refugees Social Capitalists?', in *Social Capital: Critical Perspectives*, ed. Stephen Baron, John Field and Tom Schuller, pp. 124–41. Oxford: Oxford University Press.

Navaro-Yashin, Yael. 2003. '"Life is dead here": Sensing the Political in No Man's Land', *Anthropological Theory* 3(1): 107–25.

Oberling, Pierre. 1982. *The Road to Bellapais: The Turkish Cypriot Exodus to Northern Cyprus*. Boulder: Social Science Monographs.

Palley, Claire. 2005. *An International Relations Debacle: the UN Secretary-General's Mission of Good Offices in Cyprus, 1999–2004*. Oxford and Portland, Oregon: Hart Publishing.

Patrick, Richard A. 1976. *Political Geography and the Cyprus Conflict, 1963–1971*, ed. James H. Bater and Richard Preston. Waterloo, Ontario: Department of Geography, University of Waterloo.

Scott, Julie. 1995. 'Identity, Visibility and Legitimacy in Tourism Development in Northern Cyprus'. Unpublished Ph.D. dissertation, University of Kent at Canterbury.

Strong, Paul. 1999. 'The Economic Consequences of Ethno-National Conflict in Cyprus: the Development of Two Siege Economies after 1963 and 1974'. Ph.D. London School of Economics and Political Science, University of London.

Volkan, Vamik and Norman Itzkowitz. 2000. 'Modern Greek and Turkish Identities and the Psychodynamics of Greek-Turkish Relations', in *Cultures Under Siege: Collective Violence and Trauma*, ed. Antonius Robben and Marcelo Suarez-Orozco, pp. 227–47. Cambridge: Cambridge University Press.

Zetter, Roger. 1982. 'Housing Policy in Cyprus – a Review', *Habitat International* 6(4): 471–86.

————. 1986. 'Rehousing the Greek Cypriot refugees from 1974', in *Cyprus in Transition 1960–1985*, ed. John Koumoulides, pp. 106–25. London: Trigraph.

————. 1992. 'Refugees and Forced Migration as Development Resources', *The Cyprus Review* 4(1): 7–39.

————. 1994. 'The Greek-Cypriot Refugees: Perceptions of Return under Conditions of Protracted Exile', *International Migration Review* 28: 307–22.

————. 1999. Reconceptualizing the Myth of Return: Continuity and Transition amongst the Greek-Cypriot Refugees of 1974', *Journal of Refugee Studies* 12(1): 1–22.

4

THE SOCIAL SIGNIFICANCE OF CROSSING STATE BORDERS
Home, Mobility and Life Paths in the Angolan–Zambian Borderland

Michael Barrett

When the young man Reagan arrived at the UNHCR reception centre in Kalabo Town in Zambia's Western Province in the final days of the twentieth century, he did so not merely as an 'Angolan refugee'.[1] In fact, without denying the turmoil and suffering that occasioned thousands of Angolan citizens to cross the border into Zambia, I would argue that this label obscures many facets of the predicament in which Reagan and his family found themselves in Zambia. It fails to convey that Reagan was a fiancé and a young provider for his extended family, an experienced cross-border trader, and once a member of the irregular government civil defence forces. Rather than being an indicator of shared experience, the 'refugee' label thus hides many existential components. These include cross-cutting social relationships in and of the borderland, regional historical practices of mobility and integration, ethnopolitical identification, differential economic and political power and, finally, differences related to gender and age – the particular positions of individuals in social life and in individual life trajectories.

This chapter explores the social significance of crossing state borders in Southern Africa with a particular focus on the Angolan–Zambian borderland. By comparing the fate of Reagan and other Angolans who arrived in Zambia in 1999 with established Mbunda families in Kalabo District, their family histories and social relationships, I show the inadequacies of the conventional understanding of mobility across state borders that is embedded in the humanitarian discourse on refugees. The value of anthropological analysis of these themes, I suggest, hinges on careful scrutiny of the presuppositions that we bring to the fore in trying to understand the relationships and practices involved in border crossing.

Recent reviews have clearly shown how the adoption of categories from a policy context (e.g., humanitarian aid and international law) threatens to undermine the viability of the anthropology of migration and mobility in this context (Englund 2002: ch. 1; Turton 2003). I argue that a phenomenological and intersubjective approach to mobility promises not only to reiterate the relevance of the subdiscipline but also, more importantly, to restore the agency and humanity in our portrayals of people who for any reason are compelled to leave their home.

The setting of the chapter is Kalabo District in Zambia's Western Province, where I conducted fieldwork during a total of one year spread out between 1998 and 2003. This is a region that has until recently been beset by large numbers of migrants originating mainly from neighbouring Angola's Moxico Province. The civil war in Angola raged between independence from Portuguese colonial rule in 1975 and 2002, oscillating in its intensity and in the fortunes of the warring sides – the Angolan government forces (FAA) and the rebel movement UNITA.[2] During the late 1990s, towns and areas in the eastern part of Angola were often sacked and lost and then sacked again in turn by the two overstretched armies. Although these were acts of low-intensity warfare, each created an immense chaos, sending villagers and townspeople into the bush, disrupting the cycle of agriculture and impeding livelihood.

Although dominated by the Lozi (or Barotse) chiefdom and ethnic group, who generally claim the status of 'owners of the land', Western Province is a historically multiethnic area with a large proportion of people known by the Lozi label *Mawiko*, 'peoples from the West' (sing. *Wiko*). Under this ascribed label are lumped together people who call themselves Mbunda, Luvale, Luchazi and Chokwe, and who are, to varying degrees, culturally, linguistically and historically associated with the ancient Lunda kingdom in what is today the Democratic Republic of the Congo (DRC). However, today these peoples live in three states: Angola, DRC and Zambia. Almost all of the 'Angolan refugees' in Kalabo and Western Province belong to these ethnolinguistic categories and are thus both socially and culturally related to many 'Zambians' living in the area.

Because of large-scale migrations of both seasonal and more permanent nature between areas which today belong to two different polities (Angola and Zambia), mobility has come to pervade many aspects of social life in the area. These historical circumstances are probably why a majority of migrants arriving in western and north-western Zambia over the last forty-five years have opted to stay as 'self-settled refugees' in Zambian villages rather than going to the established settlements (Bakewell 2000a; Pritchett 2001). According to Hansen, who conducted research in Zambian Luvale villages in the 1970s, 'the refugees may be seen as only the latest phase in the continuing migration of these people along the same routes throughout this [the twentieth] century' (Hansen 1979: 371).

Beyond Identity in the Borderlands

Anyone familiar with life in an African border region must be struck by the limits of the current humanitarian discourse as a model to understand people on the move in borderlands. The established terminology of 'refugees', 'repatriation' – 'voluntary' or 'spontaneous' – makes little sense to most borderland people, at least not the sense that we as external observers might expect. A review of the Southern African literature on borderlands shows that the humanitarian logic has other imperatives (and maybe rightly so) than to describe the nitty-gritty reality of the people receiving their assistance (Bakewell 2000b), that to appreciate the life worlds of refugees and migrants calls for close attention to social relationships, life trajectories and personal narratives (Englund 2002; Powles 2002), and that the very distinction between 'economic migrant' and 'refugee' is sometimes beside the point (Lubkemann 2002). Perhaps unsurprisingly, then, the language of the metropolitan system of nation-states differs significantly from the vernaculars of the world's peripheries (Scott 1998) also in Southern Africa. This type of critique amounts to an established anthropological genre with some historical record (Hansen 1979; Harrell-Bond 1986; Malkki 1992). In a parallel movement, anthropologists have highlighted the importance of transnational linkages and regional dynamics in borderlands (Alvarez 1995), where, especially in postcolonial situations, geopolitical borders are often bridged by social relations organised around ethnicity, kinship and religion (Bakewell 1999; Hansen 1979; Harrell-Bond 1986; Mamdani 1998).

Instead of viewing social belonging as necessarily and unequivocally adhering to particular places, studies on transnationalism have posited 'global ethnoscapes' as an image of the contemporary movement of people across borders and over the world (Appadurai 1991). This position has come increasingly under fire in recent years, as ethnographers have reaffirmed the reality of geopolitical borders in the life worlds of the peoples with which they work (McDermott Hughes 1999) and the psychological consequences for people dispossessed of statehood (Navaro-Yashin 2003). In the words of McDermott Hughes (1999), for the Mozambican migrants/refugees crossing into Zimbabwe during the 1990s, the politically soft and permeable border envisioned by some theorists was in fact both 'hard and constraining' and helped to further entrench established patterns of exploitation of migrants (see also McGregor 1998: 37 for the Mozambique–South African border). It would seem that the current conditions that have enabled the free movement of goods, people and ideas have simultaneously produced the circumstances for the immobility of many others (Ferguson 2002; Geschiere and Meyer 1998; Navaro-Yashin 2003).

Following these debates, we may formulate two arguments against conventional positions on displacement that have plagued not only applied and policy-oriented research but also anthropology as a whole.

Firstly, I reiterate the now familiar critique against the reductionism of the 'national order of things' in which 'refugees', defined by national identity, are simply people out of place in this order. Sometimes this line of argument leads to even more simplistic notions of a single 'refugee experience'. Secondly, I argue against the opposite view, no less reductionist in its consequences, that advances either the utter unimportance of state borders or their irrelevance in the face of alternative (primordial) identities – sometimes supported by notions of 'border cultures' spanning territories separated by state borders.

Put simply, the preoccupation with identities (ascribed or primordial) that these perspectives exhibit precludes the possibility of perceiving migrants as actors (Turton 2003). In my view, the objectives outlined in the introduction to this volume (to investigate the humanitarian assumptions of distinctions between forced and non-forced migration, the role of different forms of violence, and the relationships between place and home/belonging) call for a change of focus from identities to the actual social practices and personal relationships of borderland dwellers and their experiences of mobility as they pursue their lives and livelihoods. Consequently, I suggest that an anthropology of borderlands informed by an awareness of the potential fluidity or rigidity of geopolitical borders and the identifications associated with them, must take a two-pronged approach. In what follows, I thus analyse life in borderlands as determined, on the one hand, by the reality of borders as manifestations of an international system of 'nation-states' and, on the other hand, by political and cultural economies of regional, historical interrelationships between people that straddle those borders. Here we should also consider the relations of global capitalism, which are often starkly articulated in borderlands by these two paradoxical processes.[3]

Borderlands as Path Space

If we are to appreciate the complexity of life in borderlands in terms that highlight contradictory relationships and landscapes rather than fixed identities and territories, we need to espouse a particular view of space. Such a perspective must depart from the abstract, yet simplistic, mathematical notions of space that often dominate (among other domains) humanitarian discourse. Home, in such a view, is simply a demarcation of space, a fixed point to which people naturally adhere. That borderlands, like any landscape inhabited by humans, are constituted by social landscapes and not merely geographical (in the sense of mathematically defined) space, comes as no surprise to anthropologists (see, e.g., Cohen and Atieno Odhiambo 1989; De Boeck 1998; Ingold 2000; Jackson 1989; Lovell 1998).[4]

The concept of social landscapes refers to the potentials and the limits of social relationships in a particular social setting, the horizon of possible and culturally sanctioned relationships situated in a physical landscape (see Cohen and Atieno Odhiambo 1989; Crehan 1997: 227f.; Lovell 1998). Such a view of landscapes tries to merge the environmental aspects of particular physical places with the experiential and relational aspects of the people inhabiting them. Appreciating the social nature of space has two consequences for our understanding of migrants' experience of physical space.

First, landscapes have biographies that mediate belonging and that may be articulated by the people inhabiting and passing through them. In an article about the place of ancestors in the daily life of Igbo-speaking people in Nigeria, John McCall (1995) sketches the process by which people gain consciousness of their natural and social landscapes. He argues that for children, the cultural environment first emerges as a 'landscape of names', names attached to villages and fields and referring to both the living and the dead, 'those people who cleared the land, built the compounds, farmed the land, and conceived the people' (McCall 1995: 259; cf. Basso 1996: 85f.). In a similar way, for people in Kalabo the natural landscape evokes memories of ancestral migrations from Angola, villages and hamlets carry the names of their founders, named spirits of forebears roam the forests, making the whole landscape alive with past, current and future social relationships. In other words, the fact that places in the landscape bear the name of mutual ancestors constitutes a quality of social relationships for people in a neighbourhood, a call for mutual interest, an indication of common purpose, and a possibility of making claims on both places and people.

Second, the meaning of landscapes changes over time for particular persons in step with the varying social positions they hold through their lives. The significance of physical landscapes for human beings may thus be fully understood only when placed in the context of the life span. For it is in relation to life that the variable meanings of the landscape – as the source of livelihood, shelter and the raw material for expressing deeply felt cultural notions, as the stage of life events, and as the nexus of social relationships and communal belonging – become evident.

In order to elucidate these two points and to further illustrate the social configuration of landscapes, I turn to one particular extended family whose members consider a particular rural village in Kalabo District, Livindamo, as their 'home' (see Barrett 2004: ch. 9). Although most senior members of this family came to Zambia from Angola, the current generations are firmly established in the district and in Zambia. Livindamo village was the stage where two generations matured and established themselves during the Zambian postindependent economic growth and the base from which some family members eventually expanded into urban areas. These aspects of Livindamo, as stage of socio-ritual maturation and as base of an economic network, explain its status as 'home' to these particular people. The woman Ndombelo served as the family's genealogical focal point, a central ancestress, in the life histories that I collected during my fieldwork.

Born in colonial Angola and sold off into slavery (*bundungo*) by her stepfather while she was still a little girl, Ndombelo grew up and married far from her biological relatives. Years later, in her new village, still in Angola, and without any knowledge of her origin, Ndombelo agreed to let her daughter Susan get married to a suitor from some distance away. It so happened that the man (Kapisa) was a maternal relative of Ndombelo, and when Kapisa heard the name of his bride's mother it struck a chord in his memory. He was well aware of the fate of Ndombelo, a story that belonged to family lore. Kapisa thus called Ndombelo to come and visit them in their village. She came, but wary from earlier experiences of disclosing her slave origin (this had previously been grounds for a man to divorce her), she kept it to herself. However, when she left the village of her in-laws she unknowingly passed the graveyard where her mother, Ntumba, was resting. Right there, a whirlwind caught her and struck her to the ground. Upon hearing of this, Kapisa was now certain that he was right in his assumption. Ndombelo presently came to stay with her blood relatives and soon thereafter (in the mid-1950s) accompanied her daughter and the in-laws across the border to Northern Rhodesia (at the time a British colony, now Zambia), where large parts of the extended family had already decided to settle.

It is significant when hearing members of this family relate their life paths that crossing the border between Angola and Zambia – done at will by most of these people on numerous occasions during their lives – is narrated as a small and unimportant issue, while stirring ancestral spirits lurking by the road is certainly not. From a European/North American perspective, such an evaluation of the importance of social and political space seems strikingly different.

The second of Ndombelo's children to be born in Zambia was her son Kamana. Born in the mid-1950s, he would always describe his childhood with his extended family in the village Livindamo as a happy and prosperous period. The time was distinguished, as he saw it, by the morally satisfying, 'traditional' values of respect for authority and economic reciprocity. However, despite the prosperity offered by becoming a junior in his brothers' business ventures, education, military training and urban opportunity, which followed Zambian independence in 1964, propelled him far away from Kalabo. When returning much later from the Zambian capital Lusaka as a man of the world, even his best efforts at adapting to the familial hierarchy were thwarted and he soon came into open conflict with one of his elders. The ill feeling between the two, couched in the idiom of sorcery (*bulothi*), eventually led to Kamana's leaving Western Province and settling permanently in one of Lusaka's low-income areas. By the time of my fieldwork, Kamana's ambivalent feelings towards parts of his extended family and his lack of success in the contracting Zambian economy had turned him into an 'exile' (*chichoni*).

The experiential border that separated him from his natal village had seemingly become impermeable. Kamana's life trajectory, thus leading to exile from the village where he spent his childhood, serves well as an illustration of the temporality of home. In other words, it shows how a person's relationship to the (social) landscape – sense of belonging in a social context, engagement in mutual support, activation of resources and relations of livelihood – may change profoundly with time and with his or her position in the gendered life cycle (see also Powles 2002: 83).

Nevertheless, as was clearly demonstrated by the junior relatives who over the years sought out Kamana in Lusaka in order to enter into his large urban network (and whom he always assisted to the best of his ability), the possibility of returning to Kalabo was a living option in his mind. The social landscape centred on Livindamo village was a dormant landscape to which Kamana might still have access in the future, with a certain amount of social effort.

This example of an extended family in Kalabo District, like many others in the area with historical ties to Angola, displays some of the ambiguous dynamics of home, state borders and experiential boundaries. On the one hand, the state border between Zambia and Angola had been mainly a practical obstacle that could be transcended with ease and that promised economic opportunity for those who made the effort. It still was for some of the younger (male) members of the family who continued to engage in cross-border trading. The border to them was not a source of identification, and the word 'refugee' was not in the vocabulary with which family members described themselves now or in the past. On the other hand, Kamana's lot shows how existential borders may be erected, not between states, but between city and rural areas, as a consequence of social ruptures between siblings.[5]

Rather than taking the content of identities and experiences for granted as natural consequences of displacement, the case shows how we should make their formation the subject of study. A similar perspective has been developed, for example, in relation to refugee studies, through focusing on what Emanuel Marx (1990) has called the 'social world' of refugees. This identifies their meaningful, contextually produced, social relationships regardless of locality, as a topic of examination instead of 'displacement' (their relationship to physical space) and in contrast to a universal 'refugee experience'. Steven Lubkemann (2001) follows Marx when he employs the concept 'lifespace' in analysing the transnational migration practices of Mozambicans in South Africa. In contrast to a formal geographical concept like 'location', 'lifespace' also embraces migrants' relationships with significant persons as well as impersonal objects (resources and the natural environment). It denotes particular migrants' perception of those 'social and impersonal dimensions' of space 'within which meaningful projects are realized' (Lubkemann 2001: 6).

Drawing on an anthropological appreciation of landscapes and expanding on Lubkemann's thoughts on 'lifespace', I propose that our interpretations of mobility across borders substitute a perception of the border as 'hodological space' (Egenter 2002), i.e., the border in the context of lived reality, for the conventional notion of physical landscape (mathematical space). The former concept is derived from the Greek *hodos*, 'path', 'way', and was coined by German philosopher Otto Friedrich Bollnow (1963). According to Egenter, '[t]his is a type of space which differs absolutely from mathematical space. Path-space or hodological space, corresponds to the factual human experience during movement between two different points on a map. It is absolutely different from the geometrical line which connects two points' (Egenter 2002).

Adopting a hodological perspective reminds us of the social dimensions of mobility, something that is often obscured by notions of 'refugee flows' and 'emergencies'. It reminds us that our self-perception, who we are perceived to be by others, as well as who we are connected to (the 'know-who', as Susan Whyte [2002] would have it) determines our experience of moving from one place to another. Furthermore, because of its insistence on human experience the perspective necessitates an appreciation of time and thus a grasp of how mobility fits (or fails to fit) into people's expectations of what life at different stages should be like. Finally, and directly related to the issue at hand, the perception of borderlands as 'path space' makes us understand that the act of crossing a border *may or may not* make a significant difference in a person's life, and its significance should thus be an issue for examination.

Mobility in Western Zambia

For many people in Southern Africa mobility as opposed to immobility has often been the key to both ecological and social sustainability (Lubkemann 2002: 191; Pritchett 2001; White 1959). The mobile population in South Central Africa is part of the reason why landscapes in the region need to be seen as social, rather than geographical, entities. But as I argued above, social landscapes are possibilities and adopting a life perspective makes us mindful of how they expand and contrast with changing fortunes over time. Placing these questions in the context of the struggle for livelihood and the attainment of social recognition and personhood – after all, these are universal features of human existence – reveals some important continuities of the importance of mobility for local people over the last century.

In the western part of Zambia, as in the rest of South Central Africa (Gluckman 1950: 166–67; Kopytoff 1986; Vansina 1966), people have a strong propensity to migration, seasonally and more permanently, and this has been an integral part of everyday life over the centuries. Some researchers have thus argued for the existence of a 'culture of mobility' in the region (e.g., Hansen 1977 on Luvale speakers). This is not to imply a culturalist perspective, as if mobility were an automated behaviour obscuring other motivations for the people of the region. I will use the concept rather to evoke a historical emergence of various 'mobility practices' in the sense that people have come to view different modes of mobility as means of survival that are morally, socially, economically and politically acceptable, expected or inevitable.

Nevertheless, people of this region have developed social mechanisms as well as ritual practices to accommodate mobility. Taking Mbunda people in Kalabo District as an example, this process has been compounded by an ecologically sensitive land resource base, a politically uncertain position vis-à-vis original landholders, and wider economic and political developments. For this ethnolinguistic group, then, there are four main indicators of the paramount importance of mobility, indicators that may be descriptive of western Zambia as a whole (see, e.g., Crehan 1997; Hansen 1979; Turner 1957; White 1959).

First, Mbunda have been engaging in the form of shifting agriculture that in the regional literature is commonly labelled *chitemene* (see, e.g., Moore and Vaughan 1994; Richards 1939), involving the clearing and burning of new land, the extensive growing of cassava, millet and vegetables within relatively short cycles, and frequent relocation to new areas. Together with a seasonal reliance on hunting and fishing, often leading to long-distance travel, a high divorce rate, a flexible kinship system and methods of incorporation, and a highly adaptable traditional political system, this form of subsistence ensures a mobile population. In sociocultural terms, this mobility is illustrated in the Lunda diaspora by sophisticated rituals of relocating ancestral shrines to new homesteads (De Boeck 1998), rich symbolic elaboration of the process of transforming bush into domesticated village, and a strong normative emphasis on the maintenance of long-distance social ties (see Barrett 2004: ch. 3).

The second indicator of mobility concerns labour migration. The incidence of (in the majority of cases) men leaving their rural villages for longer or shorter periods to travel to and work in the rapidly industrialising areas of Central and Southern Africa forms a significant part of the socioeconomic history of the region (van Binsbergen 1975; Cheke Cultural Writers Association 1994). During the first half of the twentieth century, a majority of men between eighteen and forty-five in rural districts like Kalabo were involved in this highly organised circulation of the labour force, which paved the way for the massive wave of urbanisation following independence in 1964.[6] As historical studies have demonstrated, this particular system of labour recruitment (for Southern African industries) reached far into the interior of what was to become Angola (Herbert 2002).

The third aspect of mobility, trade migration, displays an even deeper historical depth. It falls back on centuries of interconnection through commerce between the Atlantic and Indian Ocean coasts and the hinterland. Mobility in conjunction with trade has thus constituted an important supplement for people in this area, for subsistence or for generating capital (Hansen 1977: 136ff.; von Oppen 1993). In Kalabo, and Western Province in general, trade has also been a matter of survival for Mbunda people, who have often been disadvantaged by land ownership rights favouring Lozi cultivators (Hospes 1999). Due to their linguistic and cultural ties with people on the Angolan side of the border, cross-border trade with Angola has been a lucrative alternative for (mostly young) Mbunda in the district.

Before describing the fourth, more recent, indicator of mobility among Mbunda, namely, what might be called 'forced migration', let me take stock of how these mobility patterns are perceived and represented by the Mbunda themselves. What kind of cultural expressions of this emergent mobile lifestyle are evident in social interaction and in the Chimbunda language?

Among Mbunda in Kalabo the importance of mobility reverberates in the social and cultural imagination. While mobility (*kwenda*, 'to move'), especially for young people, is associated with being 'clever' (*kuthangama*) or showing 'sense' (*mangana*), to be immobile implies the opposite. The stereotype of the inert, backward villager (*mukalimbo*) is frequently ridiculed among young people in Kalabo Town. It signifies a person who is 'only seated in the village' (*kutumama ngocho hembo*) and whose lack of initiative is the cause of his or her poverty. Enforced immobility thus constitutes a sadly prevalent feature, which is connected to the predicament of the current generation coming of age. It surfaces through references to the inability of young people to get wage employment and to create legitimate households, and in their inability to assist, support and even visit family and friends (see Barrett 2004: ch. 4). Moreover, as has been argued for refugees staying in camps in the region, to be immobilised and thus powerless to make life and livelihood decisions is tantamount to suffering (*kuyanda*, 'to suffer') (Barrett 1998; Hansen 1990).

Hence, mobility is intimately connected to 'going ahead in life', 'to growing' (*kukola*) and to becoming an established person. As I have argued elsewhere (Barrett 2004), seeking out opportunities found outside of the native home is considered a crucial aspect of being young and a starting point for obtaining the livelihood of an adult (*litukuka*). Conversely, 'to be seated in the village', according to my informants, can only lead to poverty and stagnation. In other words, immobility was not conducive to the gendered paths of marriage and parenthood and to establishing new households. The life histories I collected in Kalabo, being mostly records of those who stayed behind, were obviously influenced by such impediments to the ideal paths to adulthood.

However, if these expressions seem to imply that mobility has become 'normal' and even desired in this social context, it must be remembered that this is not always so. Depending on diverse contingencies, some of the common social patterns that together constitute 'the Mbunda propensity to mobility' may also be experienced as deeply disconcerting ruptures in individual lives (see Powles 2002 on displacement in everyday life). Take, for instance, the frequent predicament of young single mothers in Kalabo, who, in attempting to support their children, feel more or less forced to marry non-committal men. In keeping with the common viri-patri-local postmarital residence pattern, this usually means moving to the husband's village, where a woman with small children is perceived to be subtracting from rather than contributing to sustaining livelihood. In a vulnerable low-income environment this may have severe effects on the treatment and well-being of the in-moving woman and her children. Very often, a woman experiences such reluctant alliances as a form of displacement from her home village (*limbo lyange*, 'my village'), where stronger bonds of support and nurturing are in place. Sometimes this leads to divorce and a return to the home village, often in a repetitive serial pattern of marriages/divorces throughout the life span, but at other times it generates a different form of rupture. For in many cases when these single mothers marry into a new village their children from previous marriages are forced into yet another form of displacement by being sent away. Very frequently in this region, as in Africa more generally (see, e.g., Bledsoe 1990 for West African examples), children circulate between more or less reluctant relatives or other 'foster parents'. As Pamela Reynolds (1991) has noted for rural Zimbabwe, children frequently take a very active part in cultivating relationships with particular relatives and adults through working or running errands for them and thereby consciously facilitating such fosterage. It is thus fairly common that adults 'take' their sibling's child and care for it for longer or shorter periods.[7] However, despite what Mbunda people hold to be 'proper' rules of sociality, which equate children of close relatives with one's own, children are not always wanted or welcomed.

At an existential and emotive level, then, even when 'ordinary life' is largely devoid of violent conflict (as in Zambia) there is a continuum between what are perceived as life-sustaining and life-rupturing forms of mobility. This contention might be even clearer if we proceed to the fourth element of Mbunda mobility, the prevalence during the twentieth century of 'forced migration', mostly from Angola to Zambia. However, before addressing the paradoxical circumstance that 'forced migration' has become part of the overall propensity for mobility of the people in the Angolan–Zambian borderland, I will provide some background to these population movements. The reasons for these migrations are diverse and complex. During the twentieth century they were at first mainly found in poor economic opportunity and Portuguese oppression in colonial Angola. Later, migration was attributed to the social unrest resulting from mounting resistance to colonial rule, which after 1966 was increasingly waged with military means (see Hansen 1979). The two major Zambian refugee settlements in Western (Mayukwayukwa) and Northwestern Province (Meheba) were built to cater to the massive numbers of Angolans who crossed into independent Zambia. After independence in 1975, several new waves of people fled the country as a consequence of civil war between the MPLA in government and the UNITA rebel movement.

Viewing forced migration as part of the overall propensity for mobility in western Zambia and eastern Angola seems paradoxical, since the term 'forced' indicates that people migrate not because they deem it desirable or natural but because external factors (like the threat of violence) have eliminated all other options. In such a familiar view, Angolans entering Zambia are merely responding to conditions beyond their control, and the decision to cross the state border has little to do with mindful action outside the mere will to survive. However, in line with Turton's call for perceiving agency also in the direst circumstances of forced migration, even the extraordinary fact of people in this region leaving their homes due to violence or poverty must be understood in terms of historical modes of migration. This connection should be made, since the ways in which people understand and imagine their future life paths, as the case studies below imply, are always integral to individual decisions to migrate. Such imagined life paths (*bithinganyeka*, 'plans', 'thinking', 'intentions') are, in analytical terms, forged in social practice as composites of ideal models of gendered personhood, socioeconomic opportunity and the creativity of particular generations.[8] Fleeing violence, just like joining groups that perpetrate violence, thus also contains aspects of long-term planning of life paths, including considerations of how life will be sustained in terms of marriage, household formation, livelihood and well-being. In fact, the ability to engage these life paths, or the ability to forge new credible ones, is the key factor determining whether a person deems his or her situation as a migrant as life sustaining or life impairing.

In recent times, it is mostly Zambia that has been on the receiving end of large movements of people. Yet it is indicative of the population's favourable view of mobility that some people (mostly young men) have been engaging willingly in cross-border migration in the opposite direction, thus defying the insecurity of the Angolan situation, as soon as there have been opportunities for employment or trade (see Bakewell 1999).

Rather than leading us to celebrate mobility for its own sake, these insights allow us to shed light on Mbunda understandings of 'home'. How does a high level of mobility affect the understanding of 'home' among Mbunda people? Is what counts as home completely unimportant, arbitrary or interchangeable? Not surprisingly for an ethnolinguistic group whose members are overwhelmingly rural, their definition of home is intimately related to livelihood, village, kinship and marriage.

A person's village (*limbo*, plural *membo*) is the place where the basic requirements of food, shelter and sociality are met, and where he or she receives the means (i.e., land) from the parental generation to start cultivating for their own subsistence. According to the often idealised image presented in formal interviews, 'home' (*kwimbo*) in the recent past was invariably the place where one's mother's brother (*bananantu*) and one's matrilineage (*ng'owa*) resided. However, today home is increasingly perceived as the place where your father lives, although the place of one's maternal kin is still important. People in reality thus tend to conceive of home bilaterally (which is probably a long-standing Central African practice, see MacGaffey 1983), recognising both the village of one's father's cognates (*bakabatate*, 'the people of the father') and that of one's mother's cognates (*bakabanana*). Furthermore, the physical location of a village is easily transported through ancestral rituals and through the planting of a new *mouymbo* tree inside the village headman's courtyard.[9]

What emerges from this varied pattern of where home is located are, firstly, flexible idioms for making sense of and coping with an incessantly changing social landscape, a variability that is a result of mobility. Consequently, Mbunda people appeal to home, through the idioms of descent, kinship and friendship, in order to make political and economic claims on other people (MacGaffey 1983) in a situation characterised by constant social movement. In this sense, home is in many ways a negotiable and unstable construct. Secondly, however, there are limits to this negotiability since social belonging may not be conjured up from nothing and is predicated on memories of past and expectations of future exchange. To use the terminology of Hage (1997: 102ff.), a person needs to acquire intersubjectively a certain measure of knowledge of the social conventions, of the social and physical landscapes, and a measure of communicative agency in a particular *limbo* (village). Only then may it become the locus of his or her 'sense of possibility' and thus to be defined as *kwimbo*, 'home'.

Life Paths Crossing Borders

Having shown the centrality and historical depth of mobility for the inhabitants of this region, on both sides of the border between Zambia and Angola, I now turn to how this fact of life is manifested today. I will do this with reference to the rather large population movements that took place at the end of the twentieth century and that placed great stress on the population of Kalabo District. In particular, I will examine how three men born in Angola, all of whom at some point took recourse to the humanitarian system of refugee reception, crossed the border into Zambia.

Starting in October 1999, the arrival in Zambia of a large number of Angolans, who could not be absorbed by local villages in the established fashion, developed into what could be described as an 'emergency', partly beyond the scope of the historical experience of people in the region. The sudden influx of Angolans into Kalabo District following the recapture of Lumbala N'Guimbo by UNITA in December 1999 was arguably the largest the district had experienced in a long time. The Angolan town had previously been in the hands of UNITA for seventeen years, and dissatisfaction with its regime seems to have been behind the decision of many civilian inhabitants in the area to join the Civil Defence Force (*Defesa Civil*), irregular combatants organised by the Angolan government when the latter captured the town in October 1999. The period of government control was thus short, and the anticipated retaliation by UNITA, which during previous years had failed to arouse any but enforced support in the local population, led to quite a large number of people starting the journey across the unmarked border, into Zambia.

Within three months, twenty-two thousand Angolans fled from Moxico Province into Zambia, and although many arrived in North-western Province, as many as five thousand reached the hastily established reception centre in Kalabo and another eight thousand the one in Sinjembela further south (UNHCR 2000).[10] Due to the annual flooding of the Zambezi, which effectively stopped the distribution of necessities as well as efforts to transfer the refugees to established settlements, the national and international structures for receiving them were severely crippled. The situation was exacerbated by the fact that the refugees arrived in the lean months of December and January, which people often refer to as the months of hunger, *ndungu*, causing further pressure on local hosts.

Returning to Reagan, whom I mentioned at the outset of this chapter, he arrived in Kalabo in December 1999. He had registered with the UNHCR and had taken up residence as an official refugee with his mother and two grandparents at the Reception Centre only a few hundred metres away from our house. When he arrived in Kalabo, Reagan was twenty-one years old, unmarried, and had been living in the Angolan town of Lumbala N'Guimbo. Despite his having lived under UNITA rule his whole life, Reagan had fled the town in fear of retaliation when UNITA soldiers began to attack, since he belonged to the majority of young men who had joined the Defesa Civil. The reason he gave for joining was dissatisfaction with life under UNITA authority: their forcing people to work for them, to carry arms or sing and dance at rallies, their failure to provide food and proper schooling. He recounts:

> We had stayed with UNITA for seventeen years, when the MPLA troops came in October 1999. During those seventeen years no one volunteered to join UNITA, but when *o governo* took control over the area most of the remaining men joined them. Then UNITA returned on the first of December, around three a.m. in the morning they started shooting 'twa, twa, twa' [imitating the sound of firing guns]. The fighting went on until eight hours when everyone decided to leave.

For Reagan, this was far from the first time he had been to Kalabo and Zambia. In a long-term effort to raise money for bride wealth in order to marry a girl, he had already made five trips to Zambia. There he would sell his maize and buy second-hand clothes (*salaula*), which he would then bring back to Angola to sell for a small profit. Each trip would take about one month and was still considered hazardous, not least because of the more dangerous nature of magic in Zambia, reported by some informants. Nevertheless, according to Reagan, most *bakwenje* (young men), or at least 'the clever ones', participated in the trade, especially those who were 'orphaned' like him (his father was dead). Having come to settle in Zambia, he was looking forward to a more stable life:

> In Angola we were almost like nomads, we would always move between places. One person would have three, four villages: one month you stay here, then you're chased there. Whoever you were running with was your relative. Here, in Zambia, people stay more permanently and do their job according to their will.

This quote brings out in stark relief the paradoxical relations between 'forced migration' as it has been defined during the latter part of the twentieth century and mobility in the long-term regional practice, as described in the previous section. The sixty life histories I collected in Kalabo District demonstrate that having several villages in which residence was possible, and indeed often realised due to divorce or domestic conflict, was part of the ordinary experience of people also on the Zambian side. The difference was that, compared to Angola, the peaceful social environment in Zambia was more conducive to the fulfilment of *bithinganeyka*, life plans, and that even enforced mobility could allow these plans to continue.

Another young man of twenty-three years, Chainda, also from Lumbala, came to Kalabo at the same time as Reagan with a large extended family of young and old, as well as his wife of one year. His reason for coming to Zambia was also fear of UNITA retaliation. Chainda had similarly visited Zambia on trade business four times previously, staying with relatives in Kalabo District. During these trips he would paddle a canoe filled with maize from his own harvest and exchange it for clothes, plates and soap that he brought back to Angola. He claimed that one of these trips was enough to pay for the bride wealth (*bionda*) demanded by his parents-in-law. Although he accepted being transported with the rest of the refugees in the Kalabo Reception Centre to the Mayukwayukwa settlement, he said that it would be on the condition that he could carry out trade there. He stated quite bluntly that if he were not allowed to trade, he would take his relatives outside the settlement instead. While the Zambian policy on the subject of refugees doing business was unclear to him, he was adamant that in the future he would settle down in Zambia, where 'life is more civilised'.

In terms of the theoretical framework employed in this chapter, the 'refugee crisis' of 1999–2000 temporarily transformed the borderland of Kalabo District and thus shaped the experience of the borderland as path space for the people who crossed into Zambia. The most important consequences were, first, that the heightened presence of representatives from the Zambian government, the United Nations High Commissioner for Refugees (UNHCR), and their implementing partners, Lutheran World Federation (LWF) and Médecins Sans Frontières (MSF), imbued the social arena with the values and actions of these institutions. As often happens when an 'emergency' is announced (Bakewell 2000b), the humanitarian actors roaming around Kalabo Town began to classify the population according to the objective of dispensing aid, into 'beneficiaries' and 'hosts'. Interestingly, I heard rumours among the aid workers that Zambian villagers were among those who presented themselves as refugees at the Kalabo Reception Centre, which would not be surprising owing to the scarcity of food at the time.

Second, as a consequence of this humanitarian logic, the term 'Angolan refugee' suddenly became a viable social category to impose on other people as well. In combination with the sheer number of people who entered and the general lack of food in the area, this seemed to undermine the conventional system of support in Zambian borderland villages and to temporarily suspend the efficacy of the classificatory kinship idiom (see Barrett 2003).

Reagan's and Chainda's stay in Kalabo ended with the airlift in January and February 2000, which took twenty-five hundred refugees (the remainder transported by boat) to the provincial capital Mongu, from where they were conveyed to the established refugee settlements. Though I could neither confirm nor disprove it, in view of their prior experience as traders and their connections with partners in Kalabo, it was unlikely that these young men would stay in a refugee settlement very long. As Hansen contended long ago (1979: 371), 'refugees in camps are those who failed to find kinsmen or who could not generate enough local social and political support'. Finding kinsmen or generating support also had gender and age dimensions. For a woman, marriage would probably have been one of few avenues for creating social bonds in host villages, while this would be much more difficult for a man lacking means. On the other hand, a man was more likely to get piecework and survive through paid labour. If Reagan had arrived alone in Kalabo District (as he had done so many times before) and not in the company of elderly people, it is thus likely that he would have chosen another alternative than the reception centre, which on this occasion became the only alternative.

I end this section with the story of another male cross-border migrant, one who possessed infinitely more 'know-who' in the political and economic landscape of the borderland than the two previous cases. A few years after I met Reagan and Chainda, in 2002, the UNITA leader Jonas Savimbi was killed in action by Angolan government troops, leading to the rapid dissolution of the military wing of his organisation that had been active since 1966. Major Kasoka, a leading UNITA commander in one of the 'security zones' on the border with Zambia and Kalabo District, could have found himself in a socially insecure situation for the first time during his long military career. Former UNITA combatants who had fled across the border to Zambia were singled out and placed by Zambian government and UNHCR representatives in the Ukwimi settlement far away in Zambia's Eastern Province, awaiting transport back across the border to special containment areas in Angola. But as rumour had it, Kasoka was wanted by the Angolan government for some offence. I had met him a couple of times in Kalabo when he was on his frequent trading missions to Zambia to sell diamonds and procure fuel or other goods – mixing personal gain and official UNITA business. In these ventures he was much aided by his fictive brother, a well-connected Mbunda businessman in Kalabo whose parents were born in Angola.

When I was back in Kalabo in 2003 and I inquired about Kasoka, to my surprise, several people claimed that he had been taken to the civilian settlement of Mayukwayukwa in Western Province. I later found out that he had used his contacts and some of his wealth acquired in business to escape the classification as an ex-combatant.

Hodology and the Social Significance of Crossing Borders

In this chapter, I have attempted to discuss the implications of a shift in our view of refugees, mobility and the act of crossing state borders. The shift concerns how we conceive of human beings moving through space – as a geographical matter or as an issue of experience. The geographical perspective is inherent when we as social scientists adopt categories provided by states and the international humanitarian system as a starting point for analysis and thus reify 'refugees' as 'people out of place'. Instead, I have suggested that anthropologists embrace an experiential perspective by introducing the concept of hodology, which allows us to consider mobility as occurring experientially and existentially in 'path space' and which conceives of migrants as actors in their own life trajectories in time and space. I have employed this view of mobility in the context of Mbunda families in the Angolan–Zambian borderland and of three Mbunda men who at the end of the Angolan civil war took refuge in Zambia.

How these people experienced the borderland as path space was influenced by a number of factors. To begin with, the historical and cultural conventions of the landscape – how it had been inhabited in general through migration and land management and by whom in particular (its biography) – determine who could make claims (and through what means) on belonging to its social landscapes. Furthermore, their social position in terms of gender, age, ethnicity, wealth and 'know-who' shapes the degree of ease or resistance with which they may pass through the landscape or emplace themselves in it. Consequently, a person may perceive the landscape differently at different moments of his or her life trajectory. Finally, long-term expectations of path space in the borderlands may be suspended by contingencies like violence, poverty and political forces. As the case of Reagan illustrates, in Angola the war has long destabilised 'home' (*kwimbo*) and 'village' (*limbo*). His story alludes to a heightened (abnormal) uncertainty when everyone had many villages and 'whoever you were running with was your relative'. It is not far-fetched, however, to point out the similarities experienced by vulnerable individuals in the highly mobile and economically fragile society that was Zambia at the end of the twentieth century: although less dramatic, and devoid of the horrors of armed violence, the displacement suffered by single mothers and children in particular could well be felt as grave.

Among the contingencies that have great impact on life in borderlands must also be included the workings of humanitarian agents and the state, whose world-views and classifications tend to affect how social relations and social space are understood. All three of these Angolan men had a similar perception of the border: sometimes as a minor practical nuisance, but mostly as a source of wealth in trade in relation to their long-term plans for livelihood and existential security. At times, however, their experience of moving through the borderland was much influenced by 'the national order of things', imposing itself in terms of border enforcement, refugee bureaucracy, and the humanitarian logic of identifying 'refugees/beneficiaries' and 'hosts'. Despite their considerable experience of crossing into the familiar path space of Zambia and summoning support there, the force of the 'national order of things' made Reagan, Chainda and Kasoka into 'Angolan refugees'.

The experiences of Reagan and Chainda as young, male Angolan traders display some significant resemblances to their Zambian counterparts living in Kalabo (see Barrett 2004), like their knowledge of the long-standing economic and social integration of the region. This entailed emplacing themselves into the social landscapes (often through appeals couched in the idiom of kinship and friendship) and acquiring the 'know-who' of the politico-administrative system, which at the time basically amounted to different networks of high- and middle-ranking UNITA personnel, Zambian immigration officers and local businessmen. To know these social landscapes, as Major Kasoka obviously did, was a great advantage if a person wanted to preserve a measure of independence in the face of forceful circumstances.

For Zambian Mbunda, Angola constitutes the genealogical, and in some cases mythological, 'homeland' from where their forebears had come to settle in what today is called Zambia (Cheke Cultural Writers Association 1994). For both Angolans and Zambians living in the borderland, the country on the other side of the state border has always offered a way forward on personal life paths in terms of livelihood, adventure and marriage. It is these kinds of regional and personal dynamics that are easily lost in the process of applying the humanitarian conceptual framework in which the label 'refugee' belongs. I have demonstrated how adopting a hodological understanding of migration across state borders, or of mobility in general, allows us to investigate rather than take for granted the significance of such movements for the people under study. It forces us to consider the social qualities of landscapes and the way social landscapes may be accommodating or hostile (or something in between) to different people at different points in time. Most importantly, a hodological perspective makes us attentive to people's expectations and hopes for future lives and livelihood in decisions relating to personal mobility, even when and where such expressions of human agency seem remote or unlikely.

Acknowledgements

The research for this chapter was supported by the Swedish International Development Cooperation Agency (Sida). Many thanks to the editors and the anonymous readers for helpful suggestions. I extend my deep gratitude to the descendants of Ndombelo, who all figure under pseudonyms in this text.

Notes

1. This adopted name, quite common in the region, should be seen in the context of the sustained financial and political support that the former US president Ronald Reagan afforded Jonas Savimbi and his UNITA 'freedom fighters'. When Reagan was in his early teens, growing up in UNITA territory, the name of the US president presumably figured frequently in official propaganda. He thus took the name after completing his initiation ceremony (*mukanda*), which usually occurs around the age of ten to twelve.
2. The hostility between UNITA and MPLA actually began at the inception of UNITA as an anti-colonial movement in 1966 (Minter 1988).
3. The relations of global and national neoliberal capitalism are articulated, for instance, in the flourishing economies of extraction that are amply represented in Kalabo through the trade in diamonds, cattle, fuel and food – largely benefiting a small local elite, national urban centres and international businessmen, often to the detriment of the rural majority.
4. This holds true even for larger bodies of territory like states. State borders as social constructions thus require state-orchestrated action in order to make a difference in people's lives (see, e.g., van Schendel 2004).
5. Kamana too, as a younger man, took part in the centuries-old cross-border trade in cattle and other goods between Zambia, Angola and Namibia.
6. Although the notion of 'circulation' of the labour force is spurious and may in fact be misleading (Ferguson 1990a, 1990b).
7. At a time when death from AIDS is rampant in Zambia and Southern Africa, much research demonstrates how crucial such support networks are for the survival of so-called 'AIDS orphans'.
8. Employing this same theoretical framework, I have shown how, for instance, labour migration to Johannesburg, although the practice is obsolete in the current political economy of Southern Africa, is still a vivid symbol of male personhood for contemporary young men in Kalabo (see Barrett 2004: ch. 8).

9. The site of an abandoned village (*ngundu*) is remembered in the surrounding neighbourhood and by descendents of its prior inhabitants.
10. These numbers need to be appreciated against the fact of very low population density in Western Province and a total population of only 120,000 people in Kalabo District.

References

Alvarez, Robert. 1995. 'The Mexican–US Border: The Making of an Anthropology of Borderlands', *Annual Review of Anthropology* 24: 447–70.

Appadurai, Arjun. 1991. 'Global Ethnoscapes: Notes and Queries for a Transnational Anthropology', in *Recapturing Anthropology: Working in the Present*, ed. Richard G. Fox, pp. 191–210. Santa Fe: School of American Research Press.

Bakewell, Oliver. 1999. 'Returning Refugees or Migrating Villagers? Voluntary Repatriation Programmes in Africa Reconsidered'. *New Issues in Refugee Research*, Working Paper No. 15. Geneva: United Nations High Commissioner for Refugees.

———. 2000a. 'Repatriation and Self-Settled Refugees in Zambia: Bringing Solutions to the Wrong Problems', *Journal of Refugee Studies* 13(4): 356–73.

———. 2000b. 'Uncovering Local Perspectives on Humanitarian Assistance and Its Outcomes', *Disasters* 24(2): 103–16.

Barrett, Michael. 1998. 'Tuvosena: "Let's Go Everybody": Identity and Ambition among Angolan Refugees in Zambia'. *Working Papers in Cultural Anthropology*, No. 8. Uppsala: Department of Cultural Anthropology and Ethnology.

———. 2003. 'Social Landscapes and Moving People: The Mysterious Meaning of Migration in Western Zambia'. *New Issues in Refugee Research*, Working Paper No. 78. Geneva: United Nations High Commissioner for Refugees.

———. 2004. *Paths to Adulthood: Freedom, Belonging and Temporalities in Mbunda Biographies from Western Zambia*. Uppsala: Acta Universitatis Upsaliensis.

Basso, Keith H. 1996. 'Wisdom Sits in Places: Notes on a Western Apache Landscape', in *Senses of Place*, ed. Steven Feld and Keith H. Basso, pp. 53–90 Santa Fe, New Mexico: School of American Research Press.

van Binsbergen, Wim. 1975. *Labour Migration and the Generation Conflict: An Essay on Social Change in Central Western Zambia*. 34th Annual Meeting, Society for Applied Anthropology, Section: Anthropological Contributions to the Study of Migration, 19–22 March, Amsterdam.

Bledsoe, Caroline. 1990. '"No Success without Struggle": Social Mobility and Hardship for Foster Children in Sierra Leone', *Man* 25: 70–88.

Bollnow, Otto F. 1963. *Mensch Und Raum*. Stuttgart: Kohlhammer.

Cheke Cultural Writers Association. 1994. *The History and Cultural Life of the Mbunda Speaking Peoples*. Lusaka.

Cohen, David W. and E.S. Atieno Odhiambo. 1989. *Siaya: The Historical Anthropology of an African Landscape*. London and Athens: Ohio University Press.

Crehan, Kate. 1997. *The Fractured Community: Landscapes of Power and Gender in Rural Zambia*. Berkeley: University of California Press.

De Boeck, Filip. 1998. 'The Rootedness of Trees: Place as Cultural and Natural Texture in Rural Southwest Congo', in *Locality and Belonging*, ed. Nadia Lovell, pp. 25–52. London and New York: Routledge.

Egenter, Nold. 2002. *Otto Friedrich Bollnow's Anthropological Concept of Space: A Revolutionary New Paradigm Is under Way*. The Internet Journal of Architecture. December, 2002. E-journal: http://thedesignershub.com/archi%2Djournal/view.asp?id=40&flag=7

Englund, Harri. 2002. *From War to Peace on the Mozambique–Malawi Borderland*. Edinburgh: Edinburgh University Press.

Ferguson, James. 1990a. 'Mobile Workers, Modernist Narratives: A Critique of the Historiography of Transition on the Zambian Copperbelt [Part One]'. *Journal of Southern African Studies* 16(3): 358–412.

———. 1990b. 'Mobile Workers, Modernist Narratives: A Critique of the Historiography of Transition on the Zambian Copperbelt [Part Two]', *Journal of Southern African Studies* 16(4): 603–21.

———. 2002. 'Of Mimicry and Membership: Africans and the "New World Society"', *Cultural Anthropology* 17(4): 551–69.

Geschiere, Peter and Birgit Meyer 1998. 'Globalization and Identity: Dialectics of Flow and Closure: Introduction', *Development and Change* 29(4): 601–15.

Gluckman, Max. 1950. 'Kinship and Marriage among the Lozi of Northern Rhodesia and the Zulu of Natal', in *African Systems of Kinship and Marriage*, ed. Alfred R. Radcliffe-Brown and Daryll Forde, pp. 166–206. Oxford: Oxford University Press.

Hage, Ghassan. 1997. 'At Home in the Entrails of the West: Multiculturalism, "Ethnic Food" and Migrant Home-building', in *Home/World: Space, Community and Marginality in Sydney's West*, ed. Helen Grace, Ghassan Hage, Leslie Johnson, Julie Langsworth, and Michael Symonds, pp. 99–153. Annandale: Pluto Press.

Hansen, Art. 1977. 'Once the Running Stops: The Socioeconomic Resettlement of Angolan Refugees (1966–1972) in Zambian Border Villages'. Ph.D. dissertation, Cornell University.

———. 1979. 'Once the Running Stops: Assimilation of Angolan Refugees into Zambian Border Villages', *Disasters* 3(4): 369–74.

———. 1990. *Refugee Self-Settlement Versus Settlement on Government Schemes: The Long-Term Consequences for Security, Integration and Economic Development of Angolan Refugees (1966–1989) in Zambia*. Discussion Paper, 17. Geneva: UNRISD/United Nations.

Harrell-Bond, Barbara. 1986. *Imposing Aid: Emergency Assistance to Refugees*. Oxford: Oxford University Press.

Herbert, Eugenia W. 2002. *Twilight on the Zambezi: Late Colonialism in Central Africa*. Basingstoke: Palgrave Macmillan.

Hospes, Otto. 1999. 'The Dynamics of Conserving Movable Property in Western Province, Zambia', Sustainable Development Department, Food and Agriculture Organization of the United Nations (FAO). 2002, April 4. Posted June 1999. http://www.fao.org/waicent/faoinfo/sustdev/ppdirect/PPan0013.htm

Ingold, Tim. 2000. *The Perception of the Environment: Essays on Livelihood, Dwelling and Skill*. London and New York: Routledge.

Jackson, Michael. 1989. *Paths toward a Clearing: Radical Empiricism and Ethnographic Inquiry*. Bloomington: Indiana University Press.

Kopytoff, Igot. 1986. 'The Internal African Frontier: The Making of African Political Culture', in *The African Frontier: The Reproduction of African Traditional Societies*, ed. Igot Kopytoff, pp. 1–24. Bloomington: Indiana University Press.

Lovell, Nadia. 1998. 'Introduction: Belonging in Need of Emplacement?', in *Locality and Belonging*, ed. Nadia Lovell, pp. 1–24. London: Routledge.

Lubkemann, Stephen. 2001. *Embedded Time and Dispersed Place: Displacement and Gendered Differences in Mozambican "Lifespace"*. XXIV IUSSP Congress. Salvador, Brazil.

———. 2002. 'Where to Be an Ancestor? Reconstituting Socio-Spiritual Worlds among Displaced Mozambicans'. *Journal of Refugee Studies* 15(2): 189–212.

MacGaffey, Wyatt. 1983. 'Lineage Structure, Marriage and the Family Amongst the Central Bantu', *The Journal of African History* 24(2): 173–87.

Malkki, Liisa. 1992. 'National Geographic: The Rooting of Peoples and the Territorialization of National Identity among Scholars and Refugees', *Cultural Anthropology* 7(1): 24–44.

Mamdani, Mahmood. 1998. 'When Does a Settler Become a Native? Reflections of the Colonial Roots of Citizenship in Equatorial and South Africa', *Electronic Mail and Guardian*. Johannesburg.

Marx, Emanuel. 1990. 'The Social World of the Refugee: A Conceptual Framework', *Journal of Refugee Studies* 3(3): 189–203.

McCall, John. 1995. 'Rethinking Ancestors in Africa', *Africa* 65(2): 256–68.

McDermott Hughes, David. 1999. 'Refugees and Squatters: Immigration and the Politics of Territory on the Zimbabwe–Mozambique Border', *Journal of Southern African Studies* 25(4): 533–52.

McGregor, JoAnn. 1998. 'Violence and Social Change in a Border Economy: War in the Maputo Hinterland, 1984–1992', *Journal of Southern African Studies* 24(1): 37–60.

Minter, William. 1988. *Operation Timber: Pages from the Savimbi Dossier*. Trenton N.J.: Africa World Press.

Moore, Henrietta L. and Megan Vaughan. 1994. *Cutting Down Trees: Gender, Nutrition, and Agricultural Change in the Northern Province of Zambia, 1890–1990*. Portsmouth: Heinemann.

Navaro-Yashin, Yael. 2003. '"Life Is Dead Here": Sensing the Political in "No Man's Land"', *Anthropological Theory* 3(1): 107–25.

von Oppen, Achim. 1993. *Terms of Trade and Terms of Trust: The History and Contexts of Pre-Colonial Market Production around the Upper Zambezi and Kasai*. Hamburg: Münster.

Powles, Jullia. 2002. 'Home and Homelessness: The Life History of Susanna Mwana-Uta, an Angolan Refugee', *Journal of Refugee Studies* 15(1): 81–101.

Pritchett, James A. 2001. *The Lunda-Ndembu: Style, Change, and Social Transformation in South Central Africa*. Madison: University of Wisconsin Press.

Reynolds, Pamela. 1991. *Dance, Civet Cat: Child Labour in the Zambezi Valley*. London and Athens: Ohio University Press.

Richards, Audrey I. 1939. *Land, Labour and Diet in Northern Rhodesia: An Economic Study of the Bemba Tribe*. London.

van Schendel, Willem. 2004. *The Wagah Syndrome: Territorial Roots of Contemporary Violence in South Asia*. 8th Conference of the European Association of Social Anthropologists. 8–12 September, 2004, Vienna.

Scott, James C. 1998. *Seeing Like a State: How Certain Schemes to Improve the Human Condition Have Failed*. New Haven: Yale University Press.

Turner, Victor W. 1957. *Schism and Continuity in an African Society: A Study of Ndembu Village Life*. Manchester: Manchester University Press.

Turton, David. 2003. 'Refugees, Forced Resettlers, and "Other Forced Migrants":
Towards a Unitary Study of Forced Migration'. *New Issues in Refugee Research*,
Working Paper No. 94. Geneva: UNHCR.

UNHCR. 2000. *Briefing Notes: Zambia: 22,000 Angolans since October*. Web page.
United Nations High Commissioner for Refugees. 28 January, 2000.
http://www.unhcr.ch

Vansina, Jan. 1966. *Kingdoms of the Savanna: A History of Central African States until
European Occupation*. Madison: University of Wisconsin Press.

White, Charles M.N. 1959. 'A Preliminary Survey of Luvale Rural Economy'. *The
Rhodes-Livingstone Papers*, No. 29. Manchester: Manchester University Press.

Whyte, Susan R. 2002. 'Subjectivity and Subjunctivity: Hopes for Health in Eastern
Uganda', in *Postcolonial Subjectivities in Africa*, ed. Richard Werbner, pp.
171–90, London and New York: Zed Books.

5

Strategies of Visibility and Invisibility
Rumanians and Moroccans in El Ejido, Spain

Swanie Potot

Introduction

The violence encountered by the migrants discussed in this chapter is of several kinds: they were confronted with the 'structural violence' of poverty and economic crisis in their countries of origin (Galtung 1969), and they are now facing racist violence in the place they have migrated to in order to work. Categorised not as refugees but as economic migrants, they do not benefit from any sort of international protection regime.

This analysis will focus on the Almeria province of Andalusia, in the south of Spain, where large numbers of foreign workers from various origins are employed in agriculture. In this region, massive exploitation of cheap and reliable manpower, together with strong competition for jobs between workers, have led to severe inter-ethnic tensions. During the year 2000, these tensions escalated into riots directed mainly against Moroccan workers, causing dozens of people to be injured as they were chased down the streets of the agricultural centre of El Ejido. Since then, Moroccan workers, who for decades have been the main group of foreigners working in the area, are being steadily replaced by other migrants, among whom Rumanians are estimated to be the most numerous.

This essay explores the social relations shaped by such contestations in the context of labour migration. Agriculture is the most important economic activity in the area and the entire social life of the Almeria region seems to revolve around this sector. The sharp rise in economic productivity of the area has been the work of persons from a variety of backgrounds: Spaniards coming from other regions, Moroccans, who have been immigrating here for decades, Rumanians, relative newcomers and very much subdued, and others. But this collective activity has not given rise to solidarities or collective feelings amongst those workers. On the contrary, the pragmatics of the context have been articulated into an atmosphere of social distance and conflict, in which the various groups are in search not only of economic promotion but also of social recognition.

Xenophobia plays a key role here. While Spaniards tend to deploy it as a strategic dimension of their human resources management, Moroccans attempt to resist it in order to regain a sense of dignity, whereas Rumanians negotiate their identity as whites, intending to gain social recognition by inscribing themselves into Spanish racism. This chapter analyses such complexities of racism and their link with territory. A comparison of Moroccan and Rumanian migrants' attitudes will under-line that relations to space, composed through the history and resources of those groups, strongly condition their dealings with social exclusion. This will lead us to investigate how personal and collective histories, meanings and objectives of migration, as well as social, juridical and political contexts in places of arrival, play a role in the process of attachment to territory and the collective representations of immigrant workers.

The analysis will proceed in four steps. The first step will shed light on the social and economic context which led various populations to come to work in the area. It will show how a social scale has been built parallel to the growth of the region, placing different groups on ranking levels. The second part will explore the sources of increasing racism towards Moroccans during the last decade and their collective responses to it. The third section will deal with the recent arrival of Rumanians, considered highly desirable by many Spaniards, and their development of a very different relationship to space. The conclusion intends to explain the absence of solidarity based on class consciousness between farm labourers and the overwhelming weight attributed to origin in their self-identification.

The Colonisation of Almeria Province

Fifty years ago, the Campo de Dalias, as the region of El Ejido was formerly called, was just a windy, salty desert. As the region was the poorest part of Spain, its inhabitants would emigrate in large numbers to other European countries. The subsequent development of the area relied on a strong colonisation policy. This policy was very efficient as, today, the area has become the richest in Spain, with the highest net domestic product per person (Checa 1999).

The colonisation of the area goes back to the 1950s. Under the tutelage of the ministry of agriculture, wells were dug to make the lands arable. The government then allocated small lots to modest families, promoting familial enterprises. The aim of this policy was to stop emigration by making it possible for people to develop economic enterprise in Spain. This policy resulted in the first wave of immigration into the province: in the course of two decades, hundreds of Spaniards from close or distant provinces came as colonists, attempting to make their fortune in the farming sector.

The first greenhouses appeared in the 1960s, but it was only ten years later that this kind of cultivation became dominant. According to official data, in 1963 only half a hectare of greenhouses had been erected, while in 1984 they covered fourteen thousand hectares, including more than twelve thousand developed with government support. Financial assistance, via banks and state grants, allowed rapid access to property and agricultural equipment. The products resulting from these planta- tions – fruit and vegetable harvests – were sold to an increasingly vast region. Profits for small farmers were huge, and the region became known as the Green El Dorado. The economic growth of the area continued to be supported by the integration of Spain into the European Economic Community. Considered by the EEC, and later the European Union (EU), as a disadvantaged zone to be integrated with priority, Andalusia has benefited fully from European subsidies during the last twenty years.

But by the early 1980s, this expansion was confronted with an environmental problem, since all the water used in the greenhouses comes from underground. With time, this water had been polluted by chemical products and became far less abundant. For this reason, in 1984 the government decided to stop the colonisation process (law 117/1984), putting an end to the grants and no longer selling land.

This decision marks the beginning of the development of a new illegal economy in the province. Despite the law, greenhouses continued to be built, and wells irrigate more and more land. By the end of the century, the number of greenhouses was twice what it had been in 1984, nearly thirty thousand hectares (Checa 1999). Since the mid-1980s, all agri- cultural development in the province has been completely outside any legal control, and new farmers remain very eager. Meanwhile, farms have been restructured: intensive exploitation has slowly replaced small-scale operations, which have often gathered into cooperatives. Subsequently, rising demand from European markets, coinciding with improvements in transport, has promoted exports, which have become the most important mode of trade for Andalusian fruits and vegetables.

These changing conditions led to the recruitment of a new kind of labour force. Until the 1980s, workers were mostly family members, but with intensive agriculture the need arose for casual workers, very flexible and poorly paid, in order to maximise profits from intensive production. Initially most casual workers were unemployed people from the area or nearby provinces. But economic difficulties encountered by farmers, in contrast to overall economic growth in Spain, reduced the available reserve of Spanish workers willing to work in poor conditions, and landowners were enticed to exploit another type of labour. This led to the second wave of migration, dominated by foreign, low-skilled workers, coming mostly from North Africa, who could be paid low wages and managed in a very flexible way. This turning point occurred in the mid-1980s, when the model of the small family farm was overtaken by a more industrial mode of production.

Contributing to this process is the fact that for the last twenty years Spanish farmers have had to compete on the European market with other agricultural regions in South Mediterranean countries that enjoy climatic conditions as good as Andalusia's while labour is much cheaper. In this context, and confronted with the hegemony of a few large supermarket companies that bargain harshly on every transaction, product prices have systematically decreased while demand has steadily increased. Until the 1990s, Spain coped with this situation thanks to market protection and financial support from the European Union, but with the progressive withdrawal of import quotas imposed on non-EU members, competition is becoming very effective. Moreover, the type of sales has changed: nowadays farmers have to respond to fluctuating demands from supermarkets all over Europe, and the harvesting of produce is done almost on real-time, following requests by supermarkets for delivery in the freshest possible state.

In such a context, massive exploitation of cheap labour has become essential to keep the sector running, and it is clear that foreign workers have been playing a central role in the process of modernisation of Andalusian agriculture. Today, even more so than ten years ago, it is essential for the farmers to have, on the spot, a readily available reserve of workers who can be used and dismissed according to the unpredictable variations of activity. In this schema, the origins and statuses of foreign workers have become strongly diversified: South Americans, Filipinos, Africans and Eastern Europeans are now often hired alongside Moroccans. That is the main characteristic of the third period of immigration in the province. Job conditions are very hard: in the greenhouses the temperature is often well above 45 °C, and workers frequently handle very dangerous toxic products. Every year some of them are contaminated, sometimes fatally, while they are processing vegetables (European Civic Forum 2004). But despite all these drawbacks, the area is still a very attractive place for people from poorer countries who seek to work in Western Europe.

This third phase is also marked by the structural role played by undocumented workers. As they do not have the benefit of any protection concerning wages and dismissals, they provide to some extent the flexibility required by the farming companies (Berlan 1986). This exploitation is possible because these people are, by necessity, devoted entirely to agriculture. As Dan, one of my Rumanian informants, explained:

> Here, if you don't have legal documents, you have no choice but to work in greenhouses. In the construction sector, employers want you to be covered by

insurance; there are many accidents, so they don't want any problem. They want you to be insured, but if you are undocumented you can't get insurance. In greenhouses, what can happen to you? There is little chance you hurt your-self with tomatoes, is there? And actually, we are so many foreigners here, they don't need undocumented ones, they leave us in the greenhouses while they employ those who manage to get papers.

(Dan, interview, 19 August 2000, translated from Rumanian)

Though some documented migrants leave the province to find better jobs in the north or in the Madrid area, and a small proportion of undocumented migrants get repatriated by the authorities, the arrival of hundreds of new migrants all year long maintains the reserve of workers at a high level. Only legal migrants obtain permanent or, more often, longer-term contracts (for a few months); most undocumented foreigners are casual workers hired on a daily basis. If they have no friends who are more settled in the area and who can help them find an occasional job, they go, every morning, to a 'job-market square' where they offer their labour to potential employers. During high season – January and February, and September to November – nearly all of them find some work; but during low season, many remain unemployed. For example, during the research, Dan – quoted above – was sharing a flat with five other Rumanians, two women (a mother and daughter) and three men, of whom only the two women, who had been in the area for two years, were actually working. August being in the middle of the low season, the others were out of work. The three young men spent their time wandering, hoping for an improbable opportunity to work while waiting for the resumption of the agricultural activity in September. As they had nothing to do during this period, they would go to the beach for hours, this activity being free. This situation of temporary unemployment in the black economy is a point of tension between migrants, since it puts them in competition for jobs, while, as we shall see, the divisions and competitions between workers of different origins contribute to the implicit management of this special kind of labour power.

Political Tensions and Racist Violence

In this context of large-scale legal and illegal immigration, racism is part of everyday life, especially towards people from the Maghreb and black Africans. In February 2000, racial tensions exploded into three days of riots against Moroccan workers after a mentally ill young Moroccan killed a Spanish girl. Following these exactions, Moroccan workers went on general strike. Then, large numbers of workers from Eastern European countries arrived, who, so was it argued by journalists, had come especially to take the place of the striking Moroccan workers (*El País* 10 February 2000; *Le Monde* 13 February 2000). A deeper analysis of the situation, however, shows that coexistence of these populations dates back to a time before these events. Rumanian workers had been hired frequently in Spanish greenhouses since the mid-1990s. It was thus the increasing social and economic tensions of the sector that brought the presence of Rumanians to light. This process is of great interest, for, with no fundamental change, the strained situation to which it led made it possible to observe clearly the different ways in which the various populations related to territory, as we shall see below.

The events of February 2000 were not the first violent expressions of racism against Moroccans in the area. Two years previously, in February 1998, two workers from the Maghreb were burnt to death in their shelter. A few months later, a foreign farm worker was executed at night by a masked commando. In both cases, the matter was closed with no proceedings; police in the area are not prone to prosecuting Spaniards in cases of racist attacks.

The racist riots in February 2000 were indeed the consequence of a violent racist climate, endemic in the area, but their outbreak and the popular aspect they took on at that particular moment can be explained by related circumstances that, for several months, inflamed the situation. Two parallel processes aggravated tensions between Spanish bosses and Moroccan workers. The first is rooted in the economic quarrel between Spanish and Moroccan farmers. The second concerns the political climate during the months preceding the March 2000 elections. Let us look at both in turn.

The fruit, vegetable and fishing sectors are often sources of clashes between the Spanish and Moroccan governments. For many years, traditional modes of production did not allow Moroccans and other South Mediterranean farmers to compete with Spanish producers, but now-adays, more and more farms use modern equipment. Across the Strait of Gibraltar, Spanish farmers fear that the Moroccan trade will supplant the hegemonic position of Spain on the European market. Moreover, some huge food-processing companies have started relocating their plants to Morocco. Up to the present, import quotas of Moroccan products to the European Union are regularly determined by the European Commission after negotiations with Morocco, and each year custom rates are lowered for those quotas. Yet import into Europe is not controlled, or is badly controlled, and Spanish farmers regularly complain that Moroccan quotas are illegally exceeded, thus reducing their own opportunities to export to the rest of the European Union. Furthermore, an agreement signed in 1995 between the European Union and Morocco aims at creating, in 2012 or thereabouts, a free trade zone within the framework of a Euro–Mediterranean partnership. In that event, Spanish and Moroccan products would be in direct competition on the European market. Spanish farmers denounced this agreement, for according to them it endangers their own future. In Andalusia, and more specifically in the region of Almeria where most producers of fruit and vegetables for export are located, the fear of 'unfair' competition thus heightened feelings against Moroccans. Farmers' unions complained of the government's deserting them:

> Farmers in Almeria are being sacrificed to globalisation. The importation of tomatoes from Morocco is increasing, and in return, Spanish multinational companies have access to the [Moroccan] communications market, and an agreement with Spanish fishermen is being negotiated.
> (Extract from interview with representatives from the COAG of Almeria quoted by European Civic Forum 2004: 48, author's translation)

In El Ejido, tensions created by this situation were aggravated when, in January 2000, the Confederation of Farmers' and Breeders' Trade Unions (COAG) denounced the Moroccan export of tomatoes, which exceeded thirty thousand metric tons. In the same month, the system of import certificates installed during the previous year, and requested by Spanish farmers, was abolished, as demanded by the Moroccan authorities. In reaction, on 25 January, fifteen hundred farmers demonstrated their anger and blocked the ports of Algeciras and Cadiz. A series of violent acts against Moroccan fruit and vegetable haulers on Spanish territory followed: lorries were burnt, cargoes ruined, drivers manhandled. In Andalusia, Moroccans, be they lorry drivers or farm workers, were subjected to increasing animosity.

The situation became ever more strained since the farmers' protests found an echo among political parties now campaigning for the March 2000 legislative elections – all the more so since the electoral campaign focused attention on the new immigration law. During debates about law 4/2000, finally voted on on 22 December 1999, farmers from the El Ejido area closed ranks. The proposed law had a particular progressive aspect that could not satisfy the position of the Andalusian farmers. Its aim was to give some rights to illegal immigrants, and it included a plan, for the following years, to reduce the number of undocumented migrants by increasing the number of regularisations and making procedures automatic after a two-year presence on Spanish territory. Above all, this law sought to penalise employers that hired foreign workers illegally, which in the Almeria area meant condemning the whole economic life of the region. In the months after it passed, farmers' unions joined forces in a national debate on a scale far beyond themselves, in order to radically amend the bill submitted by minister M. Pimentel. In Andalusia, the argument reinforced resentment against Moroccan workers, who were held partially responsible for the advancement of the new law, insofar as, thanks to the Forum for the Integration of Immigrants, several associations defending immigrants' rights made their claims loud and clear.

Although the law passed, the subject remained at the core of the national debate because of the elections scheduled for March 2000. The Popular Party, which itself had created the law, promised to review it if it were reelected. The question of immigration thus became a primary theme of the campaign. Detractors of the law and xenophobic candidates ceaselessly pointed out the damaging effects of immigration and denounced problems caused by immigrants. Such rhetoric was particularly prominent in the Almeria region, where racism had already been obvious before this argument. Law 4/2000 was scheduled to come into effect on 1 February 2000; the next day, all foreigners present since 1999 would be able to start a regularisation procedure. Anti-immigration voices exceeded all predictions: they expressed the fear that the country would be rapidly invaded by immigrants who, strengthened by the new law, would not behave in accord with their 'proper' status in Spanish society anymore. Many of the media took over this point of view, stating, with pictures to prove it, that an increasing number of *pateras*[1] from the Maghreb were arriving on the Spanish coast. Again, this mainly concerned southern regions of Spain, and some voices lashed farmers who hired illegal workers and thus generated a perpetual appeal for new immigrants. In the Almeria region, the farmers' reaction consisted in demanding that immigrants behave with greater social discretion; they chased them away from public places and attacked immigrants' associations.

It is in this context of increasing racism that we must understand the riots in El Ejido. External circumstances stimulated anti-Moroccan feelings and established a climate filled with the potential for extreme violence. The smallest event was then enough to catalyse this and allow hatred of 'Moors' to erupt into violence. On 22 January a Moroccan worker killed two Spanish neighbours during a quarrel. During the following days, the town council, whose mayor, J. Encisco, is well known for his xenophobic position, organised a demonstration calling for 'justice to be dispensed'. This event, which seemed pacifist, was used as a means of expression by racist groups. Still, things might have ended there had it not been for the incident mentioned above; a few days after the demonstrations, a young Moroccan, later declared to be mentally disturbed, killed a Spanish woman in El Ejido. That triggered the riots: in the course of the next three days, racist rioters sacked the city and set upon Moroccan workers. Tension decreased only when five hundred policemen intervened and journalists arrived, bringing the situation to the attention of the rest of the world. Ultimately, about sixty Moroccans were injured and twenty-two people arrested, eleven on each side of the dividing line.

In reaction, on 7 February, Moroccan farm workers launched a strike for an undetermined period of time. This collective action had clear, concrete demands (improved living conditions, a guarantee of minimal rights) and aimed at creating a social existence for immigrants in the region. Still, this was not a general strike, as all non-Moroccan foreign workers continued their labour in the greenhouses. Hence, their shared predicament did not erase the ethnic split; rather, the opposite occurred.

Relations to Space

Though the acts of violence against Moroccans may be explained by the context outlined above, it does not help us understand the lack of solidarity among foreign workers in the area and the unwillingness of other workers, especially Rumanians, to join the demonstrations. I suggest that this atmosphere of division was due to the history and social position of the different migrant groups in this place. Because they arrived under dissimilar conditions and are in different stages of their migratory process, 'old' and 'new' arrivals have not developed the same links to territory.

Moroccans – 'Old' Migrants in a Process of Local Integration

Moroccans, geographically in close proximity and economically disadvantaged, were the first to benefit from the opportunity to work in Spain. Most of the early arrivals were men from the countryside who were sent abroad by their families to give their community the possibility of staying put (Checa 1994). Their plan was to work temporarily in Spain, even if conditions were harsh, spending as little as possible on living expenses so as to send most of their income home, which at this point in time was clearly identified as being in the country of origin. But for this first generation, most of the time, this precarious situation lasted much longer than anticipated, and permanent returns were actually quite rare. Therefore, they began to share their life between two places: the symbolic aspects of home remained in Morocco, where their migration helped them gain social consideration, but their continual presence in Andalusia, though regularly interrupted by long holidays at home, drove them to develop social relations there and, gradually, to settle in Spain. During the 1990s, we began to see, in the streets of El Ejido, some 'Arabic' coffee shops and a few Muslim butcher shops. And, whereas at the beginning of the 1980s most workers lived in slum conditions in the countryside, often using the *cortijos* – shelters in which tools are usually stored – as accommodation, by the end of the 1990s some streets in El Ejido town were known as Moroccan neighbourhoods. Some Moroccan workers still live in *cortijos*, but many have followed the same experience as Hamid:

> When I arrived for the first time, in 1992, I stayed in the greenhouses – anywhere, where I could, I had no place to go. Then, after maybe two weeks, I went to Farid's *cortijo*, a cousin of mine, we used to work for the same boss and we lived in his *cortijo*, far away from here, near Balerma. Then, when I came back in 1995, I moved into a flat rented by a man called Kamel: his roommates had left and he couldn't pay for it on his own, so he asked us, me and my friend. We said yes, because it was nicer, it's a good flat and we are in town, it's better than in the countryside. Me, I couldn't rent a flat, because I didn't have legal papers, but Kamel [who had been regularised in Spain] had papers for the

flat in his name, so we pay him and he deals with the owner. So, we live here, in this building [in El Ejido], we are four in the flat, there is also a young boy, seventeen, who arrived two months ago. He's Kamel's nephew.

(Interview in an El Ejido street, 20 August 2000)

Connections across the Mediterranean Sea increased steadily during the last twenty years and places grew closer. Links have been tightened between the province of Almeria and some Moroccan villages, which have sometimes sent nearly all their able-bodied males across the Strait of Gibraltar. Every inhabitant of these villages has heard of Andalusia, and most of them have some friends or relatives there. They also often possess some electrical appliances or clothes purchased in Europe. All of them have stories about Almeria, and even if they have never been there, they can easily imagine how it is. For decades, Spanish agriculture has been regarded as a chance to make money that would be impossible to earn in Morocco. So even though the place has always been difficult to get to (Spain, being an EU member, imposes a strict visa regime on Morocco), many young Moroccans have long considered the south of Spain as part of their personal space: it is a place where they have links and where they can plan to go sometime in the future. In this sense, we can say that these migrants constructed a 'transnational space', as Portes defines it (Portes 1996): strongly connected places joined by a multiplicity of links.

This closeness and the hopes it allows had an impact, with time, on the migratory project itself. The migrant model of a family emissary evolved into something more individualistic: instead of being sent by their kin, young people started to leave of their own will, seeking a better life in a richer country.[2] Thus nowadays many Moroccans who reach the Andalusian coast have emigrated with personal motives, not knowing when they will be able to go back and with the hope of obtaining, in time, the opportunity to stay legally in Spain. When they do, they often invite their wives to join them in Spain, making their family life in that country. In their memory, and even in their vocabulary, Morocco remains their home country, but their everyday life is clearly developing in Spain. The way they manage their earnings is significant: when a couple is reunited in Spain, less than one-third of their wages are sent back home, while the situation is the inverse when a migrant is single (Checa 1994).

This new situation changes the way these migrants consider their place in the Spanish area. As the idea of an eventual, permanent return fades away or is seriously delayed, their presence, not only as workers, but also as full persons, becomes a critical point. They no longer consider their stay as a temporary situation of hardship compensated for by the benefits gained in the home country. Social considerations are henceforth a matter that has importance in the area of immigration itself. Progressively, they seek not only better working conditions but also more respect from the local population. This is a major issue with Spaniards: having been confronted with racism for years, Moroccans now expect to be considered inhabitants of the region and part of its social life.

In contrast to the 1980s, many Moroccan workers nowadays, even if undocumented, refuse to hide away as the dominant Spanish community expects them to. While Spaniards try to contain them in areas outside town – by not renting them flats and by expelling them from Spanish bars, for example (some bars have a notice on the door saying 'Forbidden to Foreigners') – they do not hesitate to gather in the streets after work or to socialise in bars owned by compatriots downtown. In doing so, they give their presence a certain public visibility. These everyday life practices may not be considered by all of them to be acts of resistance but, in the context, they are a point of tension with many Spaniards, as these practices declare to all the presence in the region of a large contingent of people from the Maghreb. Indeed, during the last twenty years, undocumented migrants have been tolerated in the province – because they were playing a crucial role in its economic development – on the condition of discretion and social invisibility. It is this tacit agreement that is being called into question today by Moroccans, many of whom settle fully in Andalusia.

More actively, some Moroccans, in spite of their illegal situation, are getting involved in local public life, responding favourably to the invitations of Spanish NGOs (non-governmental organisations) and trade unions. The latter realised the importance of such a reserve of cheap labour in the region and understood that, if they wanted to sustain the local working class, they had to take into account and denounce the working conditions imposed on foreign workers. Meanwhile, organisations more preoccupied with racism also wished to enrol these disaffected migrants. For a long time, these invitations fell on deaf ears, but some extreme cases – injured workers thrown out onto the street because they could not work anymore, or people victimised by physical racist violence – led a few migrants to contact these organisations. The friendship they encountered and the support they received encouraged others to join when they encountered difficulties with their bosses. So, at the end of the 1990s, some Moroccans – first, legal workers and then even undocumented ones – became union members or sympathisers. Thanks to these structures, and with the support of Spaniards, these Moroccans gave voice to their social demands. Benefiting from legal support, they were able to claim their rights and make use of medical assistance or the Spanish justice system.

In 1999, unexpectedly, a few hundred Moroccan workers demonstrated in the streets of Campo Hermoso (near El Ejido) to protest acts of racism. Though they were very few relative to the number of Moroccans working in the region, this was the first time migrants had acted publicly. On this occasion, they abandoned their usual submissive attitudes to show to the Spanish population that even if they were not full citizens, they were full persons, with demands and expectations. They asked for more respect from their employers but also from the Spanish population itself, demanding rights as basic as the right to walk in public space at any hour (usually, any African or Moroccan in the streets during working hours is arrested by the police), the right to enter any shop or bar without suffering discrimination, or the right to lodge a complaint against an employer (since the police most often refuse to register it). Not surprisingly, their demands were not met by local authorities or farmers, but it was a little revolution: before this incident nobody would have thought they were capable of such a collective action.

In the same period, trade unions took a role in the political debate on foreign workers and were mobilised when the new immigration law was publicly discussed in 1999. As the quotas of legal migrants were being decided between Spain and Morocco, the unions drew attention to illegal migrants and claimed rights for them. By this action, Moroccan migrants, in spite of the fact that only a small minority of them were activists, became the centre of a national debate in Spanish public life. This situation irritated Spanish farmers, since it was the presence of a population without any rights and totally ignored by the Spanish population that guaranteed the exploitation of these workers.

In a phenomenon reminiscent of 'the cyle of racial relations' studied by Burgess and Park (1921), it was through conflict that Moroccan migrants were gaining social acknowledgement of their existence in Spain. In this recent phase, the majority of Moroccan workers did not fit the model of a 'transnational community' anymore, but seemed instead to be in a process of settlement in the country. What is meant here when we speak of 'settling' does not imply a matter of time but depends rather on the way migrants regard their own presence in the region. Through the activity of the most dynamic actors, it became clear to everybody that Moroccans were moving socially to a new position. More than a cheap and invisible labour force, they increasingly expected to achieve a symbolic and material place in the area.

This is the key to understanding what occurred in El Ejido in February 2000. Migrant claims did not fit with the economic role offered to this population and, through racist violence, Spanish demonstrators made it clear to Moroccans that they were not willing to accept them if they refused to keep their traditional place: that of very discreet and vulnerable workers. El Ejido's mayor was quite clear on this point when he declared that 'NGOs bear all the blame [for the racist demonstrations], since they taught immigrants their rights' (J. Encisco cited in *Diario 16*, 11 February 2000). It is the evolution of their social status that was the target here. Spanish demonstrators were asking Moroccan migrants to return to their previous attitude of total submission. Responding to this demand, Moroccan workers, documented and undocumented, intended to show their economic power and collective solidarity by going out on strike. At stake was the new social place they intended to occupy, low on the social scale but at least recognised and respected.

It is clear that these events did not result suddenly from one particular event – even though a tragic one – such as the murder of a Spanish girl by a Moroccan. Rather we must make sense of them in a longer process of settlement from the earliest immigrant workers in the province onwards. The racism expressed by Spanish farmers towards Moroccans has its own logic in this process: it orders a certain hierarchy between social groups. This explains why Moroccans were not joined, during the strike, by migrants of other nationalities. The latter have different immigration histories in the area and, while they do share similar working conditions, they do not share the same social relation to the place.

Rumanians – Unsettled and Anchored in Mobility

After Moroccans, Rumanians appear to be the second largest group of foreign workers in Almeria, though we must be careful with our estimates because a large majority of these workers are undocumented. Migrants from Rumania are of diverse social backgrounds: some come from collective farms in the south of Rumania, which have partially collapsed since the end of Ceauşescu's[3] dictatorship in 1991, but there are also people from towns, relatively educated, who see work in Spain as an opportunity to improve their living conditions in Rumania. For example, during my fieldwork I met a doctor from Rosiori (a town on the Danube plain) working with her two daughters in the greenhouses. Different generations are represented, but two groups predominate: young people between twenty and thirty years old without dependants, and older people with adult children. Though their social backgrounds are diverse, many hail from the same region of Rumania, the department of Teleorman, as they use their social networks to facilitate their migrations.

Rumanians are the main competitors with Moroccans for jobs, and in the context of racism described above, they appear to be the employers' favourite foreign workers nowadays. The first Rumanians to be hired arrived in the mid-1990s, and the group grew very rapidly. Again, their undocumented status makes estimates approximate, but during the high season in 2005 there were probably between seven thousand and ten thousand in the province of Almeria (still a minority compared with Moroccans, of whom there are believed to be between twenty thousand and twenty-five thousand). During the events of 2000, Rumanians were far less numerous, no more than a few thousand, but they represented a point of crystallisation for the attention of external observers, such as journalists, because they played a crucial role in the reorganisation of foreign labour in the Almeria province.

Parallel to the steady arrival of Moroccans, the end of the century was marked by a diversification of foreign recruitment. Farmers enrolled people from South America, mainly Ecuador and Colombia, from sub-Saharan Africa, from the Philippines and from Eastern Europe. Obviously, this turn to new sources of recruitment was not due to a lack of potential

Moroccan workers but can be understood as an answer to the reluctance Moroccans were showing during the same period towards being submissive. In such a situation, Rumanians are particularly appreciated, for the attitude they present is just the reverse of the Moroccans'. This characteristic is due not only to the fact that they are more compliant because they are in an earlier phase of migration, like Moroccans in the 1980s, but they also regard their presence in Spain in a different way.

Until the year 2000, Rumanian workers played the game of invisibility expected from this kind of labour force perfectly: with the exception of their employers, nobody had noticed their presence in the area. This is why the newspapers later wrote that Rumanians had been sent from their country to Andalusia for the purpose of breaking the Moroccans' strike. Their appearance is probably partly responsible for the success of this discretion: being white-skinned and dressed like the Spaniards, they can walk through the streets without being spotted as foreigners. The presence of a large proportion of women (around 30 per cent) also tends to make this group less suspicious to the local population: these migrants do not congregate in 'worrisome' male groups in public spaces. During interviews, Spaniards often postulated that Rumanians did not need to assimilate, as they were already close to the Spanish population in many ways, culturally as well as morally. Of course, we know from inter-ethnic research that closeness and cultural differences between groups do not rely on any essential characteristic but depend on the situation and the relations between groups (Barth 1969). Moreover, Rumanians are very circumspect about their presence because they do not want to be noticed by the local population. I suggest that this attitude is due mostly to the way they envisage their migration. This is how Iliena sees her situation:

> You know, here, you cannot be integrated; Spaniards don't want foreigners to settle here, they just want us to work. But it fits what we want, we don't want to stay here, we don't care about Spain; we are here because we can work. If there are jobs here, we come here. We go where we can earn some money, here, in Castellón or in France, everywhere there is something to do ... I have friends all over Europe and I go where it's good for me, for jobs ... It is easy for us to find jobs, because we don't ask much, because what is a small wage for you or for a Spaniard is a big one for Rumania.
>
> (Iliena, interview in Balerma, 19 August 2000)

I have conducted parallel fieldwork in Spain, France and Great Britain on the same kind of Rumanian migration, and these different situations seem to propose a new model of migration, quite distant from either assimilation or transnationalism as Portes defines it. Rumanian migrants are not successors to a long tradition of international mobility: most of them started to move after the end of the Ceauşescu dictatorship, not because they were marginal in their own country but because the 'transition' to capitalism had such a social cost that it pushed the middle classes into a state of poverty that had been unknown to them before. It is in reaction to this social disqualification that people of various social origins decide to go abroad to earn wages no longer available at home. But most of them have not emigrated properly – rather, they use the wealth differential between geographically close countries to improve their lifestyle at home, becoming international commuters. As in other Eastern European countries (Morokvasić 2004), many of them became petty traders at the beginning of the 1990s, selling cheap Rumanian goods abroad and importing any kind of foreign products. In a second period, this model of temporary migration has been extended to more distant lands and longer periods (Diminescu 2003). Visa regulations imposed by EU members until 2002 and the possibility of obtaining – legally or on the black market – a tourist visa for up to three months has certainly encouraged these back-and-forth movements. Since 2002, this tendency has been reinforced as Rumanians no longer need visas to travel to the EU, but they are obliged to return to their home country every three months or they can have their passport withdrawn. It is thus much more attractive for this population to commute than to settle in a place abroad. Unlike Moroccans who, after taking high risks to reach the Spanish coast, intend to stay as long as they can on the other side of the Mediterranean, Rumanians are pushed, by institutional arrangements, towards a continuing mobility between places.

In such a context, Rumanian workers develop original practices that consist not of reinforcing their presence in one territory but of accumulating places where they can find temporary jobs in social migrant networks. When a person discovers a new destination where foreign workers are welcome, she or he exploits it and will often tell a few friends about it. By doing so, the discoverer makes an appeal to compatriots who are connected, even if not directly, to his or her social network. Meanwhile, she or he might learn from compatriot migrants that an interesting work opportunity exists in another country and will then forsake the first destination for a new one. Communication between migrants from the same area of origin is stimulated by frequent returns, as, in home cities or villages, migrants constitute a social group who do not hesitate to go out collectively, showing off their social success due to migration (Potot 2002). Thus, these migrants are more connected to a network of mobility in which several places are exploited at the same time, than anchored in a particular territory of immigrant arrival.

This is quite clear in Andalusia, where many Rumanian migrants explained that it was not their first destination of migration. Some of them had worked in Italy before, where they were employed in restaurants or hotels; others had worked in construction in France or Germany, and so forth. It emerged that these routes were dependent on connections and bridges they could rely on, a function of the people they knew all over Europe. Consequently, these people are not willing to struggle for their rights in one place: their mode of resistance is mobility. When a situation is worsening in one place, or if they simply find a better opportunity, they just keep moving to another niche (Waldinger 1994) already 'domesticated' by colleagues. In a situation of conflict they are more inclined to *exit* than to *voice*, as Hirschman would put it (Hirschman 1970). The costs of these movements, psychological and financial, are minimised by reliance on compatriots to find work and shelter. This does not mean that a strong sense of solidarity exists between all Rumanian migrants – arrangements are made only between persons who know each other or if somebody is recommended by a friend – but on a large scale, this kind of organisation appears to be a solid social background that favours international migration, at least throughout the EU. Of course, these observations should not lead us to suppose that not a single Rumanian will settle in the south of Spain, but only that there is little chance, for now, of seeing collective Rumanian action erupting, since the strength of the group comes more from its scattering than from its capacity to organise demonstrations.

Apart from the fact that they have not developed the same attachment to territory as Moroccans, another motivation led Rumanians not to join the latters' demonstrations. Their social proximity in Spain has clearly not developed into a resource of collective identification. It is important for Eastern Europeans not to appear too close to people from Africa, primarily because this is what their favourable position in the competition for jobs relies on. If they had voluntarily joined the protest, they would have lost their qualities in the employers' eyes, mainly their perceived reliability, and would then be relegated just like the others. This situation of competition for jobs sustaining racism resonates with Bourgois' description of racist tensions between recent and older immigrants in New York City (Bourgois 2002). Yet the second reason, less pragmatic and more symbolic, appears to be essential in our case study. Rumanians, overwhelmingly, share the racist perceptions that many Spaniards have of Moroccans. In their representations, ethnic closeness is much more important than social or conjectural proximity. It is true that they share the same job conditions with Moroccans and are as such situated in the same place on the labour social scale. However, they see themselves as being much closer to Spaniards, sharing a 'Christian culture' and expecting to live by the same standards. In doing so, they tend to wholeheartedly make theirs the Spanish xenophobic representations of Moroccans. This attitude can be related to the strong racism existing in Rumania towards Gypsies (Trandafoiu 2003). Stereotypes seem to be translated from one population to another, without taking into account the differences between both situations. Rumanian workers explained to me that a fundamental distinction between them and Moroccans came from the fact that Moroccans were originally nomadic, while Rumanians were not. There is nothing in the Moroccans' background that supports such notions of a supposed Gypsy-like nomadic origin, and even Spaniards do not share this view. Another racist stereotype imported from Rumania relies on the idea that Moroccans were afraid of water and avoided it. This attitude is usually attributed to Gypsies who, in the nineteenth century, were systematically expelled from sources of water in Rumania because they were suspected of polluting them and who, as a consequence, took up the habit of camping far away from wells or rivers.

During my fieldwork, the harshest xenophobic talk did not come from Spaniards but from Rumanians. While Spanish racist enunciations would always be preceded by 'I am not racist but ...', Rumanians would never take this kind of precaution, speaking as if racism was a universal point of view. In such a context, joining Moroccans in demonstrating against Spaniards and denouncing racism would not only have been meaningless, but being associated with them would even have been depreciative with regard to their own identity. Rumanians thus prefer to preserve representations of themselves by sharing the Spanish position. This attitude places them in the camp of the white majority and, at the same time, gives them the opportunity to take up better jobs by replacing relegated Moroccans.

Conclusion

This chapter has shown how racism appears as a practice of division not only between Spaniards and foreign workers but also between workers of various foreign origins. In this sense, it is quite clear that it is an important element of the management of manpower (De Rudder, Poiret and Vourc'h 2000). Origin being a factor of division, it reinforces the atmosphere of competition between workers and militates against any general collective action. Solidarity or even identification along class lines, common to all farm workers, cannot emerge as long as these ethnic identities remain stronger. With each group of origin intending to promote its own position, it seems that these differentiations are not likely to disappear. Moreover, this organisation around group identities is exacerbated by the employers' attribution of specific qualities to each group and by their ranking on scales of value.

Coming from different backgrounds, each migrant group then develops its own view of its role and prospects in the area. For Moroccans, even more than better job conditions, a key issue is to obtain social acknowledgement and to be accepted as being part of the local population. Meanwhile, Rumanians are not so much attached to territory and could leave the place rapidly if the atmosphere became harsher for them.

Thus, it is clear that the social action of the workers does not depend on objective conditions of labour but more on social representations and on resources available. The core question, for these economic migrants, is to maintain a positive self-identification, in spite of their lowly role in the labour market. For Moroccans, who are more involved in a process of settlement, this search for respectability passes through a struggle for their rights and against racist representations. For Rumanians, their way of resisting social depreciation due to their migration is to align themselves symbolically with the dominant group, depreciating others. We can suppose they will keep this attitude as long as Spaniards privilege them. But if the situation was to change, for example if new migrants from elsewhere were to be favoured instead of them, it is improbable that they would be categorised with Moroccans. In such a situation, which is very likely to appear in a context of harsh competition for jobs, it is probable that Rumanians would leave for other places in Europe, making use of their particular relation to space, since their main resource consists not of a capacity for collective protest but for transnational networks.

Notes

1. Small boat used by migrants to reach the Spanish coast illegally from Morocco.
2. This evolution has been very well described by Sayad (1977) in the case of Algerian migrants in France.
3. Nicolae Ceauşescu, president of the 'People's Republic of Rumania' from 1965 to 1989.

References

Allen, Tim and David Turton. 1996. 'Introduction: In Search of Cool Ground', in *In Search of Cool Ground*, ed. Tim Allen, pp. 1–22. Oxford: James Currey.

Barth, Fredrik. 1969. *Ethnic Groups and Boundaries. The Social Organisation of Culture Difference*. Oslo: Universitetsforlaget.

Berlan, Jean-Pierre. 1986. 'Agriculture et migrations', *Revue Européenne des Migrations Internationales* 2(3): 9–32.

Bourgois, Philippe. 2002. *In Search of Respect: Selling Crack in El Barrio*. Cambridge: Cambridge University Press.

Burgess, Ernest and Robert Park. 1921. *Introduction to the Science of Sociology*. Chicago: University of Chicago Press.

Checa, Francisco (ed.). 1994. *Invernaderos y inmigrante. El problema de la adaptación de un colectivo marginal*. Madrid: MAS.

———. 1999. 'De la Andalucía de los emigrantes a la de los inmigrantes – Diez años para la reflexión', *Demófilo Revista de cultura tradicional de Andalucía* 29: 211–55.

De Rudder, Véronique, Christian Poiret and François Vourc'h. 2000. *L'inégalité raciste. L'universalité républicaine à l'épreuve*. Paris: Presses Universitaires de France.

Diminescu, Dana (ed.). 2003. *Visibles mais peu nombreux. Les circulations migratoires roumaines*. Paris: Maison des Sciences de l'Homme.

European Civic Forum. 2004. *Rapport sur la situation actuelle à El Ejido et dans la province d'Almeria*.

Galtung, Johan. 1969. 'Violence, Peace and Peace Research', *Journal of Peace Research* 6(3): 167–91.

Hirschman, Albert O. 1970. *Exit, Voice, and Loyalty: Responses to Decline in Firms, Organizations, and States.* Cambridge, MA: Harvard University Press.

Morokvasić, Mirjana. 2004. '"Settled in Mobility": Engendering Post-Wall Migration in Europe', *Feminist Review* 77: 7–25.

Portes, Alejandro. 1996. 'Global Villagers: The Rise of Transnational Communities', *The American Prospect* 7: 25.

Potot, Swanie. 2002. 'Les migrants transnationaux: une nouvelle figure sociale en Roumanie', *Revue d'Etudes Comparatives Est-Ouest* 33(1): 149–77.

Sayad, Abdelmalek. 1977. 'Les trois âges de l'émigration algérienne en France', *Actes de la recherche en sciences sociales* 15: 59–79.

Trandafoiu, Ruxandra. 2003. 'Racism and Symbolic Geography in Romania: The Ghettoisation of the Gypsies', *Global Built Environment Review* 3(2): 6–12.

Waldinger, Roger D. 1994. 'The Making of an Immigrant Niche', *International Migration Review* 8(1): 3–30.

6

A New Morning?

Reoccupying Home in the Aftermath of Violence in Sri Lanka

Sharika Thiranagama

We had lost the most, Amma [Mother] and I, but we couldn't come back. How could we come back to this house? We were forced to stay in Jaffna. But we kept the land in Colombo. They asked us to sell, there were offers from Colombo. Amma refused to sell. She had revenge in her heart still.

Malathi's tone was measured.[1] We were sitting in the kitchen of the house she had just moved into. It stands in one of Colombo's busy, thriving old neighborhoods, one of the first on the sandy road that leads off a main street to this cluster of houses jostling for space. Malathi is a Jaffna Tamil in her mid-thirties living in Colombo, the capital of Sri Lanka, with her mother, her husband and her two daughters, Ovia and Rosa. She was born in Colombo but in 1983 her father and eldest brother were murdered in the worst anti-Tamil riots in Colombo to date, when two to three thousand Tamils were killed. Malathi, her brother and mother were displaced to the Tamil majority Jaffna peninsula in northern Sri Lanka. In the 1990s, after Malathi's remaining brother, a member of the Tamil militant movement EPRLF (Eelam People's Revolutionary Liberation Front), died in combat and after the newly supreme Tamil nationalist group the LTTE (Liberation Tigers of Tamil Eelam) began to arrest members of other Tamil militant groups, dissidents and their families, Malathi and her mother were displaced back to Colombo. This mapped Malathi's journey from Tamil nationalist politics to profound disillusionment with its consequences. In Colombo the family lived in a variety of rented houses until, twenty years after the riots, Analuxmi, Malathi's mother, insisted on rebuilding their original house in Colombo in order to pass it on to her granddaughters, Malathi's children. This house, in which we sit, is the same house and neighborhood in which Malathi's father and brother were murdered in 1983. The twenty-two years between Malathi's departure and her 'return' to this house form a life history that emplaces the ongoing war in Sri Lanka. Through this individual life story, this chapter seeks to tell a larger story about Sri Lanka's civil war and think through issues of memory, violence, belonging and 'home'.

The war fought between the Sri Lankan government and the Tamil separatist guerrillas, the LTTE, now spans over two decades. It has completely transformed the lives of ordinary people living in the primary battlefields of the north and east – the Tamil and Muslim majority regions that are the basis for separatist claims for an ethnically Tamil homeland. The result has been massive internal and external displacement as well as the complete reordering of physical and social landscapes. For Sri Lankans, displacement has become a characteristic way of inhabiting the world: one in two Sri Lankan Tamils has been displaced, and nearly one in four lives outside the country (Sriskandarajah 2004).[2] The title of this chapter partially quotes the written response of a young Jaffna Muslim, 'When will there be a new morning for us?', to a 1991 RAAF[3] question-naire asking northern Muslims about their life in the refugee camps after their 1990 expulsion from the north. Because I cover that expulsion extensively elsewhere (Thiranagama 2006, 2007), here I focus on the desire this man expresses for the future. For the young Muslim refugee, the question draws on the understanding that a new morning where ethnically cleansed refugees can belong is necessarily a new morning for Sri Lanka. It states what is obvious for most Sri Lankans living through the war: personal and larger collective political futures, as well as personal and collective displacement, are inextricably linked. The struggle of an individual, whether Tamil or Muslim, to find a place to live is both a personal story and a collective story. The violent making and unmaking of place and 'home' in Sri Lanka is also about the right to belong as members of a minority. Thus I suggest that the relationship to what was once 'home' is not just one about relationships to the *past*, but about the possibilities of belonging in the *future*, the possibilities of finding a future in which one can flourish personally and collectively.

This emphasis on the future is important. Sri Lanka struggles under the weight of 'expectation for the future', a desire for social transformation that still remains unrealised.[4] This desire most brutally shows in the two insurrections in the south and the ethnic conflict and war in the north and east. They form concrete measurements, if tragic and most often repressive, of popular desires and mobilisations for political change. This desire, as it emerged in my life history interviews with displaced Tamils and Muslims from the north, strongly conditions the ways people regard the past. All of the people I interviewed had been displaced, undergone traumatic experiences over the past twenty years, and lost their homes, but recounted these experiences through their constant attempts to imagine (or even fear) what the future would look like. Where could one belong in the future? How could one pass on land, stories, food, material and non-material sustenance? Is return possible? How could one imagine 'home' until the violence stopped, until a future could be ensued where one did not have to flee again? I found one theme reiterated in individual stories: the relationship to the future was as problematic and in as much need of construction as the relationship to the past. This was linked to the perception that only large-scale political change could effectively actualise and frame the unceasing attempts of individuals to try to move into a desired future. Perceptions of political stasis are woven into individual stories of personal fortunes and possibilities.

New trends in anthropology focusing on suffering and violence and on the individual traumas of living through (and engaging in) violence often talk of the relation of individuals to the past, to their former experiences, and to their attempts to work through, to mourn, to reinhabit the world (e.g., Das et al. 2002). This literature fails to fully mark that in situations of ongoing violence, as is the case in Sri Lanka, the necessity of 'working through' and 'surviving' is well understood but the desire to not have to survive in this manner is of equal importance. The necessity of the constant work of repair is not so much valorised, but instead read as the result of ongoing acts of violence. In my attempt to understand 'reinhabitation' I wish to go further, to understand the desire not only for the subject to reinhabit the world but also for the world to change for the subject.

Within my larger research on the internally displaced, their stories of 'home', and the ongoing brutal war in Sri Lanka, Malathi's story is a particularly good illustration of the ways in which the notion of 'home' is made and unmade through both larger social and political structures of belonging and personal affective relations of family, kin, and house. Here, through elaboration of Malathi's life story, I trace two different kinds of movements and ways of making home. The first centres on place, the movement between two locations in Sri Lanka – Colombo to Jaffna and back to Colombo – memories of the 1983 riots, the harsh unforgiving face of the militancy of the LTTE, the ethnic polarisation of the country, and the ongoing civil war. Thus, I consider belonging and the complexities of memory and inheritance through place. The other story that I introduce is the story of 'home' through kin, specifically through the relationships of different generations and of mothers and daughters. It may seem a truism to suggest that individual memories continually shift in relation to other events in life. However, because we continue to ascribe causal relationships between particular cataclysmic events and subsequent attitudes and behaviours, I argue that this needs to be restated. Therefore, this chapter traces a second movement. Through Malathi's journey through the 1983 riots and back to her original home, I draw out her complex relationship to Tamil nationalist politics. If we know that understandings of the past are constantly shifting, this must inform our analyses of the long-term legacies of events in that past.

In examining Malathi and Analuxmi's rebuilding of their family home twenty years after the riots, I try to explore how families deal with loss and how they store memories and secrets. What happens when one returns to the place that was once 'home' and attempts to make 'home-in-the-future'? The last section deals with the question of 'return' and what this question asks of the future. I track the transformation of place and imagination of 'home' over time, as well as the constantly changing relationships we have to those people, dead or alive, through which we mediate and understand feelings of 'being-at-home' in the past and the future (see Hage 1997).

Childhood

> I was close to Appa [Father]. He didn't help out at home at all … It was Amma [Mother] who cooked and cleaned and looked after us, but I was closer with Appa. Until he was dead, I was his pet. Amma was more attached to my broth-ers … I used to go out with Appa all the time, not with the boys … Amma was open and closed at the same time. I was more attached to Appa.

Malathi's family was from Sri Lanka's northern Jaffna peninsula, which was economically marginal to the emerging plantation economy of the island, had a chronic land shortage and intense population pressure that led to consistently high rates of out-migration throughout the colonial and postcolonial period (Bastin 1997).[5] Malathi's father, a civil servant, moved his family to Colombo after he was posted there. Colombo was a classic site for migrants from the Jaffna peninsula throughout the twentieth century. Don Arachchige notes that Jaffna–Colombo was one of the most consistent migration routes in the twentieth century, chiefly for employment (1994: 30). Colombo was a city of many minorities, especially Tamil-speaking ones, including recent Sri Lankan Tamil (SLT) migrants from the north and east; SLT who claimed distant heritage in the north and east; Tamils from Colombo itself who did not claim origin anywhere else; Malaiyaha/hill-country Tamils (descendents of Indian Tamil plantation labourers brought to Sri Lanka in the nineteenth century by the British); recent Tamil migrants from India; and (Tamil-speaking) Sri Lankan Muslims, Malays, Borah Muslims and so forth. In fact, as Tambiah (1986) points out, the effects of the 1956, 1958, 1977, 1981 and 1983 anti-Tamil riots in southern Sinhalese majority areas were possible because Tamil minorities (SLT from all areas and hill-country Tamils) were found in large numbers throughout the island, not just in the 'Tamil areas' of the north and east.[6] It is the movement of people – as was Malathi's case – during riots and the civil war that has polarised Sri Lanka into more clearly defined Tamil- and Sinhala-speaking areas (ibid.).

In 1983, Malathi's mother Analuxmi was away, abroad. Malathi and her two brothers were at home with their father when rioting began. The 1983 riots were prompted by the LTTE killing of thirteen Sri Lankan soldiers in northern Jaffna and the return of their bodies to Colombo. Violence occurred in many phases. The army and the police watched without intervening. High-profile government members were implicated in the violence and there is considerable evidence that some action against Tamils was preplanned because in the second phase rioters came armed with voting lists and addresses of Tamils (Tambiah 1986, 1996). The riots spread from Colombo up through the country, affecting both Sri Lankan Tamils and Malaiyaha Tamils. Tambiah reports that, despite the officially reported death toll of 470, around two thousand to three thousand were murdered and thousands displaced, ending up in a few quickly assembled refugee camps (1996: 94). In Colombo, more than half of the city's Tamil population, around 100,000, were displaced (ibid.).[7] Malathi recounted:

> The thugs on buses, with their voters lists, they knew how to find the houses, particular houses, particular numbers. Even I didn't know the other Tamil people in the neighborhood. They had spotted them; they came with their voters lists. If the government had not assisted there is no way that they could have done such mass destruction in three days … It was obvious to us that it was a well-planned and government-aided massacre.

It was the thirteen-year-old Malathi who found the charred bodies of her father and eldest brother in the hallway of their house. Malathi and her other brother hid with one neighbour and watched their house being looted by others. They then lived in the makeshift refugee camps set up in temples and schools in Colombo where refugees were housed and then sent in boats to the north and east. Malathi and her brother eventually went to her father's village in Jaffna, where her mother joined them. In the camps, the refugees made new alliances, friendships, and kinships, telling stories of their experiences of the riots to each other and helping each other in camp life. Thus, when refugees arrived on the ships in the north and east with nothing but their stories, they were not only transformed themselves but they also transformed those who listened to their stories.

The 1983 riots represent the cataclysmic event of the ethnic conflict. The riots made a feeling of besieged Tamil-ness possible across caste and class lines and comprehensively transformed Tamil public support and recruitment for newly emergent Tamil militancy. In the 1970s, Tamil militant groups of many names and ideologies had sprung up in the north and east in response to the evident failure of Tamil parliamentary parties to resolve ongoing discrimination against Tamils by the state. After 1983, Tamils lost faith in the Sri Lankan state, given clear evidence of state collusion, cover-ups, and support for 'keeping the minorities in their place'. Recruitment to the militant groups swelled, increasing members from tens to thousands.[8] The riots were also the impetus for the geographic polarisation of Sri Lanka, with Tamils fleeing to the north and east and large numbers going abroad and forming a major Tamil refugee diaspora (McDowell 1996). Large-scale displacement, that has since characterised the conflict, began in earnest in 1983. Significantly, the 1983 riots continue to be cited as grounds for the insistence of the LTTE that Tamil people must have their own state, that they can never live at peace with the Sinhalese in a Sinhalese-majority country. Malathi and her brother, like all the others who lost family and property, were displaced to Jaffna, which has become a larger 'home' and place of refuge for Tamils. She and her brother were among the thousands of people who joined militant groups.

I belonged in Jaffna

[In Colombo] one day there was a big trouble in our house because Anna [elder brother] was running around with the movement [EPRLF] and Appa had found out … They had such hopes for him, he was so clever and studied hard. … Appa hit him and then cried, and then we all went to sleep. But Anna did not give up on it.

Malathi's brother had already been a member of one of the many Tamil militant movements – the Marxist EPRLF – in Colombo but Malathi, a schoolgirl then, now joined the EPRLF women's wing in Jaffna. The militant movements were youth movements openly rebelling against the confines of a gerontocratic kinship system and exalting inter- and intra-group sibling relations. The dominant image presented was one of a horizontal family, of brothers and sisters, fighting for the same cause. After the riots, Malathi fully identified with this cause:

After we went to Jaffna, I became more concerned and I supported him [brother] fully. What happened in Colombo pushed us to think then that we can't live with the Sinhalese and we have to have autonomy. We were so young then, but I had a feeling of revenge.

For Malathi, Jaffna, the site of her growing political awareness, becomes 'home'.

I gained a sense of identity in Jaffna … I loved being in Jaffna, that was the main time for me. In Colombo I was only there as a small child, only up to thirteen years … When you are thirteen, fourteen, then you start looking at the world. Until then you need your family. That I had. But when that time came I had lost everything. I think that it was then in Jaffna that I filled this need. Then it was only Amma, Anna, and I. At that time Anna was involved and people were coming in and out. From thirteen to twenty-two, until I came back to Colombo … In that time you have a need, you know, as an individual it is a confusing moment. You are not a girl nor a woman, not a big person but not a child, you are in between. At that time what I needed, or what gave it to me … it was Jaffna society that fulfilled me. I feel more like I belonged there.

In Malathi's story, Jaffna presents itself as a choice, a desire, or, as she says, 'an identity'. It centres on a community and a society. In Jaffna, she and her family lived in her father's natal village and it continued to provide her with a sense of connection and belonging traced through her father, who appeared socially present even though he was physically absent. Often at odds with her mother, Malathi's attachment to Jaffna was not only about belonging to a family or household, but also about having ties to school, friends and neighbours, that actually provided refuge from her troubled family. After the experience of the 1983 riots, Malathi emerged with a new sensation of what it meant to be Tamil, and she tells me that she filled loss and liminality with a feeling of society, collectivity and growing political awareness. Jaffna became for Malathi that which brought her 'into the world'. When I asked, 'Why belong in Jaffna and not Colombo?' she replied immediately that Colombo never felt like her city.

In saying this, she is part of larger Tamil conversations about Colombo as a city of minorities but not *for* minorities. Colombo was a difficult place to be Tamil. It is in Colombo that the major anti-Tamil riots began. Up until the 2002 ceasefire, Tamils from the north and east were subject to special regulation. Northern and eastern Tamils had to register their addresses with local police stations and carry a police certificate at all times; they were liable to arrest if they were found at a different address. Sinhalese were encouraged to report on 'strange Tamils' in their area. The Tamils I interviewed in Colombo told me of the years during which they were afraid to wear the *pottu* (the vermilion mark on the forehead) or speak Tamil on the streets. Lodges, temporary housing where Tamils rented rooms, were regularly raided by the police at night. Colombo was for many Jaffna Tamils a transient city, a marginal waiting place. Most of the Tamils I interviewed in Colombo in 2003 had come there in order to find a way to leave the country and go abroad. Some had been 'waiting' for over ten years. Everyday exclusions reinforced a feeling of not being able to be at home in Colombo if one was a minority Tamil.

However, by 1991 Malathi had returned to Colombo and to date she has not been able to return to Jaffna. Through focusing on this I wish to show that the consequences of events on personal lives should be seen within long-term life and political processes: home making depends on the interplay between places bringing together both political and intimate relations of belonging. Furthermore, homeliness also depends on the possibility of finding a home-for-the-future.

Malathi's story of leaving Jaffna strikes at the heart of the political awakening, community, and sense of being Tamil she acquired in that town. In 1985 cracks had begun to show among the militant movements and rumours of internal killings abounded. In 1986 internecine fighting took a new inter-group turn when the LTTE banned all militant groups not allied with it, first TELO (Tamil Eelam Liberation Organisation), and then EPRLF and so forth. They even exhibited the bodies of TELO members in the street and some were publicly burned with tyres around their necks. Hundreds from the other movements were arrested and/or killed, and many members and their families were increasingly persecuted. For Malathi, who had come from Colombo in search of some sort of community, Tamil nationalism was increasingly showing its LTTE face. Then another blow struck her family. Malathi's only remaining brother died in a military operation at sea. She and her mother were the only two left from a family of five.

In the years following 1986 and the LTTE's combat and eventual victory over the Indian Peace Keeping Forces in the 1987–90 war, the organisation consolidated its power. Assuming full control over Jaffna in 1991, the LTTE continued to eliminate anyone considered a political dissident and or associated with other militant movements and their families.[9] Malathi left Jaffna for Colombo because she feaed for her life, as people even peripherally involved with alternative political movements were in danger. Many of those she knew were killed or arrested, most by the LTTE,[10] some by the Sri Lankan Army, and some by wartime bombing. EPRLF carried on, but after the LTTE's ban of other movements, the EPRLF women's wing was deactivated. Malathi had intended to go back to Jaffna, but it became clear after 1992 that the LTTE had taken Jaffna as its own, and her exile from the place 'she belongs to' began.

In writing about the implications of Malathi's departure from Jaffna, I seek to engage Koselleck's notion of 'the temporal structures of experience' and consider experience as that which continually 'leaps over time' (2004: 260). As Koselleck suggests,

> Events ... have occurred once and for all, but the experiences based upon them can change over time. Experiences overlap and mutually impregnate each other. In addition, new hopes or disappointments, or new expectations, enter them with retrospective effect. Thus experiences alter themselves as well, despite, once having occurred, remaining the same. This is the temporal structure of experience. (2004: 262)

Malathi's experiences and evaluations of the 1983 riots shift continually with respect to her relationship with her mother and her daughters (which I will discuss in the next section) and through her relationship with Tamil nationalism. There is nothing straightforward about these shifts. The short-term effect of her experience of the 1983 riots was her move towards Tamil nationalism and militancy. Now, more than twenty later, she still bears the scars of the event. Her family and her sense of belonging have been restructured but she no longer affiliates herself with Tamil militancy in the same way, having been expelled by the LTTE from Jaffna. Thus, the place of the riots in her own personal life story, and a larger collective story of how Tamils came to identify with a collective discrimination and fear, as time passed, came to intertwine in a less than predictable way. It is important to mark the different ways in which particular events are rephrased in individual lives in order to acknowledge the expansive and changeable nature of the life process and also to be cautious about attributing clear causality between events and attitudes. As Jansen (2002) argues, explanations that posit straightforward causality between present conflict and recollections of past events and traumas run the risk of such events becoming 'canonised', retracing resignification without critical examination of how collective memories and nationalist narratives can intertwine (see, e.g., Amin 1995). Recollections of 1983 have to be reinserted into the changing parameters of nationalism, belonging, militancy and personal histories in Sri Lanka. By telling a story of a life-in-progress and Malathi's move towards, and alienation from, the nationalist movement – which itself was built on memories of 1983 – I wish to show that a radically different account of '1983' is possible in place of the one written through immediate multiple recollections. Academic accounts often move from accounts of particular events to theorising the political effects of those events as self-evident emotional and traumatic consequences. However, the legacies of particular events over time, both short- and long-term, are not self-evident. Instead, they actually have to be continually reshaped and reconstructed by political groups in order to be maintained.

Moreover, the ways in which such moments of violence are written into experiences of place, family and self mean that understandings of 'home' and homeliness are also constantly shifting. Therefore, I now complicate the picture I have drawn hitherto of 'being-at-home' as being one of 'community', where Jaffna represents 'community' and Colombo 'alienation'. As Hage argues, 'it is forgotten in many theorisations of homely structures that home has to be a space open for opportunities ... so that one can perceive opportunities of "a better life": ... to develop certain capacities ... personal growth ... the availability of opportunities for "advancement"' (1997: 103). This sense of possibility is what I attribute to making home-in-the-future. How then is 'home' made meaningful in a war fought for 'homeland', in which, as one person told me, 'we have no home or land anymore'? Most Jaffna Tamil migrants in Colombo come there because they cannot live in Jaffna anymore; it no longer offers them a future. Ongoing war, recruitment of their children by the LTTE, and a lack of resources and facilities mean that many leave Jaffna, where they are the centre of the imagined Tamil nation. Almost two-thirds of those from Jaffna now live outside the peninsula. Jaffna, as 'home' and specifically a 'home' for Tamils, offers a story about former sociality and emotional and spiritual sustenance, but Jaffna is also a place that people continue to attempt to leave because it cannot offer them a future. Those who remain in Jaffna are most often those who are unable to mobilise the resources to make it out of Sri Lanka. Colombo was a transient place where people felt they did not belong, but it also offered them relief from the war and, most importantly, an airport out of Sri Lanka to dream of 'foreign' overseas destinations that might offer Tamils some sort of future. Homeliness, of the past and the future, was discussed through the interplay of these places: Jaffna, Colombo and 'abroad'. Katy Gardner points out in her discussion of *desh* (home) and *bidesh* (abroad) for Sylheti migrants from Bangladesh that 'localities' are more than physical places; these places are used to 'discuss both the past and contemporary change and the future' (1993: 1) and are associated with different power and socioeconomic relationships. For Tamils 'home', as a place where one could belong, was not always synonymous with a Tamil homeland where the future was bleak and uncertain. The paradoxical effect of the fight for a Tamil homeland has been the constant stream of Tamils attempting to leave that 'homeland'. Thus, conversations about 'home' and belonging are also conversations about 'senses of possibility', about the expectations and possibilities of flourishing in the future. As Hage points out, these are conversations about ideal-types, approximations, because homely structures, far from existing in reality, are also aspirations and 'ideal goal guiding practices' (1997: 104).

However, 'home' and homeliness are also produced through our interactions with others, kin and intimates, those others with whom we share houses and neighborhoods. I now move to look at mothers and daughters living through the aftermath of violence and massive loss.

Mothers and Daughters: The Living and the Dead

> Amma was not there for the riots. She was abroad, so sometimes I used to think she didn't understand what had happened to us … the importance …

Analuxmi and Malathi's relationship with Jaffna and Colombo were quite different. Analuxmi had sold her dowry property in Jaffna and bought the house in Colombo. In Sri Lanka, dowry – the passage of land from mother to daughter – is a significant way of imagining belonging. Dowries represent future continuity, and Analuxmi's was moved to Colombo. In Jaffna, Malathi recalls,

> We ended up in Appa's ur [home], they were not kind to her … We were sur-rounded by his people. Everyone in ur is related to us. Amma was the outsider. It would have been easier for me than for her. Everyone liked me because I was his daughter; people would take me and give me food … I was one of them. She was an outsider.

Malathi's relationship with her mother also became tense in Jaffna because of her brother's involvement in EPRLF:

> Amma used to have arguments with Anna about being in the movements. 'What does it mean you are in a movement and you are still going around with them? Why don't you go abroad? I have some money saved too.' Amma would tell him, 'You have a little sister, you are responsible for her.' I used to tell Anna, 'You go and do what you want.' Amma was so angry with me because she was trying to stop Anna and using me as the reason. If you have a sister in our nor-mal Jaffna society it is the brother's responsibility, if there is no father, for giv-ing dowry and for looking after her. She used to tell him, 'I only have your father's pension. If you go and die in the movements, what are we to do? Aren't there enough deaths in the family?'

Because I was in full support of him Amma was so angry with me. And then he died of course. And then Amma was even angrier with me. If I hadn't given Anna such support maybe he would have gone abroad, maybe he would have lived.

Malathi's sense of sorrow and memory of guilt forced on her by her mother, lingered in her tone:

She can be very arrogant and rude, but now I can see her reasons behind it and the way she was with me. Because I supported Anna, Amma may be blaming me inside. Now she is okay with me, him [Malathi's husband], and the children. But those days she was really angry and took it out on me. Sometimes she would not cook for me. I used to be very angry with her.

By withholding food, Analuxmi withheld nurture from Malathi. Malathi tells me this as we sit in her kitchen and she cooks for her own daughters. She puts food in my mouth as I help. She talks of her mother and herself, and the different things the same ghosts and places say to them.

Malathi's changing relationship with her mother mediated her understandings of herself and facilitates the constant revaluation of her experiences. Each noticeable phase that she introduced in her story of how 'she was coming to be' was also an introduction of another phase of her relationship with her mother, who withheld nurturing but still represents the unbreakable bond of family. Analuxmi and Malathi's relationship breaks, and is continually reconciled, around 'inheritance' – shared families and memories that could be moved into the future. These were tied integrally together by their understanding of belonging through people in place. For Analuxmi especially, belonging and continuity were also phrased through the idealised inheritance of land passed down through mother and daughter as dowry. It is this idea of inheritance and projected continuity that I will discuss next.

Malathi's already difficult relationship with her mother turned into full estrangement when, after Malathi left Jaffna for Colombo, she married Ketheswaran. Analuxmi and her siblings could not fully locate Ketheswaran's caste, and imagined that this meant he was of a lower sub-caste. Malathi, for whom caste was not a concern, told me how her uncles and cousins had threatened to break Ketheswaran's legs. For Analuxmi, Malathi symbolised the only child who would receive all of the family property, the only child for whom responsibility could be borne, the only child for whom a marriage could be arranged, the only child whose children would perpetuate the family, and the only child for whom dowry must be provided. It is a heavy set of inheritances to bear and the mother–daughter relationship broke after Malathi defied Analuxmi. After marriage, Malathi and her husband moved away from Colombo to eastern Sri Lanka. There she found a job, became pregnant, but missed her family; though the relationships were uneasy, this family was still a part of her life that she needed. Being cut off from her mother's family also meant that the remembered relationship between herself and her father and brothers became blocked. Malathi's recollection of this time is not happy: 'Amma cut me off completely and refused to give me dowry. I was very isolated and depressed for a long time then.'

By severing dowry transmission through Malathi, Analuxmi had signalled her attempt to end the relationship. Property, land and inheritance are polysemic 'goods' in Sri Lanka – they represent the possibility of making relationships of continuity and transmission as well as of status, both material and non-material relations of sustenance. The desire for transmission finally became the basis of Analuxmi and Malathi's reconciliation, around Malathi's two daughters, Ovia and Rosa, to whom Analuxmi decides to give dowry.

Malathi began to reevaluate her relationship with Analuxmi after she became a mother:

> Then I didn't understand. Now I am a mother I can see, think about her feelings. Now we talk about things that we never talked about before. Now she tells me that those days, people were jealous that she had two sons, among our relatives. In her family there are five girls and one boy, so that when she got two sons right away there was jealousy. And then she ended up with only the girl. And we also didn't do counselling or anything, we didn't know about things like that. Maybe someone should have talked to Amma about these things.

For Analuxmi, her granddaughters presented to her the possibility of passing on inheritance. She sought to reintegrate Malathi's daughters into the family, gifting them the dowry she refused Malathi and taking them with her to commemorate the dead family that they did not know. Thus Analuxmi tied the children into her own family through the commemoration of the 1983 riots, known as 'Black July' for Tamils, in which they lost a grandfather and an uncle. Thus, she substantialises the relationships between the children, herself and those absent.

> On the annual date we do something at the temple. Amma does it for Appa [Father]. When a young unmarried male or female dies, you can only give in their name once ... so that these young men and women will be born somewhere else. If we carry on giving, it will be like they have not been released from this life. Their 'soul' [atma] will struggle ... So Amma gives not for my brothers but for Appa. These two [daughters] go to those. So Amma does one for July twenty-fifth and she makes ten or twenty food parcels for beggars on the road ... When she goes to the temple she takes the children and they know. The little one knows 'Black July'. 'That's when something happened to your father, isn't it Amma?' she'll ask me. I started to tell them little things now and then. Then they used to look sad. I don't tell them much. They know about me going for Anna's thing. They don't know much about it, so the sad thing is that if it is only Prabhakaran [the LTTE leader] that tells them 'this is what happened', that will go into their heads, no? ... They are small still. But I will tell them later what happened, they should know their roots. We must not forget these things. Thirteen, fourteen, they might understand better.

The children present the possibilities of renewal to Malathi and Analuxmi, a perpetuated and whole family, pulling them towards the future and away from the past. Ovia and Rosa make it possible for Malathi and Analuxmi to begin new relationships.

The two girls also reorder relationships to the dead. Malathi sees telling stories to Ovia and Rosa about her dead father and brothers as a way of remaking the relationship bridging the gap between material and non-material webs of relationships. There have never been any funerals in Malathi's family. The bodies of her father and brother were not officially cremated, and her other brother's body was never recovered – a commonplace occurrence in Sri Lanka, where war ensures that bodies are rarely recovered. Rituals that most people carry out to commemorate the dead also 'create' the dead for Malathi and Analuxmi. However, as Malathi points out, while there is no permitted commemoration of her unmarried brothers' deaths, their names unspoken, that does not suspend the relationship between them and herself. This also indicates the disjuncture between the ritualisation of deaths and how unmarried men and women continue to be remembered by the living. The inability to acknowledge them in ritual does, however, point out how – in contrast to the acknowledgement of her father – relationships to those young and unmarried, and thus without children to remember them, are always more partial. Thus remembering her brothers by tying them to their nieces is very significant. However, the reverse is also true: ways of remembering the dead still remake relationships for the living.

> I had some differences of opinion with Amma and I did not go there for a while. Then I went once when she had called the *aiyer* [Brahmin priest] for the twenty-fifth of July. She was doing it in Appa's name, she keeps my brothers' photos there but the *aiyer* will not say their names. Three kilos of rice and seven kinds of vegetables are given, and when she gives, Amma says the name and gives; 'I am giving this for the *atma* of ...'
>
> I went after a long time and then I saw the photos and then I started crying. As soon as these two little ones came home, they told their father, 'Amma saw a photo and she cried.' From then I was able to talk to them about this more ... I didn't know that they had observed it for so long. In one sense I was happy because I knew they share my feelings; it has affected them that I cried.

Memories of riots, defiance and neglect irretrievably pull Malathi and Analuxmi together towards a family that only they are left to remember. Though they do not speak the names of the dead in order to release their souls, the dead have not released the living yet. Malathi's children's observance of her grief gives her the hope that they will understand her later on. Analuxmi and Malathi are reconciled again, tied together by relationships to the dead and to the living: each to the other and to Malathi's children.

Malathi and Analuxmi, who saw themselves as a family only through others, are forced to construct a relationship as those others who could have defined them as a family die and new ones are born. As relationships with the dead collapse or disappear in the tangible present, the mother and daughter reassemble themselves and entomb the lost relationships within their remaking. These constantly negotiated relationships bearing the knowledge of loss coalesce around the possibility of new life for Analuxmi and Malathi: Ovia and Rosa, watching, observing, and puzzling through their family.

These two little girls run in and out of the kitchen whenever I talk to Malathi. I often wonder exactly what they think of all these secrets that they do not 'know' about people and the house they live in, which nonetheless structure their lives. For Ovia and Rosa memory is being passed as allusions, secrets and absences. Between generations, memory is being handed down without direct speech but rather through the contours of relationships and interactions. Their watching and listening ears, knowing without being told, and the patchy histories they must be putting together force us to think about the multiple ways in which families transmit knowledge and memories. How will they, when they grow up, understand all of this? Moreover, how will they understand the house that they are inheriting from their grandmother as dowry, the house in which their grandfather and uncle were murdered? This is how I come to 'return' and how Malathi and her family took the almost unheard-of step of coming back to the house that Malathi fled when she was thirteen.

Return

Amma said she was going to save her money and started to build a new house. I knew nothing of this, for a long time no one told me. But I had nothing to do with it at all, she was the one who built it up.

Malathi had heard from others that Analuxmi had begun rebuilding the house in Colombo. She describes Analuxmi's actions ambiguously. On the one hand, she expressed admiration for Analuxmi's gesture of defiance that it was her house, her dowry, and she would not give it up because of the neighborhood. She talked of Analuxmi's pain at not being there in 1983 and returning to find everything gone. However, Malathi is constantly conscious of the fact that Analuxmi was absent for the riots. It is part of the tangled knot of misapprehensions and recriminations between mother and daughter. Malathi tells me she herself would not have chosen to return to the neighborhood and the house. 'She [Analuxmi] said from the time she went back, people were talking, passing comments, staring at her. Now she says there is nothing, she says that some neighbors are even good to her now. It must be the guilt, I think.'

Becoming permanent residents in that neighborhood and assuming ownership of land was, as she recalls, the issue that had provoked hostility twenty years earlier:

The neighbor from that house [in front] came to talk to me. I told him, 'So you thought in 1983 that the troubles would be solved by threatening us and sending us all back to Jaffna. Have the troubles been solved?' He told me, 'I never did anything to your father. If I had been there I would have looked after your father. He was such a nice man, I knew him.' He is a cunning man, just trying to tell me tales. ...

"They had many of our house possessions in their house ... Now when they see me they are feeling guilty ... Now he is a little like a snake with its fangs drawn because he is old. But I knew that we would have trouble from him one day. When Appa used to go by on his bike, he would look at us with hostility, and he would tell tales. He was not at all happy with us. We were the first Tamil people to buy land there and build a house. There were other Tamil families after a while, but we were the first, so he always had a problem with us ...

He said, 'It seems like you are a familiar face, like I have seen you before.' I told him, 'Why are you even thinking about it, I am the daughter of ____.' Then he asked me, 'Who was that?' He had understood, his face changed when I said it. I said, 'You killed him didn't you? I'm his daughter.' He said, 'I was not there, I wouldn't have done something like that, I was somewhere else. If I had been there it would not have happened.' I said, 'You would have gone somewhere else to cut somebody else up.'

Malathi cannot forget that this man led the mobs in her area in 1983. The riots draw neighbors into histories that cannot be disentangled from each other. 'When they see me then they start to be anxious. Amma was not there then, but I was there. But also I know, Amma is old now, but I am young, and if I go and live there ...'

Malathi makes many trips back to the house as it is being rebuilt, and as she points out, the Sinhalese neighbors are anxious about her presence for two reasons. First, she reminds them of a past they wish to forget, and second, as a young woman she represents a future of residence, of ownership, and possibly continuity that they wish to avoid. The neighborhood is willing to accommodate an elderly woman living out the rest of her life. Malathi and her family, however, are young, like the family they were when they first resided there. They have children, to whom the house and the land will pass on. They represent the past to the neighborhood, and they represent the future through the possibility of their continued residence there. Their presence reminds the neighborhood of a guilt it cannot contain.

Riots happen in localities, concrete places; they tear apart intimate, face-to-face daily relations. Memories of neighbors acting on neighbors, from direct physical violence and looting to standing silently by, reside in such sites. 'Returning' not only stirs these memories, it forces neighbors into an unwilling confrontation with the past and the necessity of repair for the future. Malathi's experiences illustrate this 'after', when the dust has settled and people cope and create new lives and new histories. In addition, if not in Malathi's case then in other stories I recorded, for many this is made easier by memories of those Sinhalese neighbors who braved the mobs to protect and give shelter to strangers and friends. These are the other memories of riots. Malathi's experiences were less positive.

> He [the neighbor] had said in Amma's hearing to someone else, 'The children are lovely and innocent but their mother is a real trouble maker.' Because I had scolded him … They want to forget. Even we Tamil people have that too … We want to hide it and forget about it all … In 1988 to 1989 there was a huge massacre here [in the south] with the JVP [Janatha Vimukthi Peramuna], sixty thousand people, but nobody is talking about that. Everybody wants to forget the past. Our people [Tamils] keep memories alive for a little, but who talks about the TELO massacres now? We still remember a little more, though. So much we don't forget … It may be easier if we forgot a little bit.

In Sri Lanka in the south, as Malathi points out, sixty thousand went missing between the years 1987 and 1989 as a result of fighting between the Sri Lankan state under the UNP (United National Party) and the southern insurrectionary group, the JVP. Both the UNP government and the JVP were in parliament at the time we spoke. What Malathi alludes to is not the failure of the mechanical retrieval in memory, but the operation of memory within the larger political context of the present and also the future. For Malathi, the neighborhood's reluctance to recognise her and its asking her *to forget*, is not their tacit and unspoken silent acknowledgement that the riots will never happen again and thus a sign of reconciliation and moving on. For her, their desire that *she forget* and not 'make trouble' is their attempt to avoid a future that acknowledges this past. These are the difficult memories of violence that local(e)s contain and that only large-scale political change, still unavailable in Sri Lanka, can make into stories of the past.

The failure of all the three peace processes in Sri Lanka and thus the constant anticipation of future violence mean that, despite Malathi and her family's return to their former house, the possibility that violence may once again tear open their lives is always on the horizon. What 'return', 'reinhabiting', 'working through' – the favoured subjects of innumerable articles on individual trauma – often elide is that in situations of ongoing war and violence for those like Malathi, what is desired, in order to make these histories memories of the past and not expectations of the future, is some transformation of the political structures. Those people whom I interviewed in Sri Lanka repeatedly told me that the past was the past, it had happened and, unable to do anything else, they were dealing with it and carrying on. What they wanted to know was that it would not happen again. Until Sri Lanka finds a new morning, individual 'repair' can always be undone. Thus, the intimate lives of Tamils always beckon to the intimacy of the effects of the riots and the war, forcing new reimaginings of feeling-at-home through place and through people.

Through Malathi's life story, I have discussed the transformation of feeling 'at home' with people and places over a life course, marked and constituted by a series of violent experiences and multiple displacements. In doing this I suggest that home- and place-making practices are far from fixed on one place and that these experiences and understandings of 'home' are temporally structured. I have discussed here the ways in which different places, Jaffna and Colombo, offer different belongings, possibilities and experiences of the future. I de-essentialise the links between certain peoples and particular places that emerge through nationalist struggles, to show the complex ways in which violence, political struggles and personal life processes come together to make and unmake 'home'. I stress that stories of home do not just reflect on the past, but envision and dream of the possibility of a flourishing future. The experience of the 'return', which Malathi and her family undertake, leads not to an account about individual trauma but to the necessity of imagining the transformation of collective political structures to accommodate belonging for people in the future. Through employing one life story, I have sought to show several things: first, how structural and physical violence continually remakes places and people in Sri Lanka; second, that feelings of belonging to a community and a place are not synonymous with being able to be-at-home but instead need to be understood through complex political and social histories of inclusion and exclusion; third, that one's relationship to events, to 'home', to place is rarely frozen in time but constantly shifts and is re-embedded in narratives in relation to other experiences, events and people; and, finally, that 'home' is not only about place but also about the people through whom we feel-at-home, and uneasy and constantly renegotiated relationships. Relationships with place and people constantly need to be remade; they are never just natural and given identifications. These narratives, even while they talk about the past and memory, are instead constantly concerned with looking forward and imagining continuity in the future.

Acknowledgements

I wish to thank the ESRC (Economic and Social Research Council of Great Britain and Northern Ireland) for their postgraduate scholarship 2001–5 and postdoctoral fellowship 2006–7). Many thanks also to Stef Jansen and Staffan Löfving, several anonymous reviewers, and Thomas Blom Hansen for their much-appreciated comments and encouragement on an earlier draft of this chapter. I am most grateful to Malathi and her family who generously shared their stories with me.

Notes

1. Pseudonyms have been used for all names. Interviews were conducted by the author in a mixture of Tamil and English. Translation of the interviews has been done by the author.
2. Muslims are not left unaffected either: all northern Muslims were forcibly expelled in the space of forty-eight hours in October 1990 by the LTTE and the numbers of eastern Muslims displaced are rising as a result of communal tension between Tamils and Muslims in the east. Moreover, most Tamils have experienced multiple displacements; the Danish Refugee Council (2000) estimates that since 1983 around 1.7 million have been displaced one or more times.
3. Research Analysis and Action Forum, a northern Muslim NGO based in Puttalam district.
4. I suggest in invoking the future, following Koselleck, that 'the presence of the past is distinct from that of the future' (2004: 260). For Koselleck 'the space of experience' and 'the horizon of expectation', while conditional, are also fundamentally of different orders. By this he means that experience is the past incorporated into the present – its events can be remembered – whereas expectation directs itself to the 'not-yet': '[E]xperience once made is as complete as its occasions are past; that which is to be done in the future, which is anticipated in terms of an expectation, is scattered among an infinity of temporal extension …' (ibid.). It is the not-yet that exceeds experience and occupies ideas of the future for civilians in Sri Lanka.
5. This was enabled by the presence of one of the most comprehensive networks of schools in Sri Lanka, and the value that Jaffna Tamils placed on education and migration as the prime means of social mobility (Arasaratnam 1986 [1982]). After independence, one of the key resentments articulated by the Sinhala nationalist movements was the seeming dominance of educated Jaffna Tamils within the colonial economy.
6. Attention has always been focused on the experience of northern and eastern Tamils, whereas the riots also affected Malaiyaha Tamils of Indian descent and Tamils from Colombo – the groups left out of the 'liberation struggle' for autonomy of the north and east.
7. See Tambiah (1986) for an excellent comprehensive account and analysis of the 1983 riots.
8. Subsequent to 1983, the Indian central government began secretly training and arming Tamil militants (Krishna 1999: 123).
9. See for example the UTHRJ (University Teachers for Human Rights–Jaffna) reports from 1991 on (available at www.uthr.org).
10. LTTE is a quasi-state actor; it manages a large network of prisons, camps, a judiciary, and a court system. It also manages border patrol and has its own bureaucracy and forms one has to fill out when crossing borders.

References

Amin, Shahid. 1995. *Event, Metaphor, Memory: Chauri Chaura, 1922–1992*. Berkeley: University of California Press.

Arasaratnam, Sinnapah. 1986 [1982]. 'Historical Foundation of the Economy of the Tamils of North Sri Lanka', in *Chelvanayagam Memorial Lectures, Thanthai Chelva Memorial Trust*, pp. 1–44. Jaffna: Saiva Press.

Bastin, Rohan. 1997. 'The Authentic Inner Life: Complicity and Resistance in the Tamil Hindu Revival', in *Sri Lanka. Collective Identities Revisited*, ed. Michael Roberts, vol. 1, pp. 385–438. Colombo: Marga Institute.

Danish Refugee Council. 2000. Program Document, 2002–2003. http://www.db.idpproject.org/Sites/idpSurvey.nsf/AllDocWeb/B10B95B330791E C1C12569990052D57D/$file/DRC_May+2000.pdf

Das, Veena, Arthur Kleinman, Margaret Lock, Mamphela Ramphele and Pamela Reynolds (eds.). 2002. *Remaking a World: Violence, Social Suffering, and Recovery*. Berkeley: University of California Press.

Don Arachchige, Neville. 1994. *Patterns of Community Structure in Colombo, Sri Lanka: An Investigation of Contemporary Urban Life in South Asia*. Lanham, MD: University Press of America.

Gardner, Katy. 1993. 'Desh-Bidesh: Sylheti Images of Home and Away', *Man* (N.S.) 28(1): 1–15.

Hage, Ghassan. 1997. 'At Home in the Entrails of the West: Multiculturalism, "Ethnic Food" and Migrant Home-building', in *Home/World: Space, Community and Marginality in Sydney's West*, ed. Helen Grace, Ghassan Hage, Leslie Johnson, Julie Langsworth, and Michael Symonds, pp. 99–153. Annandale: Pluto Press.

Jansen, Stef. 2002. 'The Violence of Memories: Local Narratives of the Past after Ethnic Cleansing in Croatia', *Rethinking History* 6(1): 77–93.

Koselleck, Reinhart. 2004. *Futures Past: On the Semantics of Historical Time*, trans. Keith Tribe. New York: University of Columbia Press.

Krishna, Sankaran. 1999. *Postcolonial Insecurities: India, Sri Lanka, and the Question of Nationhood*. Minneapolis: University of Minnesota Press.

McDowell, Christopher. 1996. *A Tamil Asylum Diaspora: Sri Lankan Migration, Settlement and Politics in Switzerland*. Oxford: Berghahn Books.

Sriskandarajah, Dhananjayan. 2004. *Sri Lanka Research Guide. Forced Migration Online*. http://www.forcedmigration.org/guides/fmo032/fmo032.pdf.

Tambiah, Stanley. 1986. *Sri Lanka: Ethnic Fratricide and the Dismantling of Democracy*. Chicago: University of Chicago Press.

———. 1996. *Leveling Crowds: Ethnonationalist Conflicts and Collective Violence in South Asia*. Berkeley: University of California Press.

Thiranagama, Sharika. 2006. 'Stories of Home: Generation, Memory, and Displacement among Jaffna Tamils and Jaffna Muslims'. Ph.D. dissertation, University of Edinburgh.

———. 2007. 'Moving On? Generating Home in the Future for Displaced Northern Muslims in Sri Lanka', in *Ghosts of Memory: Essays on Rememberance and Relatedness*, ed. Janet Carsten, Oxford: Blackwell.

7

LIBERAL EMPLACEMENT

Violence, Home and the Transforming Space of Popular Protest in Central America

Staffan Löfving

From the perspective of a participant observer in anti-regime demonstrations in Serbia in 1996, Stef Jansen notes how demonstrators 'disentangled and re-entangled power relations through oppositional spatial practices ... , inserting their bodies into public spaces, and thereby probing the limits of regime control' (Jansen 2001: 40). This chapter draws inspiration from such a focus on spatiality and meaning in and of protest, making the relation of public space to regime control in Europe speak to the relation of rural territories to state power and national space in Central America (see Stepputat 1994, 2001). In contrast to spaces where different truth claims collide and feed on face-to-face confrontation, the place in focus here was militarily sealed off during the 1980s when the guerrilla hunt of the Guatemalan army escalated into a scorched-earth mayhem. In a remote mountain region, surviving rebels of the Guerrilla Army of the Poor (EGP)[1] and displaced non-combatants gradually built up a society in resistance, a state within the state with its own institutions like health clinics, schools, an organisation for female political participation, a tax system, and defence, thereby probing the limits of national security doctrines.

While declared a 'liberated space' (see Jansen 2001; Routledge 1994) by its people, this area was also effectively kept in isolation by the army until the beginning of the 1990s, when an international presence made it possible for people to cross the front line. Regardless of the degree of actual liberation, however, the place remained a bastion of resistance in the political imagery of opposition to the state and the army in Guatemala throughout the war. And, as we will see, regardless of their stated pride in being liberated, its inhabitants were torn between a revolutionary commitment[2] and paralyzing uncertainties. This chapter is about those uncertainties and the political context in which they grew. It is based on my anthropological fieldwork between 1995 and 1998 in the *Comunidades de Poblaciones en Resistencia* (CPR)[3] – the resistance communities – and on two visits to Guatemala in 2006. I observed local political consequences of regional transformations as the peace agreement was signed in December 1996, the guerrillas were demobilised in the spring of 1997, and people were being split up and relocated, or 'redisplaced' (see below), one year later.

While some in the resistance communities occasionally referred to themselves as being displaced from their native communities or from their land of origin – most came from the Maya Ixil town of Nebaj, and now they lived on lands belonging to the neighboring town of Chajul – I never met anyone who saw herself or himself as a helpless victim of army atrocities. Rather, acknowledging a displaced status was posed as an argument against those who during the peace process accused them of illegally occupying the land of others.[4] 'Being in resistance' meant being in that very place, but it also implied being victorious over, if not the enemy, then at least over his intentions, and over recruitment into the paramilitary civil patrols in Nebaj and Chajul. 'Being in resistance' also marked something highly existential – it meant still being alive.

'Home' figures here in complex ways. I subscribe to Ghassan Hage's (1997) conception of home as a place and condition of physical security (cf. Bauman 1999), where familiarity marks processes of emplacement (Hillier and Rooksby 2002), where we are part of a community (Douglas 1991), and where we are 'certain' of our place in social structures to the extent that we can actually make plans for the future, both near and distant. But instead of deductively attaching a specific spatiality to such a set of aspirations and social conditions, I would like ethnographically to explore its possible scale and location. In the resistance communities, home emerged more as a 'struggle' (to use an emic label) for large-scale societal changes than as the defence or reconstruction of family, house, or even community.

The championing of home as household is part of a project of emplace-ment in the neoliberalising states of Central America.[5] As argued by Bourdieu (1998) and others (e.g., Larner 2000; Peck and Tickell 2002; Wacquant 1999; see also Kalb 2005), a globally encompassing 'deepening' of neoliberalism not only promotes the extension of market logics to all spheres of human life but also, politically, restrains contentious movements by providing the terms of the debate, or 'setting the stage', and thereby producing the very conditions for its own opposition (Gledhill 2005; Žižek 2002). In the postwar republics of Nicaragua, El Salvador and Guatemala, household sociality and economy have reemerged as the shelters, refuges and strategies of survival they once were. Movement as exit, rather than voice (see Hirschman 1970), has become an ever more attractive option to 'avoid' poverty and despair. I will come back to this point later.

Eulogised Space and Domicide

Before presenting my ethnographic case in more detail, let me briefly discuss the history of home and violence among mobilised villagers in the Ixil region of Guatemala and how to conceptually approach the destruction of home – referred to by Porteous and Smith (2001) as 'domicide' – during the wars of Central America. Greg Grandin writes:

> The military's 1981–83 scorched-earth campaign [in Guatemala] – which razed hundreds of Mayan communities, committed over six hundred massacres, murdered over a hundred thousand indigenous peasants, tortured thousands more, and drove, in some areas, 80 percent of the population from its homes – was specifically designed to destroy rural support for the powerful insurgent group known as the [EGP]. (2004: 127)

More than ten years later, people in the resistance communities revealed to me the details of how they had survived this campaign. The military destruction of homely spaces occurred in waves – rather than in a singular event of destruction – so that the families who escaped in time could, when possible, return to resume their lives in between recurrent army sweeps. Homes thus turned from shelters into temporary hideouts, bases for revolutionary organising, and the exceptionally harsh practices of wartime everyday life. When eventually these hideouts were burned to the ground, many claimed to already have been 'on the move' and that such movement had a political purpose: they were now continuing on the road to freedom and they were not coming back. They were anxious to explain that they did not perceive home as lost, nor that home was awaiting them in a different place, but, rather, that it had to be fought for *on a different scale.*[6]

The strategic secrecy surrounding the issue of guerrilla affiliation in Guatemala did hide its history from most observers, including most ethnographers during the late 1980s and early 1990s, with unhappy consequences in the narrow circle of anthropological debate. Some justified guerrilla violence by claiming that the rebels rose to defend people against unprovoked repression. Others reversed that argument and held the guerrillas responsible for having provoked an excessive yet legitimate military response.[7] My ethnography does not support either of these positions. Indeed, ambulant army units in the service of the local landowning elite were present in the Ixil region before the war, and they did contribute to the quelling of workers' protests on the estates by private security guards and the police (Löfving 2005; cf. Stoll 1993). But rebel mobilising built on a broader conceptualisation of violence than sheer military repression. Therefore, many of my informants, among them the ones I refer to below as the 'revolutionary committed', were engaged in a future-oriented project of remaking, not their own subjective worlds previously 'unmade' by violence, but, rather, society itself. They were realists in that sense, seeing revolutionary violence as a continuation of politics by other means (Clausewitz 1976; see Hardt and Negri 2004: 15).

The narratives of the revolutionary committed resemble a radical political philosophy of home, territory and emancipation. Jacques Lacan conceived of 'territorialisation' as the process by which parental care-giving charges specific organs and corresponding objects with erotic energy and value. Territorialisation programs desire to valorise certain organs and objects at the expense of others. For Deleuze and Guattari (1977), in their reading, both psychological and political, of Lacan, deterritorialisation implies both the process of freeing desire from the nuclear family *and* the process of freeing labour power from specific means of production. Since the 1950s and early 1960s, modernisation has brought new sectors of the Latin American population – women and landless peasants – into the labour force, enabling the expansion of transnational companies into Latin America as well as stirring revolutionary uprisings. In response to this emergence of threatening spaces of popular organising, the US-designed and US-funded counterinsurgency regimes of countries like Guatemala and El Salvador set out to conquer new territory, with people's homes being the primary targets.

Where others are concerned with the repressive qualities of the family (see Deleuze and Guattari 1977; Engels 1972), Jean Franco (1985) emphasises its sheltering power. Drawing on Bachelard (1994 [1958]), she defines the home of the family as a eulogised or moral space, capable of resisting state intervention. This notion of home as sanctuary, especially when compared with 'church space' (see Franco 1985: 416) must not be confused with divine protection. On the contrary, it is in spheres of high levels of familiarity and mutuality that the power to protect and the trust in the power of others can be felt and built upon. Whereas national armies and paramilitary organisations – upon targeting and rebuilding it – have converted the sanctuary into a base of operations, insinuating themselves into the most intimate spheres of social power (Feldman 1991), the relationship of sanctuary to revolution was different. Recruitment into the EGP usually occurred at night, within the shelter of the house of the person to be mobilised. Traditions of cooking and serving food, the order in which guests and hosts consumed it, and so forth, were often said to have informed those meetings. I would go as far as to argue that this approach was a precondition for a translation of home into society, making it possible to resist the insecurity of an actual or pending domicide, allowing a 'sense of possibility' to partake in the construction of a 'secure' alternative (see Hage 1997). On the basis of Franco's state-sanctuary model, I argue that rebel-controlled areas emerged as safe havens, as themselves morally inscribed sanctuaries (rebel-cum-sanctuary as opposed to state-versus-sanctuary) – a point to which I return below. Suffice it to say here that whereas *en vogue* strategies for the construction of peace would treat the function of violence in society to be the same regardless of the identity of its subjects and objects (see, e.g., Borneman 2002), my approach in this chapter attempts to qualify not only violence but also the relationship of violence to place in transforming political contexts from open state repression to liberal peace.

Time and Reemerging 'Senses of Impossibility'

To me, Pablo[8] qualified as one of the revolutionary committed in the CPR, but in 1997, time, memory and a transforming political context were challenging his pride and self-perception. He had been a militarily active member of the EGP since the late 1970s but was working in the health sector of the resistance communities at the time we met. In the early 1980s, in the midst of the army's scorched-earth campaign, Pablo found himself running and hiding, looking in vain for a safe haven:

> When I eventually returned to Nebaj to stay with my parents, my father said to me, 'Don't come back here, they [army soldiers] have already returned to look for you. ... They were armed and they threatened me, they tied me up.' They thought that my parents were the ones who kept me hidden. So they hit my poor father and my poor mother. And my father told me that it was better to keep away from home. That's what he told me. What I did? I left Nebaj. I went to a small hamlet on the outskirts of town where I stayed a couple of weeks, or months. I don't remember. Since the town does not stretch that far, I thought that they would not come. That nothing would happen. They did come, but later, to commit some massacres. They burned houses. They killed all the hens and chickens ...

The army cleared the inhabited region of hiding places and Pablo was eventually captured. He was held at an army barracks for a period of time he biblically referred to as forty days, and he was tortured and maimed for life before he managed to escape. This part of his story was obscure and the details hidden from me. Once back with his *compañeros* in the resistance, it turned out that he was not trusted: under suspicion of having turned army informant, he was reemployed not as a fighter but as a health worker without access to information sensitive to the insurgency.

Throughout the 1980s, army surveillance of the Ixil towns and villages was based on controlling people by keeping them indoors, suspecting them of subversive intentions and contacts if they were 'outside home'. Pablo said:

> My mother knew that it was very dangerous during this time to speak about whoever roams the mountains, or who isn't in the house – he will be taken for a guerrilla. My mother could not tell this to my brothers. So when we met [during a 1992 reunion in Nebaj], one of my younger brothers said, 'I don't think we are brothers. Perhaps you are my father's brother, because you look a lot like my father.' My mother cried. We were many that time, nine buses. And a lot of people ... it was a very big reunion. Many met for the first time in ten

years, in twelve years. It was then that my mother told me that my father had passed away one year before. I didn't see my father before he died. Because ... I'm sure that the army would have killed me, if I had gone to Nebaj in those days. At that time the army never bothered to find out about where you were from. The thing was that they killed whom they saw. Many friends of mine died. They settled down in Nebaj and thought that the army would not touch them, but yes, they died.

On a later occasion, when we were discussing suicide, Pablo said this was completely non-existent during the years of heavy repression, and that it seemed to reappear when military pressures eased. 'For example, my father, he committed suicide,' he said,

> My mother gave me one reason why he poisoned himself. She said that I am responsible. To tell you the truth, this thing really gets to me [nervous laughter] ... He had been tortured eight times by the army ... in their search for me. My father was horrified by this. That is why he killed himself. That's what they say. That's what my brothers are saying. Now, my mother says she doesn't know the reason. While the neighbors tell me that my father got drunk and that he didn't get along very well with my mother, they say. So, to this day I don't know the real cause.

Not knowing 'the real cause' of his father's suicide does not seem to exempt Pablo from the burden of responsibility and guilt. On the contrary, this uncertainty becomes a constant reminder of Pablo's possible role in the suffering of his family members, not exclusively in relation to past events but also with repercussions into the present. Hence, if 'home' is *made* of hope and capacities to aspire (see Appadurai 2004), home can effectively be *unmade* by fear and anxiety. Reflecting on the effects of torture, Pablo said:

> They tied my arms, they beat me, and finally they broke my bones. And nine days in that position, with broken arms that later healed without any medical attention, left me with deformed shoulders. That is one thing I will never forget. And the other thing is that when I talk to certain people, if I talk about the torture that I've experienced, sometimes I lose track of time. ... I remember the past, or I think that if those bastards had got me killed, I wouldn't have had my three children. Now I have my three children, I have one daughter. I didn't have them yet when I was captured. If they had managed to kill me, I would not have had my three children. But I lived through it, got my children ... I come to think about too many things ... And then I come to think about the fact that, shit, I had to abandon my father and my mother [silence]. And not just that, but ... I wasn't there when my father died. I wasn't present at the funeral. I come to think about too many things [his voice is about to break into weeping; he speeds up his talking and laughs nervously]. It isn't easy, as I just told you, to live in the mountains, without proper food and housing. However, one has to fight the army. If the EGP hadn't done it, I don't think that in any case they would have respected the rights, the ones they keep talking about right now, the human rights.

Living with a sense of guilt, of having failed or sacrificed too much along the revolutionary road, seemed to be intrinsic to the war experience of people in the resistance communities. As expressed in Pablo's tale, such 'failures' were often 'ours' and explained through reference to an over-whelmingly powerful enemy. Yet, at times, failures appeared individual and both violence and blame worked through the fragile social tissue of the resistance communities to individualise responsibilities for past losses and present weaknesses.

'Guilt' is conventionally conceived of as a personal thing, that is, an inner, individual agony that is not addressed in social communication, whereas 'shame' is a social emotion (see Obeyesekere 1980). In a Mesoamerican context, this divide between the self (guilt) and the social (shame) is complicated by Farley's take on the sociocentricity of 'the Mesoamerican Self' (1998), which, by disqualifying the distinction and instead of viewing shame and guilt as conceptually separated would see guilt as a likely consequence or dimension of shame. The 'social' for sociocentric selves is by necessity also inner or personal. Even if Farley problematically encapsulates the self within a paradigm of timeless culture, he interestingly highlights cultural and historical specificities of the relationship between self and sociality and thus adds to our understanding of the revolutionary experience of war–peace transforma-tions.[9] The question whether grievances and accusations against the guerrillas were delivered from within or outside the sphere of the social (i.e., if my 'judge' was my mother or the army) was crucial to their emotional-cum-political effect. It determined whether intended shame would effectively be transformed into disempowering guilt (in the conventional sense of the terms) or would, instead, enforce the division between 'a community of rebellion' on the one hand and the army – whose evilness explains its atrocities without justifying them and legitimises any actions against it – on the other. The army had effectively diminished the sphere of the social throughout the war by killing kin, breaking up social networks, and relocating survivors under its control. But not to the extent that it won the war. Pride, not shame or guilt, had characterised the revolutionary commitment. At the war's anticipated end the revolutionary self was repositioned in wider, or 'trans-frontline' social contexts, making people receptive to a moral judgement that previously had remained powerless outside the social.

The guerrilla projects in Central America viewed the historical predicament in which the poor found and still find themselves as a condition *not* of their own making (see Brockett 2005; Morán 2002; Wood 2003). The propaganda-like ending of Pablo's narration, where the ter-mination of war and the present-day emphasis on human rights exemplify some of the EGP successes, demonstrates a move away from traditional morality in the highlands, where misfortune has generally been conceived as an effect of the immoral deeds of the unfortunate themselves (see Colby and Colby 1981). His storytelling usually began in a similar fashion. But in between the politically correct beginning and end, the story gravitated towards a theme that he said 'really got to him,' towards an accusation from as close a social distance as his mother. This made him repeat statements in sentences like, 'And my father told me that it was better that I kept away from home. That's what *he* told *me*.'

Despite its isolation, leaflets with anti-guerrilla propaganda were distributed from helicopters over the area throughout the 1980s, and on the roads and markets where pro-guerrilla villagers resumed their market exchanges in the 1990s. Innumerable drawings and statements that told about the evils of guerrilla warfare and the role of the resistance communities in its continuation had been delivered to everyone by the civil patrol on the front line. In her ethnography, Judith Zur includes drawings depicting the EGP as the embodiment of the devil, with tail and horns, and the soldiers pushing him back with Christian crosses (1998: 265f.). I was given a similar drawing at a roadblock close to Nebaj in the early 1990s. After having body-searched all the men on the bus, the soldiers gave all the passengers a small drawing of a gang of thieves running away from a cosy hamlet. On their backs was written EGP and CUC (the name of the radical peasant league). Soldiers were chasing the group.

Several stories I heard during my fieldwork indicate that such messages assisted the army project of ideologically reconstructing Ixil sociality on both sides of the front line. The weekly town square speeches of the army-backed mayor of Chajul were coloured by poetic allusions to rebel 'inhumanity'. When, in the early 1990s, the CPR members were finally able to pass army-controlled front lines for the first time and go to the market in the town of Chajul, they stood out as the most ragged and skinny people on the scene. They were thus easily identified as the people who had been living in the mountains, *like animals*. For a decade, the propaganda-fuelled rumours had been saying that life in the wilderness had affected the guerrillas to the extent that they had even *turned into animals*. They were no longer humans with the capacity to switch between good and evil. They had transformed into evil. To their surprise and grief, the visitors noticed how people in Chajul tried to get a glimpse of their behinds in order to find out if they had really grown tails.

Regardless of how stubborn their resistance to a far more powerful enemy had been, I argue that events like this contributed to a gradual change in people's perception of themselves. New patterns of movement during the peace process diminished their space of autonomy and opposition by bringing the army-dominated national society closer, both geographically and socially. This process represented a war-peace continuum: when the army acquired new information from captured guerrillas, it informed the relatives who remained in the resistance by broadcasting speeches in Ixil through megaphones from helicopters that circled the area. By making the messages personal, the army insinuated itself into communal spheres of social power by violently exploiting the notion of familiarity. Hence, military demonstrations of power and successful attempts to demoralise the resistance resulted in what we may call the inner, personal emotions of guilt.[10]

Liberal Emplacement

Whereas military authority sought to violently control or close spaces of popular protest, thereby generating a certain kind of resistance, armed and non-armed, the current era of liberal democratic reform in postwar Central America confronts its opposition in a different way. In this section, I focus on people's relation to politics and place in those transformations, before I return, in the next section, to the literal break-up of the Guatemalan resistance communities.

The concept of emplacement has only recently received some anthropological attention. In an effort to come to terms with the role of place for ethnographies in contexts of global flows, Englund argues that neoliberalism itself is 'emplaced', which to him means that it can only be understood if viewed as 'embodied and situated practice' (2002: 261). Here, I shift the focus to see how subjects become emplaced in and by the neoliberal regime. With this I resort to a more conventional connotation of the term 'emplacement'. By far the most common usage of the concept today is in the field of geology. Emplacement designates the intrusion of igneous rocks into particular positions, or the development of an ore deposit in a particular place. Being emplaced could accordingly mean to be spatially fixed to degrees far beyond sedentarism (see the introduction to this volume) – roots in earth become stones or minerals in rock. The other conventional usage of the term 'emplacement' is military – it means a clearing on which heavy artillery is placed. If we combine these meanings, emplaced people become part of a political 'battle' with very specific aims. What stands out in contexts like the Guatemalan one is a lack of opportunities for the poor to position or place themselves in a political structure of influence (see Badiou 2001; Colburn 2002; Löfving 2006c). What remains is the possibility of moving to make a living rather than staying to make a political change. Being emplaced thus means 'being placed by others' and becomes a direct counterpart to displacement. Emplacement is redisplacement.

The 'warring parties' in Central America perceived violence as instrumental. It was a means towards an end. They turned to it with the alleged purpose of ending war – of disorder and revolution as seen from the perspective of the authoritarian state, of poverty and exclusion as seen by the state's opponents. But the international blueprint for the contemporary post-Cold War architecture of peace has it differently. Here, violence is not the instrument but the cause; not the road to peace but itself the vicious circle. What ends war is neither the eradication of poverty nor the defeat of rebels, but instead the *departure* from violence, and more specifically the departure from military violence in increasingly transparent polities (see, e.g., Borneman 2002; Collier et al. 2003). This approach presents an attractive third way, not only to policy makers in national and international contexts, but also to people in war-torn societies who might prove ready to try other routes, or who reject the terms in which the conflict has been construed and their own alleged association with a military organisation.

Such war fatigue was prevalent in Nicaragua, El Salvador and Guatemala at the time their presidents signed the 1987 Esquipulas II Accord, emerging from the troubled Contadora process in which Cold War divisions had hampered any real progress (Chernick 1996; Child 1992). The accord called for a ceasefire, national reconciliation, amnesty, democratisation, termination of external aid to insurgency movements, and free elections. As more or less direct results of 'Esquipulas', settlements were eventually reached between the Sandinista government and the US-funded Contras in Nicaragua in 1989; between the right-wing government of El Salvador and the FMLN guerrilla in 1992; and between a neoliberal business coalition then governing Guatemala, its oligarch-backed army, and the guerrilla movement in 1996.

Just like the civil wars themselves, the war–peace transition was part of an international process. However, the obsession with security embedded in Cold War geopolitics gave way to a more explicitly economic incentive for external involvement. Despite their many differences, the UN-monitored peace-building operations in the world from 1989 onward all initiated transformations of war-shattered states into liberal market democracies (Paris 2004).

Enlightenment philosophy is at the roots of this model, and in particular Kant's 1795 essay in which he envisions three 'building blocks' of peace: a republican constitution to protect citizens from both despots and anarchy, alliances between such republics for collective security and cooperation, and free flows of people and goods between them in a true 'spirit of commerce' (Kant 1995 [1795]: 114; see also Doyle 1983; Parish and Peceny 2002). These elements found their way to the post-Cold War reconstruction of war-torn societies by way of the 1919 Paris Peace Conference, where Woodrow Wilson 'became the first statesman to articulate what is now called the liberal peace thesis, … including the assumption that democratisation and marketisation foster peace in countries just emerging from civil war' (Paris 2004: 41). No peace conference ever ended the Cold War, but the influence of Wilson's approach is obvious. Hence, the Central American peace process beginning with the Esquipulas II Accord and culminating in the Guatemalan Peace Accords of 1996 was only the first part in the double transformation of Central America, the second being the economic structural adjustment of the region (see McCleary 1999).

In Nicaragua, following the 1990 electoral defeat of the Sandinistas, the Chamorro government immediately embarked on a program of economic reform. This included extensive layoffs of government employees, privatisation of most state-owned enterprises, reductions in social spending, and so forth. And while successful in restoring fiscal balance and economic stability, and also hailed as a 'remarkable success' by the World Bank, the International Monetary Fund and the USAID (United States Agency for International Development), which had jointly designed the structural adjustment program, the austerity measures deepened inequalities and played a significant part in the declining living conditions of many Nicaraguans (see Veltmeyer, Petras and Vieux 1997). The rapid increase in crime rates and social fragmentation has since continued more or less unabated and is continuously posing a serious threat to peace in the country, challenging the liberal peace assumption that economic liberalisation and political stability go hand in hand. The Salvadoran scenario of the past ten years is remarkably similar. Liberal orthodoxy has thus not only neglected the issues that once sparked the civil wars of Central America – poverty and inequality – in favour of macroeconomic stability and growth but has actually exacerbated social cleavages (see Robinson 2000; Vilas 2000).

Guatemala, the last Central American country to sign a peace agreement, has been able to learn from the mistakes of its neighbors. As a result, and under pressure from the United Nations, a so-called socioeconomic agreement was signed as part of the peace treaty. It endorses liberalisation, but it also commits the Guatemalan government to increasing the levels of social welfare spending (Jonas 2000: 167). However, the socioeconomic agreement was soon up against apparently irresistible pressure from the domestic business sector (Krznaric 1999; Stanley and Holiday 2002). As a result, the government fulfilled its commitments to liberalise the economy while failing to make headway in redressing social inequality. Guatemala has recently seen the resurfacing of paramilitaries (Sáenz de Tejada 2004) and is experiencing unprecedented levels of criminal violence. The phenomenon of lynching suspected troublemakers is not new to the Guatemalan highlands, but its frequency has become a phenomenon suspiciously connected to the postwar situation (see Remijnse 2001, 2005).[11]

In an early work on the magic of state power, Taussig (1992) explores the fetishism whereby the state itself becomes an object of desire, magically holding out the promise of change. He writes, '[By State fetishism] I mean a certain aura of might as figured by the Leviathan in Hobbes' rendering as that "mortal god", or, in a quite different mode, by Hegel's intricately argued vision of the State as not merely the embodiment of reason, of the Idea, but also as an impressively organic unity, something much greater than the sum of its parts' (ibid.: 111f.). Hage's view of society as that which produces and distributes hope is perhaps a more straightforward phrasing of what is at stake, and it comes very close both to the magicality of profane power and to people's attempt in the Guatemalan resistance communities to attach previous expectations of the sheltering power of home to society at large (2003). According to Hage, in shrinking the shared space of 'the public', neo-liberal policies also shrink the domain of hope, which in turn foregrounds paranoid social tendencies like xenophobic nationalism and gated communities in wealthier countries. In Guatemala, currently the third poorest country in Latin America and with a public sector yet to be built, citizens' *hope* for radically different opportunities in peace seems to be what in fact eventually brought the revolution to an end (Löfving 2004). Disappointment with the lack of concrete steps towards a true 'implementation of peace' has not led to new popular uprisings but to unprecedented social fragmentation.

The End of the Road

Back in 1996, the guerrilla leadership, soon to become a legitimate political party leadership, presented its position at the negotiating table as a very strong one when it sent information to what it perceived as its future constituency in the resistance communities. Every step in the negotiation was being discussed and debated in homes and political meetings during the first part of my fieldwork, and it is fair to say that the optimism many expressed (see Pablo's discussion of human rights as proof of an EGP success, above) took on a certain power of its own – a peace fetishism, perhaps. However, once in the implementation phase, peace and the government's tempting offer to award a limited number of rebels an economic compensation for surrendering their arms created enmities within past alliances. In this section I will present what actually took place in 1997 and 1998 when people negotiated their future residence with the government, when they eventually headed for other places, and when most of them, against the will and intention of their political leaders, returned to Nebaj.

People invoked a variety of reasons when I inquired about why they had opted for their respective future settlements. Below, I discuss the incentives associated with the four options available to them: first, migrating to new land by the coast, with prospects for maintaining their political organisation; second, migrating to new land in the highland areas, also with prospects for a sustained organisation; third, remaining in the area occupied up to then by the resistance communities, and coexisting with settlers from Chajul who in the peace talks had managed to establish their right to a previously forested mountain area, now cleared and cultivated by the resistance communities; and, last, returning to prewar settlements primarily in and around Nebaj.[12]

Those in favour of the first option, the coast and a communal resettlement on the level of organisation (not family), argued that there were likely to be roads by the coast due to the flat topography. This was connected to hopes for improved infrastructure in general and access to nearby markets, which would promote 'development' – a concept that was used with notably greater frequency in local postwar political rhetoric and seemed, along with 'democracy', to be the most recent code word, replacing 'negotiation'. What emerged was a chronological sequence in which each core political concept was replaced by a new one. It read: revolution, resistance, negotiation, development and democracy.

The people who favoured resettlement with a sustained political organisation seemed to be motivated by violent experiences in the past as well as by their revolutionary commitment to societal change. Many interviewees expressed a fear of going back to their land of origin due to 'mortal enemies' in army-controlled areas. When asked to specify this fear, people referred to an array of accusations and past threats from patrollers and the military. Another reason to opt for the coast had pragmatic undertones: a growing number of heirs in refuge and resistance left people with tiny landholdings with bad prospects in Nebaj. In contrast, the negotiations provided opportunities to start afresh with a certain area/territory for each household. This led people to divide households in order to maximise the amount of arable land for family members. If a father and one son returned to Nebaj, it was likely that the other sons turned to the other offerings of the deal with the government. Gaspar, my neighbor, decided to follow his politically active peers to the coast, and his daughters and wife went with him. His two eldest sons, however, were to take care of the small landholding inherited from Gaspar's father in the Nebaj village of Palop (see the fourth option below). Throughout the conflict it had been guarded and cultivated by Gaspar's two brothers and his mother. The geographical division of the extended family was a common sacrifice to secure a maximum amount of land.

Those in favour of the second option migrated to nearby *fincas* (estates) in Cobán and Uspantán, emphasising the familiarity of highland ecology. They too had mortal enemies in Nebaj. Moreover, when pragmatically dividing their present households in order to maximise land tenure (like those favouring the first option), members of these soon-to-be-divided families would be able to maintain contact and meet frequently because Cobán and Uspantán were nearby. This 'closeness' was also related to the land of origin of the many Maya Quichés in the area of the resistance communities known as Xeputúl. The new fincas were thus seen as strategic new locations in the political project of connecting past struggles with the present and the future.

Impatiently waiting for their new life to begin in another place, few devoted their efforts to agricultural production in the spring of 1998. Francisco, in the resistance community of Pal, could ascertain that his coffee plantation would give him a good yield. The profit would be divided between himself, his family and all the *mozos* (day-workers) who waited to be paid for the processing of the plants. And Francisco had already planted new fields. He belonged to the core of revolutionary committed who had faithfully served in the various committees over the years and who now planned to follow the organisation to one of the new settlements. The newly planted trees would not bear fruit for another four years, but Francisco hoped to be able to use them in the bargaining with the incoming *Chajuleños*. Others were cleaning their *cafetales* (coffee plantations), also with the goal of using them as economic assets when the negotiations got under way. Yet others were weaving baskets or making furniture that was easy to dismantle and transport to a new location.

Those in favour of the third option, remaining in the area of the resistance communities, also based their planning on a continued political project, though without a military wing. The expected wave of 'army-indoctrinated' *Chajuleños* – so the argument went – had to be met by organised communities. The elders remembered the lowland heat, the mosquitoes, and the hardships of seasonal work on the coastal plantations. 'Never again' was a phrase invoked in the motivation of a decision to stay put. And people who had invested much time and energy in the very practical construction of the new communities were reluctant to leave and start all over again. For example, the carpenters whose profession was in a sense their home, decided to stay put. In their case, there was usually no land and no 'back home' in Nebaj left to return to. Home villages had been erased, reconstructed and repopulated with new settlers.

Finally, those choosing the fourth option, the 'returnees', represented a growing number among the CPR villagers; among them was Pablo, now hoping to be able to continue with his health work and to move back with his wife and three children to live close to his brothers in Nebaj. Two years earlier, in 1996, my other neighbor, Juan, had shown me his field of pineapple plants. He was then scheduled to harvest in three to four months and was very satisfied with his previous initiative of creating a more diversified stock of crops. For me, this was an excellent opportunity to confront him with the CPR plans to move everybody to new settlements, and, surveying his piñas, Juan claimed that he would never ever abandon what he had built up here in the resistance community of Cabá. 'If the authorities force us to leave, there will be problems,' he said. At that time Juan calculated that at least half of the people in resistance shared his opinion.

This was in 1996, when a final solution was being worked out in political meetings and in the homes, and the equation between an identity of resistance and the territory where resistance 'took place' was striking. To return to Nebaj still implied selling out the struggle, and it represented a contradiction to the notion of a revolutionary commitment. Two grand estates, one by the coast and one close to the Ixil region, were finally bought with government funds in February 1998 for the relocation of about four hundred families on each. The search for purchasable estates had been under way during 1997, but due to the delays, the original number of one hundred families that chose to return to their 'original land' in the town of Nebaj had increased to nearly four hundred by April

1998. The need to sow in the spring forced people to return without guarantees of access to land. This often led to conflicts between spouses. My host family became a telling example of this. The elder couple, as well as the overwhelming majority of their generation, had decided to go back to Nebaj and their land of origin. This was met with tensions between men, who seemed to be eager to go to the coast with the organisation, and women, who as eagerly wanted to follow their parents and older relatives (and each other). My host planned for migration with his brother, while his wife had already gone with her mother and grandparents back to the old village. Empowered by the presence of her family's elders, she simply left. When he was on his own in a nearly deserted community in 1998, my host finally decided to follow his wife, and he too returned to Nebaj to try to save his marriage.

Returnees emphasised the bad prospects of the other alternatives, in much the same vein as others had done. The new experience of being disarmed and thereby defenceless did play a role, but 'the object of fear' differed. Whereas all the others seemed to fear their ethnic compatriots back in Nebaj, the returnees invoked fear of the coming *Chajuleños*. People were thus locked in a precarious situation. Wherever they turned, they would face enemies. There was simply no place for them, and with a disarmed resistance, neither the peace nor the future looked promising.

Hence, it was no longer the struggle to prevail as a revolutionary example that motivated people's decision about final settlement after the break-up of the resistance communities from the region. The principal focus of identification and the object of economic maximisation was not the individual, nor the political community of resisters, but rather the extended family. At the end of the revolutionary road, the road to liberal peace effectively closed this space of popular organising and protest.

The Transforming Space of Popular Protest

'Home' is one pole in a spatial opposition. 'Home is "here", or it is "not here"' (Douglas 1991: 289). But, as has been argued in the essays of this volume, 'home' is also one pole in a moral opposition. 'Coming home' is a moral movement, 'building a home' is a moral act, and when homes turn bad they become unhomely. I have not taken the spatiality of this morality as a given, but have instead explored how scales are shifting over time and how the conditions for people's ability to conceive of home as a eulogised, moral space in social spheres wider than family and household was challenged by war but undermined and ultimately destroyed by liberal peace.

As the spatiality of moral space seems to be shrinking, in Guatemala as elsewhere, I am going to end my tale with a perspective on youth, life trajectory and contemporary migration. Both young people and the image of a rebellious youth informed the Central American revolutions.

Materialist explanations of the revolutionary potentials of disgruntled youngsters emphasise the limited access to land that by virtue of its relative abundance had constituted the local power base of the elders in previous generations. Demographic expansion presupposed territorial expansion, and the division of plots among heirs remained possible in the Guatemalan highlands as long as new land could be cleared on the outskirts of villages and towns. The changes brought about by an earlier wave of liberal capitalist penetration of the peripheries in the late nineteenth century put an end to this development. The privatisation of communal land was a precondition for the inclusion of Guatemala in the then expanding global economy. By the mid-twentieth century, indigenous communities were thus territorially curtailed and overpopulated to the extent that the local institution of the gerontocracy lost the very condition of its own reproduction. The massive mobilisation of young people like Pablo into the rebel ranks during the 1970s was part of a double logic of this economic change on the one hand, and of geopolitical concerns on the other. In support of both the regimes and the big corporations operating in Central America, the USA turned the region into one of the hottest spots of the Cold War – its main enemies being the Central American young people who had recently revolted, primarily against their own elders.

However, neither agricultural space constraints nor the economic incentive alone can explain the phenomenon of revolutionary mobilisation in Guatemala (cf. Collier and Hoeffler 1998). The revolutionaries in the resistance communities shared and nourished a number of human ideals, one of them centering on youth – *purity* free from the falsehood of tradition and corruption and *strength* required to construct a new society. But as the members grew older, central facets of the political structure established in war by the once pure and strong did not stand the challenges posed by the expectations of peace. In the resistance communities, for example, a political class, clearly marked by higher levels of literacy, networks within and beyond the revolutionary movement, and a political know-how that guaranteed their continuous political reappointments, maintained its leadership positions, indeed marginalising its own youth and, for this reason among others, seeing its popular support gradually diminishing (Löfving 2002a).

Parallel to the weakening of the revolutionary project in Guatemala, a different kind of popular mobilisation began. This one built on an opposed project of culture instead of class, and of constitutional reforms instead of revolution. Many activists within the movement of Maya revivalism in contemporary Guatemala do in fact have a history in the rebel movement. Many of them found it necessary to reevaluate the aims, means and content of struggle as times changed, and eventually they replaced an ideal of youth and purity with one of old age and ancient wisdom – a development coinciding with their own life cycles.[13]

So, what is the role of 'place' in this change, and what about young people today? In cultural and social ways, the perceived distance between an affluent society up north and the economically downtrodden 'home countries' of Central American youth has shrunk dramatically since the 1970s and even the 1980s. During the past fifteen years remittances developed into the single most important source of income for millions of Salvadorans, Guatemalans and Hondurans in particular. These three countries alone received US\$7.23 billion in remittances in 2005, a sum equivalent to 10 per cent and 17 per cent of Guatemala's and El Salvador's GNP, respectively (Latin American Regional Report 2006) and the numbers have kept growing ever since. There are currently around 1.2 million Guatemalans working in the USA, 60 per cent of whom are illegal immigrants. During visits to villages in Sololá in 2006 and 2007, people told me about the necessity and the difficulties of illegal migration. Every village had stories of failures – people who had died during the journey or been sent back, now ruined by having sold their properties to afford the trip – and every village had one or two families who were much better off than their neighbors due to a successful journey of a family member across two state borders.

Remittances are thus interesting, not only from an economic but also from a social point of view, because they *preserve* household economies precisely by *breaking up* households both geographically and socially (see Hamilton and Stoltz Chinchilla 1991). Young people leave their homes with, if nothing else, the promise of contributing to their families' income once they have settled in the USA. Along with the consumption of North American popular culture in Central America, this pattern of migration generates stories, images and experiences of a different and more attractive life than the one they can lead 'back home'. If *society* is the distributor of hope, and the health of society is measured by the success of this distribution (Hage 2003), then hope in contemporary Central America is associated with the possibility of *escaping* from society in order to save the household.

The liberalisation of politics means, apart from the promotion of elections, also the advancement of basic civil liberties such as freedom of speech, assembly and conscience. I have argued in this essay that the parallel processes of political and economic liberalisation in postwar Central America are undermining these latter aspects of the liberal project (Chase 2002; see also Kalb 2005). The apparent closeness to prosperity is a deceptive one. Legally excluded from the licit market and the social advantages of North American citizenship, Central Americans in the USA and on the roads connecting these two nodes in the economy of the Americas turn to the illicit means of income available to them. While contraband activities involving drugs, weapons, and bodies, and work opportunities in the USA for illegal immigrants make some people better off than they were before, they represent the antithesis to citizenship and the social contracts and safety nets of the welfare state (Zilberg 2004). This speaks in dismal ways to Hirschman's now soon to be forty-year-old analysis. The units in his focus – firms, organisations, and states – depended on 'voice' to prevail and declined when members opted for 'exit' (Hirschman 1970). In a contemporary contrast, 'exit' from semi-sovereign polities now works to stabilise an ongoing liberalisation of world economy while simultaneously undermining political opposition in such polities, creating in the process the very semi-sovereignty on which liberal globalisation depends.

Acknowledgements

Special thanks for astute commentary on this piece to Stef Jansen, Fernanda Soto, Magnus Lembke, and Iris Jean-Klein. For perceptive engagement, I also thank seminar participants at Stockholm University and at the University of Edinburgh.

Notes

1. Ejército Guerrillero de los Pobres, one of the four member organisations of the National Revolutionary Unity of Guatemala (URNG). For introductions to the history of the EGP, see Brockett (2005: 119–22) and Löfving (2006a).
2. In involving decisions with practical social consequences, what people referred to as 'sacrifices', a revolutionary commitment transcends the related notions of revolutionary consciousness, ideas and convictions.
3. For a history and ethnography of the Comunidades de Poblaciones en Resistencia, see Löfving (2002a, 2002b, 2005, 2006b).
4. At the time, the mayor of Chajul belonged to the army-supportive political party Frente Republicano Guatemalteco (FRG) and drew popular support from anti-guerrilla agitation combined with promises of guaranteeing people land in the region now allegedly occupied by the CPR.
5. As John Gledhill (1997) notes, liberalism is far from a uniform doctrine and encompasses a wide range of perspectives on the role of state and politics in controlling market dynamics and on the relation of the economy to social justice (see also Burchell 1996: 21–30). In this chapter, I use 'liberal' when referring to the literature on current peace building and its often implicit economic precondition for political reform, whereas I use 'neoliberal' for a more aggressive and politically far-reaching individualism. For neo-liberalism, Burchell notes, 'the rationality of government must be pegged to a form of the rational self-conduct of the governed themselves [like for classical liberalism], but a form that is not so much a given of human nature as a consciously contrived style of conduct' (1996: 24; see also Gledhill 2005; Paris 2004).
6. This experience is not representative of the majority of victims of army atrocities in Guatemala. Doing fieldwork among the displaced people in the Ixil highlands implied spending time with a 'selection' of those who had survived to tell, and those who had stayed defiant of the state and its army

for ten to twenty years. While an estimated number of twenty thousand people abandoned the resistance communities during the first half of the 1990s, approximately ten thousand remained until the war's end (Löfving 2002a). Thus, it was not surprising to find an unprecedented 'revolutionary commitment' among them.

7. For this latter view in the case of El Salvador, see Grenier (1999), and in the case of Guatemala, see Stoll (1993).

8. People do not appear with their proper names in this chapter.

9. Hannah Arendt (1958) famously assessed the relationship between individualism and social solidarity in her discussion of the modern divisions of society and the simultaneous emergence of the public sphere. Similarly universalist, the liberals in political philosophy would see individuation as a precondition for the emergence of rights-bearing individuals (see Taylor 1989), while their critics (see Grandin 2004) single out individuation as a precondition for the rise of oppositional mass politics. My take on 'the Self' here is aimed rather at understanding the fluctuating spheres of social solidarity in a specific place over time and the relation of individuation to violence.

10. Elsewhere, I analyse the remaining tensions between the civil patrol in the village of Chel and CPR members passing the frontline on their way to Chajul, and what those tensions meant in terms of a preserved military might in 'peace time' (Löfving 2004).

11. Guatemala has become a showcase in a more general discussion on postwar violence, lynchings, 'popular justice' and economic decline in Latin America (see, e.g., Handy 2004; Snodgrass Godoy 2004, 2006).

12. Overlapping and conflictive legal systems inform land conflicts in many parts of Latin America. The CPR evoked traditional law (the rights of the users of untitled land) whereas the mayor of Chajul capitalised on promises to the people in his overcrowded municipality that the CPR were occupants and that the territory, even if previously uninhabited, belonged to the municipality and was his to distribute. The government, the army and eventually the guerrilla leaders signed up for this perspective in the negotiations of 1996 and 1997. The CPR dissolved and their members had to move.

13. For a critical analysis of the ethnification of politics in Guatemala, and of the relationship between 'the Maya movement' and the resistance communities in the mid-1990s, see Löfving (2002b, 2006b).

References

Appadurai, Arjun. 2004. 'The Capacity to Aspire: Culture and the Terms of Recognition', in Culture and Public Action, ed. Vijayendra Rao and Michael Walton, pp. 59–84. Stanford: Stanford University Press.

Arendt, Hannah. 1958. The Human Condition. Chicago: Chicago University Press.

Bachelard, Gaston. 1994 [1958]. The Poetics of Space: The Classic Look at How We Experience Intimate Places. Boston: Beacon Press.

Badiou, Alain. 2001. Ethics: An Essay on the Understanding of Evil. London and New York: Verso.

Bauman, Zygmunt. 1999. In Search of Politics. Cambridge: Polity.

Borneman, John. 2002. 'Reconciliation after Ethnic Cleansing: Listening, Retribution, Affiliation', *Public Culture* 14(2): 281–304.

Bourdieu, Pierre. 1998. *Acts of Resistance: Against the New Myths of Our Time.* Cambridge: Polity.

Brockett, Charles D. 2005. *Political Movements and Violence in Central America.* Cambridge: Cambridge University Press.

Burchell, Graham. 1996. 'Liberal Government and Techniques of the Self', in *Foucault and Political Reason: Liberalism, Neo-liberalism, and Rationalities of Government*, ed. Andrew Barry, Thomas Osborne, and Nikolas Rose, pp. 19–36. London: UCL Press.

Chase, Jacquelyn, ed. 2002. *The Spaces of Neoliberalism: Land, Place, and Family in Latin America.* Bloomfield, CT: Kumarian Press.

Chernick, Marc W. 1996. 'Peacemaking and Violence in Latin America', in *The International Dimensions of Internal Conflict*, ed. Michael E. Brown, pp. 267–307. Cambridge, MA: MIT Press.

Child, Jack. 1992. *The Central American Peace Process, 1983–1991: Sheathing Swords, Building Confidence.* Boulder, CO: Lynne Rienner.

Clausewitz, Carl von. 1976. *On War.* Princeton: Princeton University Press.

Colburn, Forrest D. 2002. *Latin America at the End of Politics.* Princeton and Oxford: Princeton University Press.

Colby, Benjamin N. and Lore M. Colby. 1981. *The Daykeeper: Life and Discourse of an Ixil Diviner.* Austin: Texas University Press.

Collier, Paul and Anke Hoeffler. 1998. 'On Economic Causes of Civil War', *Oxford Economic Papers* 50: 563–73.

Collier, Paul, V.L. Elliott, Håvard Hegre, Anke Hoeffler, Marta Reynal-Querol and Nicholas Sambanis. 2003. *Breaking the Conflict Trap: Civil War and Development Policy.* Washington, DC and New York: World Bank and Oxford University Press.

Deleuze, Gilles and Félix Guattari. 1977. *Anti-Oedipus: Capitalism and Schizophrenia.* Minneapolis: University of Minnesota Press.

Douglas, Mary. 1991. 'The Idea of a Home: A Kind of Space', *Social Research* 58(1): 287–307.

Doyle, Michael W. 1983. 'Kant, Liberal Legacies, and Foreign Affairs: Parts I and II', *Philosophy and Public Affairs* 12(3–4): 205–35 and 323–53.

Engels, Friedrich. 1972. *The Origin of the Family, Private Property, and the State in the Light of the Researches of Lewis H. Morgan.* New York: International Publishers.

Englund, Harri. 2002. 'Ethnography after Globalism: Migration and Emplacement in Malawi', *American Ethnologist* 29(2): 261–86.

Farley, Brian P. 1998. 'Anxious Conformity: Anxiety and the Sociocentric-oriented Self in a Tlaxcalan Community', *Ethos* 26(3): 271–94.

Feldman, Allen. 1991. *Formations of Violence: The Narrative of the Body and Political Terror in Northern Ireland.* Chicago: Chicago University Press.

Franco, Jean. 1985. 'Killing Priests, Nuns, Women, Children', in *On signs*, ed. Marshall Blonsky, pp. 413–20. Baltimore: Johns Hopkins University Press.

Gledhill, John. 1997. Liberalism, Socio-economic Rights and the Politics of Identity: From Moral Economy to Indigenous Rights', in *Human Rights, Culture and Context: Anthropological Approaches*, ed. Richard Wilson, pp. 70–110. London: Pluto Press.

———. 2005. Citizenship and the Social Geography of Deep Neo-liberalization', *Anthropologica* 47: 81–100.

Grandin, Greg. 2004. *The Last Colonial Massacre: Latin America in the Cold War.* Chicago: Chicago University Press.

Grenier, Yvon. 1999. *The Emergence of Insurgency in El Salvador: Ideology and Political Will.* Pittsburgh: University of Pittsburgh Press.

Hage, Ghassan. 1997. 'At Home in the Entrails of the West: Multiculturalism, "Ethnic Food" and Migrant Home-building', in *Home/World: Space, Community and Marginality in Sydney's West*, ed. Helen Grace, Ghassan Hage, Leslie Johnson, Julie Langsworth, and Michael Symonds, pp. 99–153. Annandale: Pluto Press.

———. 2003. *Against Paranoid Nationalism: Searching for Hope in a Shrinking Society.* Annandale: Pluto Press.

Hamilton, Nora and Norma Stoltz Chinchilla. 1991. 'Central American Migration: A Framework for Analysis', *Latin American Research Review* 26(1): 75–110.

Handy, Jim. 2004. 'Chicken Thieves, Witches, and Judges: Vigilante Justice and Customary Law in Guatemala', *Journal of Latin American Studies* 36: 533–61.

Hardt, Michael and Antonio Negri. 2004. *Multitude: War and Democracy in the Age of Empire.* New York: Penguin Press.

Hillier, Jean and Emma Rooksby. 2002. *Habitus: A Sense of Place.* Burlington, VT: Ashgate.

Hirschman, Albert O. 1970. *Exit, Voice, and Loyalty: Responses to Decline in Firms, Organizations, and States.* Cambridge, MA: Harvard University Press.

Jansen, Stef. 2001. 'The Streets of Beograd: Urban Space and Protest Identities in Serbia', *Political Geography* 20(1): 35–55.

Jonas, Susanne. 2000. *Of Centaurs and Doves: Guatemala's Peace Process.* Boulder, CO: Westview Press.

Kalb, Don. 2005. 'From Flows to Violence: Politics and Knowledge in the Debates on Globalization and Empire', *Anthropological Theory* 5(2): 176–204.

Kant, Immanuel. 1995 [1795]. 'Perpetual Peace: A Philosophical Sketch', in *Kant: Political Writings*, ed. Hans Reiss, pp. 93–130. New York: Cambridge University Press.

Krznaric, Roman. 1999. 'Civil and Uncivil Actors in the Guatemalan Peace Process', *Bulletin of Latin American Research* 18(1): 1–16.

Larner, Wendy. 2000. 'Theorising Neo-liberalism: Policy, Ideology, Governmentality', *Studies in Political Economy* 63: 5–26.

Latin American Regional Report. 2006. Caribbean and Central America, RC-06-01, 'Record Remittances to Central America.' January 2006. London: Latin American Newsletters.

Löfving, Staffan. 2002a. 'An Unpredictable Past: Guerrillas, Mayas, and the Location of Oblivion in War-torn Guatemala'. Ph.D. dissertation, Uppsala University.

———. 2002b. 'Post-rebels and Maya Mobilization: On the Ideology of Culture in Guatemala', in *Banners of Belonging: The Politics of Indigenous Identity in Bolivia and Guatemala*, ed. Staffan Löfving and Charlotta Widmark, pp. 121–44. Uppsala: ULRiCA, Uppsala University.

———. 2004. 'Paramilitaries of the Empire: Guatemala, Colombia, and Israel', *Social Analysis* 48(1): 156–60.

———. 2005. 'Silence, and the Politics of Representing Rebellion: On the Emergence of the Neutral Maya in Guatemala', in *No Peace No War: An Anthropology of Contemporary Armed Conflicts*, ed. Paul Richards, pp. 77–97. London and Athens: James Currey and Ohio University Press.

————. 2006a. 'Guerrilla Army of the Poor – Ejército Guerrillero de los Pobres (EGP)', in *Encyclopedia of the Developing World*, ed. Thomas Leonard, pp. 726–28. New York: Routledge.

————. 2006b. 'War as Field and Site: Anthropologist, Archaeologists, and the Violence of Maya Cultural Continuities', in *Warfare and Society: Archaeological and Social Anthropological Perspectives*, ed. Ton Otto, Henrik Thrane, and Helle Vandkilde, pp. 469–79. Aarhus: Aarhus University Press.

————. 2006c. 'Poverty on the Rebound: The Work of Models', *Iberoamericana: Nordic Journal of Latin American and Caribbean Studies*, 35(2): 211–33.

McCleary, Rachel M. 1999. 'Postconflict Political Economy of Central America', in *Comparative Peace Processes in Latin America*, ed. Cynthia J. Arnson, pp. 417–35. Washington, DC and Stanford: Woodrow Wilson Center Press and Stanford University Press.

Morán, Rolando. 2002. *Saludos revolucionarios: La historia reciente de Guatemala desde la óptica de la lucha guerrillera, 1984–1996*. Guatemala: Fundación Guillermo Toriello.

Obeyesekere, Gananath. 1980. *Medusa's Hair: An Essay on Personal Symbols and Religious Experience*. Chicago: Chicago University Press.

Paris, Roland. 2004. *At War's End: Building Peace after Civil Conflict*. Cambridge: Cambridge University Press.

Parish, Randall and Mark Peceny. 2002. 'Kantian Liberalism and the Collective Defense of Democracy in Latin America', *Journal of Peace Research* 39(2): 229–50.

Peck, Jamie, and Adam Tickell. 2002. 'Neoliberalizing Space', *Antipode* 34(3): 380–404.

Porteous, J. Douglas and Sandra E. Smith 2001. *Domicide: The Global Destruction of Home*. Montreal: McGill-Queen's University Press.

Remijnse, Simone. 2001. 'Remembering Civil Patrols in Joyabaj, Guatemala', *Bulletin of Latin American Research* 20(4): 454–569.

————. 2005. *Memorias de violencia: Patrullas de autodefensa civil y la herencia del conflicto en Joyabaj, Quiché*. Guatemala City: AVANCSO.

Robinson, William I. 2000. 'Neoliberalism, the Global Elite, and the Guatemalan Transition: A Critical Macrosocial Analysis', *Journal of Interamerican Studies and World Affairs* 42(4): 89–108.

Routledge, Paul. 1994. Backstreets, Barricades, and Blackouts: Urban Terrains of Resistance in Nepal. *Environment and Planning D: Society and Space* 12: 559–78.

Sáenz de Tejada, Ricardo. 2004. *¿Víctimas o vencedores? Una aproximación al movimiento de los ex PAC*. Guatemala City: FLACSO.

Snodgrass Godoy, Angelina. 2004. 'When "Justice" is Criminal: Lynchings in Contemporary Latin America', *Theory and Society* 33: 621–51.

————. 2006. *Popular Injustice: Violence, Community, and Law in Latin America*. Stanford: Stanford University Press.

Stanley, William and David Holiday, 2002. 'Broad Participation, Diffuse Responsibility: Peace Implementation in Guatemala', in *Ending Civil Wars: The Implementation of Peace Agreements*, ed. Stephen John Stedman, Donald Rothchild, and Elizabeth M. Cousens, pp. 421–62. Boulder, CO: Lynne Rienner.

Stepputat, Finn. 1994. 'Repatriation and the Politics of Space: The Case of the Mayan Diaspora and Return Movement', *Journal of Refugee Studies* 7(2/3): 175–85.

————. 2001. 'Urbanizing the Countryside: Armed Conflict, State Formation, and the Politics of Place in Contemporary Guatemala', in *States of Imagination: Ethnographic Explorations of the Postcolonial State*, ed. Thomas Blom Hansen and Finn Stepputat, pp. 284–312. Durham: Duke University Press.

Stoll, David. 1993. *Between Two Armies in the Ixil Towns of Guatemala*. New York: Columbia University Press.

Taussig, Michael. 1992. *The Nervous System*. New York: Routledge.

Taylor, Charles. 1989. *Sources of the Self: The Making of the Modern Identity*. Cambridge: Cambridge University Press.

Veltmeyer, Henry, James Petras and Steve Vieux (eds.). 1997. *Neoliberalism and Class Conflict in Latin America: A Comparative Perspective on the Political Economy of Structural Adjustment*. New York: St. Martin's Press.

Vilas, Carlos M. 2000. 'Neoliberalism in Central America', in *Repression, Resistance, and Democratic Transition in Central America*, ed. Thomas W. Walker and Ariel C. Armony, pp. 211–31. Wilmington, DE: Scholarly Resources.

Wacquant, Loïc. 1999. 'How Penal Common Sense Comes to Europeans: Notes on the Transatlantic Diffusion of the Neo-liberal Doxa', *European Societies* 1: 319–52.

Wilson, Richard. 1993. 'Anchored Communities: Identity and History of the Maya-Q'eqchi', *Man (N.S.)* 28: 121–38.

Wood, Elizabeth J. 2003. *Insurgent Collective Action and Civil War in El Salvador*. Cambridge: Cambridge University Press.

Zilberg, Elana. 2004. 'Fools Banished from the Kingdom: Remapping Geographies of Gang Violence between the Americas (Los Angeles and San Salvador)', *American Quarterly* 56(3): 759–79.

Žižek, Slavoj. 2002. 'The Prospects of Radical Politics Today', in *Democracy Unrealized: Documenta 11 – Platform 1*, ed. Okwui Enwezor et al. pp. 67–85. Ostfildern-Ruit: Hatje Cantz Publishers.

Zur, Judith N. 1998. *Violent Memories: Quiché War Widows of Guatemala*. Boulder, CO: Westview Press.

POSTSCRIPT

Home, Fragility and Irregulation:
Reflections on Ethnographies of Im/mobility

Finn Stepputat

My reflections on the contributions to this volume will not add many new points, but will rather, drawing upon my own experience in the field, restate and tie together some of the points which to me are the most important ones brought forth in the volume. While doing this I will also elaborate on the points that I find particularly promising in terms of directions for future research.

The volume deals with the dynamics and effects of violence and movement as two of the most obvious processes challenging the meaning and taken-for-granted-ness of 'home'. Together, the chapters represent a laudable attempt to lay out the ground for analysing and discussing home and home making without taking sendentarist notions of home as their unquestioned point of departure. Instead, contributions deal with the ways in which power informs notions of home and belonging, and deal with important issues of power that necessarily permeate processes of movement and violence. Rather than constituting an independent focus of analysis, states and other forms of authority are mostly present in the texts as part of decisive horizons informing actions, dreams and nightmares of the protagonists of the stories put forth in the volume.

Put briefly, my comments will deal with: (1) the relationship between politics and personal experiences of fragility and loss of home; (2) the place of movement and violence in relation to state and other forms of authority and regimes of regulation; (3) confinement as a particular form of displacement; and (4) the experience of loss of home as simultaneously destructive and potentially liberating.

Fragility and Politics

Having recently been struck by the fragility of life, by the thinness of the line that separates life and death, fortune and misfortune, one of the themes that stands out for me in this volume is the experience of misfortune and great sorrow, of the loss of house, job and dear ones, but also of rights, predictability and ontological security. All of these dimensions are tied into the metaphor of home as it is used in the collection. Throughout the chapters, Hage's notion of home as 'a space of possibilities' runs as a red thread. The life-changing events may be sudden or may build up over a long time, but the result is the same: people have to find ways of 'getting over' the losses, managing a new set of conditions, making life meaningful, and rebuilding confidence in their own ability to predict, plan and secure their life ... if they ever had it, that is.

Maybe most importantly, people have to defeat the stifling fear that death and misfortune may strike again in order to invest themselves in rebuilding home. Life is understood 'backwards', but we have to live life 'forwards' as Søren Kierkegaard put it. However, contrary to 'ordinary' experiences of premature death which may produce this kind of fear, the cases explored in this volume are all related to political events. As Thiranagama shows in her insightful contribution, relationships to lost homes are as much about hope and imagination of ideal-type futures as about memories and relations to the past. But given the overtly political nature of misfortune in the case she explores, the fear that violence and displacement may strike again is likely to persist as long as no pervasive political restructuring is occurring in Sri Lanka. Thus, the memories will continue to be associated with the future as much as with the past.

Such highly politicised and politicising contexts characterise most of the cases analysed in the volume, but we learn about the politics through critical events that represent hard choices and dilemmas to individuals and their families, such as processes of return or resettlement in Bosnia, Palestine, Guatemala and Sri Lanka, voting for a referendum in Cyprus, or being forced into public exposure by acts of violence in Spain. Methodologically, such events render explicit many of the otherwise submerged calculations, hopes, worries, tactics and strategies of individuals and families. They also enable researchers to identify the contours of the political communities that people form part of, as well as the major fault-lines, hegemonic processes and exclusionary moves at work in these communities. As the introduction notes, the political communities are formed as much (or more) by the inclusion of people in a common, state-defined category and bureaucratic regime – be it refugee, displaced person or migrant – as by common experiences of violence and displacement.

Loizos points out that these occasions articulate splits or clashes between the 'experiential time' of people slowly adapting to changing conditions, and the 'protracted time' of exile, which is the time of the political communities and issues at the heart of the conflicts and displacements. These communities are often organised around notions of victimhood, the right to return, the temporariness of exile, and other notions drawing upon sedentarist imaginaries. As one of the defining features of this volume, all authors take a highly analytical approach to these naturalised imaginaries, turning them into objects of analysis rather than ontological grounds or tools for the analysis. And it appears that sedentarist discourses play a huge role in the political-moral struggles over belonging, rights and entitlements.

In the political communities of refugees and other groups of victims, memories of violence and relations to places are represented in highly 'cooked' versions (Zur 1998) with certain hi/stories being canonised as the true versions and certain cohorts of refugees being represented as more authentic and more deserving than others (see Loizos). During critical events of choice and representation in particular, hegemonic groups police the boundaries of political community through social surveillance, shaming, violence and ostracism. Contributing to such dynamics are the juridical and moral frameworks for regulation of movement which legitimise the experience of political violence (as opposed to economic hardship, or criminal or domestic violence) as the defining criterion of who deserves support and access and who does not (see Jansen and Löfving). Potot and Barrett both do a good job of showing the difficulties of upholding the political/economic distinction in regard to conditions and motivations of spatial moves, and overall – if implicitly maybe – the volume argues for a method of studying mobility and conflict that does not privilege narratives of violent events by focusing on these in interviews and representations. Thus, in terms of methodological approach, their analyses illustrate that it is a good idea to elicit stories of changing places of residence, work and movement in order to decentre discourses of political violence and to get different perspectives on the relations between personal experience and the political.

Authority and Regimes of Irregulation

The ways in which power works through em- or displacement beyond the field of formal politics is a strong issue that gives coherence to this collection. A series of writers such as Foucault, LeFebvre, de Certeau, Harvey and Massey – who are surprisingly absent from the contributions – have amply shown that space is socially constituted. There are three implications of this: (1) Changing political economies leave their marks on existing territorial regimes (Wilson 2001) as Jansen and Löfving suggest when they discuss particular neoliberal forms of emplacement. (2) To the extent that power and authority is invested in reproducing spatial boundaries, the containment or movement of bodies across such boundaries articulate and make visible relations of power. And (3) social and political conflicts are also and always conflicts over the organisation of space. This is a vast analytical area, but, taken together, the contributions to this volume point, I think, towards at least three promising avenues for future research on the issue.

Firstly, anthropological approaches are useful for further exploration of the ritualisation and regulation of mobility and spatial boundaries, as well as of the authority produced through such practices. Modern states have been intimately associated with the regulation and registration of identity, residence, property and movement to such a degree that some writers such as Foucault have held almost romantic pictures of pre-modern times when people were free to wander (Featherstone 1997). But different forms of authority have always sought to control movement. Even today, the state is far from being the only sovereign entity that regulates and authorises movement and residence, as militias, village defences, market queens, vigilantes, illicit trade networks and many others feed off movement and containment. Hence, we should take note, as Barrett does in his contribution, of other forms and techniques of keeping track of moving subjects, such as, as Moore (1996: 11) suggests, mutilations and circumscriptions in 'ritual political economies'.

Apart from striving for monopolies of the legitimate use of force and taxation, the state's representatives also attempt to establish a ceremonial monopoly, and more so the more contested and hollow the sovereignty of the state becomes (Mbembe 1992). This is evident, for example, in the wake of armed conflicts when refugees return and Internally Displaced Persons (IDPs) are resettled. These events are often turned into public spectacles for national or international consumption, showing off the strength and crafts of the state, its public support and legitimacy, and the effects of peacebuilding, which are implicitly produced since war-displaced populations constitute challenges to normalised visions of peace.

The ritualisation is also evident at some border crossings, according to McMurray's analysis of the rituals of submission and state recognition that poor smugglers have to go through in order to pass the otherwise permeable border of the Spanish enclave Melilla, in Morocco: 'The state is not there to prevent border passage – but to require a show of recognition of the state's right to dominate … The border is thus more of a stage upon which the state's violence and pageantry play themselves out' (McMurray 2003: 142). Other border crossings are less playful although equally ritualised, such as the checkpoints in occupied territories, or the rites of reinclusion of suspected guerrilla supporters into the Guatemalan polity where they passed through centres of interrogation and reeducation after being caught in the wilderness (Stepputat 1999).

Following the ideas of Jansen and Löfving on the particular spatial implications of neoliberal forms of governance, I would suggest the further study of some of the associated ritualising practices. For instance, a new regime of mobility control is being developed by the European

Union in parts of Africa and Eastern Europe, including extraterritorial border control and other practices of sovereignty. While celebrating and operationalising good governance, accountability, transparency and human rights as means of reducing the migratory pressure on its borders, the EU seeks to establish or boost systems that permit the screening and registration of refugees and asylum seekers in their 'region of origin'. Thereby the EU will enhance their 'traceability' (to borrow a notion from the realm of value chain analyses) and the possibilities of returning them in case they reach the shores of Europe and fail to pass the tests of admission.

The second avenue for future research concerns the darker side of the regulation of movement. Kelly (in this volume) writes about the 'incompleteness' of practices that attempt to relate people to places and notes how they simultaneously act as sources of constraint and open up new spaces for movement. Against the iron-cage images of modern society of Weber and Foucault I would suggest exploring 'regimes of irregulation': whereas one may discern specific rationalities in the conception and design of the regulation of movement, these regimes invariably coproduce 'irregular movements' in the same way that attempts to regulate and formalise economic activity produce 'informal economies' (Hart 1973, 2004). This brings movement into a vast grey area between legal and illegal domains where different (but discernible) logics and dynamics shape practices. As many writers have observed, the legal and illegal domains – as well as state and non-state domains – are not working separately but are closely related at different levels and scales, a fact which also holds for the way in which irregular, cross-border movement is organised (see for example Ruggiero 2000).

Furthermore, the everyday retailing of rules and regulation by public servants or private subcontractors of the state often leaves room for a certain arbitrariness, discreteness and negotiation in decision making. This volume gives examples of the discretionary power of officials to apply the law unevenly and to make exceptions from the law which, as Schmitt observed, is a basic dimension of sovereignty that takes the bodies of subjects beyond the realm of rights and citizenship and makes them amenable to arbitrary abuse: this is the case of Israeli officers controlling Palestinian workers at checkpoints in the West Bank (Kelly). The same feature, writ large as it were, has characterised the tacit acceptance of illegal Moroccan workers entering Spanish territory (Potot).

The third important avenue of future research that comes out in this volume concerns the role of violence in the reorganisation of space, patterns of mobility and access to citizenship. Löfving deals with the issue in his chapter, where he elaborates how we may understand linkages between the destruction of homes ('domicide') and the following displacements of people as well as politics. In the early days of studies in forced migration there was a tendency to regard displacement as collateral damage in the context of armed conflict. But during the 1990s, and in particular in the cases of ethnic cleansing, it became painfully clear that domicide and displacement of civilian populations would often be carefully planned operations with the aim of changing the contours and nature of the body politic through changes in the spatial organisation of populations (Jansen, this volume; Stepputat 1999).

Displacement and destruction of homes is usually preceded by the identification of certain areas, groups or networks as representing particular threats to a given political/moral community (the nation, religion, state, ethnic group, town, brotherhood) and its political, economic or moral projects. This is the speech act that Wæver refers to as 'securitisation', an act that places the identified subjects within the domain of security where certain solutions and means become legitimate because of the alleged danger represented by the subjects (Wæver 1997). As Löfving rightly points out, violence and threats of violence have achieved a privileged place in neoliberal discourse. In the 'repertoires of violence' of the current era (Wieviorka 2003) we are witnessing a trend towards securitising issues and groups which used to be considered problems of development, inequality and lack of integration. Whereas the nexus between development and security is by no means a new one – consider counterinsurgency programs of the wars of decolonisation and the Cold War – it is worthwhile exploring how the nexus is developing currently. One suggestion for interpreting current forms of violence would be that the contested and partial nature of the sovereignty of the state as well as the contending forces of de facto sovereign entities increases the use of violent exclusion, containment and displacement of bodies as a means of producing political community and effects of sovereignty (Hansen and Stepputat 2005).

Confinement and Displaced Livelihoods

As mentioned above, the volume is consistently analytical about sedentarist notions of home without embracing the celebration of mobility and borderlessness that has characterised too many contributions since the 1990s. At one end of the continuum of mobility, Kelly's chapter in this volume very explicitly addresses the problems and effects of confinement in a world where mobility is often celebrated as an indicator of progress. In Hirschman's classical terms, we are dealing here with people who have not experienced a choice between loyalty, voice, and exit, unless exit is understood as a kind of mental exit from an impossible *cul-de-sac* (Hirschman 1970). As many humanitarian organisations have experienced, the privileging of refugees and internally displaced people as victims of violence and deserving recipients of aid qua their displacement is resented not only by 'host communities' but also by the people who stayed put in zones of conflict and who become neighbours to privileged, returning refugees in the wake of the conflict.

Without elaborating on the issue of aid and 'post-conflict' reconstruction as such, I would like to raise the question of how to deal conceptually with the issue of confinement-in-conflict, or, more generally, of the violence-in-place that displaces rights, entitlements and livelihood practices for confined populations. As the present volume shows so convincingly, conceptualisations of displacements and confinements are intimately linked to the definition of rights and entitlements, and while legal categories such as 'refugee' or 'immigrant' can be hard to bear for those included, Kelly's case leaves no doubt that the pervasive anxiety of legal indeterminacy represents an even greater challenge to livelihood and personal integrity.

People who 'stay behind' and endure the hardships of armed conflict witness how free movement is one of the first victims of conflict, which is no surprise considering the strategic importance of movement in conflict zones. Apart from being subjects and objects of cultures of violence, people lose their access to land, markets, education facilities, labour migration, sacred places, et cetera, and, combined with the fact that transported goods become scarce and expensive, such confinements result in severe impoverishment of a majority of the population.

In an attempt to de-essentialise categories of post-conflict intervention, I have suggested the notion of 'displaced livelihoods' which should denote the effects of disrupted spatial mobility, a condition that in many ways is common to refugees, IDPs and 'stayees' (Stepputat 2002; see also analyses of refugee camps inspired by Agamben, such as Turner 2005). By focusing on displaced livelihoods rather than displaced people, the notion does not a priori privilege those who have moved over those who have had their livelihoods destroyed by being confined. In addition, the notion elicits historical analysis of confinement and mobile livelihood practices, as well as struggles for spatial mobility. However, it is a problem that 'displaced livelihoods' is premised upon an understanding of livelihoods as almost always comprising different forms of mobility, an understanding which is behind the development of the notion of 'mobile livelihoods' (Olwig and Sørensen 2002). This obscures the use and understanding of the notion of displaced livelihoods outside the narrow circles of researchers, but I still think that the issue begs conceptual development and points towards one important research agenda coming out of this volume.

As a point in case, confinement and displaced livelihoods are very much a reality for Moroccan youth unable to go to Europe, but also for those who, as Potot describes it, have made it to Almeria where their illegal status severely confines their ability to move around freely. Another case would be the confinement of refugees to certain places and limited zones, often in marginal areas. New (or rather recycled) strategies of international assistance aim at helping the refugees to become self-reliant and integrated in local development, but often the main resource for economic self reliance would be the freedom of movement while in-place livelihoods are almost impossible to develop. Host governments have various reasons for insisting on the confinement of refugees, and as long as the governments of donor countries uphold very restrictive migration policies, it is hard for them to argue against the policies of confinement of host governments.

Liberty and Homelessness

Both in personal and collective lives, displacements and the loss of homes may have liberating effects. The untying of social obligations that are bound to places and rhythms is never a given effect of displacement, nor is the alienation from repressive political domination. As amply shown in the literature on transnational social fields, systems of long-distance social control are remarkably strong, and repressive political cultures and antagonisms die hard and tend to be reincarnated in new guises. However, displacement involves options and necessary choices in which personal desires for freedom and escape from oppressive family relations, in the shape of a violent husband, for example, can be decisive. At the collective level, as we see in some of the cases described here, displacement can lead to the encounter and cultivation of new ideas of gender relations, production systems, ethnicity or national identity that may be experienced as liberating for those who have struggled within and against former hegemonic ideologies and practices. That some of these freedoms can be hard to uphold when returning to former places of residence has been documented in several cases, such as the return of Guatemalan refugees when women experienced a disappointing trend towards the reinforcement of former gender relations (Pessar 2001).

Somewhat along the same lines, we have seen several decades of philosophical debate over home, homelessness and cosmopolitanism discussing the liberating effects of displacement and loss of home and homeland. Whereas a sound scepticism towards the uncritical celebration of transnationalism, mobility and cosmopolitanism permeates this volume, I would like to finish this postscript with two comments on the issue. The first one borrows from Brudholm's (2005) essay on the Jewish exile and writer Jean Améry, who against lofty ideas of cosmopolitanism insisted that 'one must have a home in order not to need it'. Or, as Said put it: 'Exile is strangely compelling to think about but terrible to experience' (2001: 173, n.15).

And secondly, the feelings of sorrow over lost relations and irreversible displacements on one side, and of the expectations related to new horizons, opportunities and challenges on the other side, are much too often set up as being at odds with each other. Rather than either-or, we should think of the ambiguous and contradictory experiences of loss and liberation as often coexisting in the difficult and tormenting processes of adjustment to the loss of home. The problem, however, is the fact that so many people do not experience any new senses of possibility but rather new varieties of confinement, dispossession and displacement. As this volume shows convincingly, the 'sense of possibility' is not something people just have; rather the quest for achieving this sense is something they live by.

References

Brudholm, Thomas. 2005. 'A Confiscated Past: Jean Améry on Home and Exile', *The Hedgehog Review* Fall: 7–19.

Featherstone, Mike. 1997. 'Travel, Migration, and Images of Social Life', in *Global History and Migrations*, ed. Wang Gungwu, pp. 239–78. Boulder, CO: Westview Press.

Hansen, Thomas Blom and Finn Stepputat (eds.). 2005. *Sovereign Bodies: Citizens, Migrants and States in the Postcolonial World*. Princeton: Princeton University Press.

Hart, Keith. 1973. 'Informal Income Opportunities and Urban Employment in Ghana', *Journal of Modern African Studies* 11(1): 61–89.

———. 2004. 'Formal Bureaucracy and the Emergent Forms of the Informal Economy', EGDI and UNU-WIDER Conference. Unlocking Human Potential: Linking the Informal and Formal Sectors, 17–18 September 2004, Helsinki, Finland.

Hirschman, Albert O. 1970. *Exit, Voice, and Loyalty: Responses to Decline in Firms, Organizations, and States*. Cambridge, MA: Harvard University Press.

Mbembe, Achille. 1992. 'Provisional Notes on the Postcolony', *Africa* 62(1): 3–37.

McMurray, David. 2003. 'Recognition of State Authority as a Cost of Involvement in Maroccan Border Crime', in *Crimes Power: Anthropologists and the Ethnography of Crime*, ed. Stephanie Kane and Philip Parnell, pp. 125–44. New York and Basingstoke, Hampshire: Palgrave Macmillan.

Moore, Henrietta L. 1996. 'The Changing Nature of Anthropological Knowledge: An Introduction', in *The Future of Anthropological Knowledge*, ed. Henrietta L. Moore, pp. 1–15. London and New York: Routledge.

Olwig, Karen Fog and Ninna Nyberg Sørensen. 2002. 'Mobile Livelihoods: Making a Living in the World', in *Work and Migration: Life and Livelihoods in a Globalizing World*, ed. Ninna Nyberg Sørensen and Karen Fog Olwig, pp. 1–19. London and New York: Routledge.

Pessar, Patricia. 2001. 'Women's Political Consciousness and Empowerment in Local, National, and Transnational Contexts: Guatemalan Refugees and Returnees', *Identities* 7(4): 461–500.

Ruggiero, Vincenzo. 2000. *Crime and Markets. Essays in Anti-Criminology*. Oxford and New York: Oxford University Press.

Said, Edward. 2001. *Reflections on Exile and Other Literary and Cultural Essays*. London: Granta.

Stepputat Finn. 1999. 'Politics of Displacement in Guatemala', *Journal of Historical Sociology* 12(1): 54–80.

———. 2002. 'The Final Move? Displaced Livelihoods and Collective Returns in Peru and Guatemala', in *Work and Migration: Life and Livelihoods in a Globalizing*

World, ed. Ninna Nyberg Sørensen and Karen Fog Olwig, pp. 202–24. London and New York: Routledge.

Turner, Simon. 2005. 'Suspended Spaces – Contesting Sovereignties in a Refugee Camp', in *Sovereign Bodies: Citizens, Migrants and States in the Postcolonial World*, ed. Thomas Blom Hansen and Finn Stepputat, pp. 312–32. Princeton: Princeton University Press.

Wieviorka, Michel. 2003. 'The New Paradigm of Violence', in *Globalization, the State and Violence*, ed. Jonathan Friedman, pp. 107–39. Lanham, MD: Altamira Press.

Wilson, Fiona. 2001. 'Territorializing Regimes and Mobility in the Andes: A Community History, 1940's–1990's', *CDR Working Paper* 01.8. Copenhagen: Centre for Development Research.

Wæver, Ole. 1997. 'Conceptualizing Security', Ph.D. Dissertation, University of Copenhagen.

Zur, Judith N. 1998. *Violent Memories. Quiché War Widows of Guatemala*. Boulder, CO: Westview Press.

Notes on Contributors

Michael Barrett is an anthropologist working at the Museum of Ethnography in Stockholm, Sweden. His research has revolved around the social relationships of adulthood, livelihood and mobility, primarily through extended fieldwork in Zambia. His publications include *Paths to Adulthood: Freedom, Belonging and Temporalities in Mbunda Biographies from Western Zambia* (2004).

Stef Jansen is Senior Lecturer in Social Anthropology at the University of Manchester, UK. His research centres on critical ethnographic investigations of home and hope with regard to nation, place and transformation. Based on fieldwork in Bosnia-Herzegovina, Croatia, Serbia and Kosovo, he has published numerous journal articles and book chapters on these themes, as well as the monograph *Antinacionalizam* (2005).

Tobias Kelly is Lecturer in Social Anthropology at the University of Edinburgh, UK. He has carried out fieldwork amongst West Bank Palestinians, concentrating on issues of citizenship and labour regulation. His ongoing research focuses on the UN human rights system and the legal recognition of suffering. He is the author of the monograph *Law, Violence and Sovereignty Among West Bank Palestinians* (2006).

Staffan Löfving is Assistant Professor at the Institute of Latin American Studies, Stockholm University, Sweden. He is currently engaged in a research project on paramilitarism and neoliberal government in Colombia and Central America. Among his publications is *Peopled Economies* (2005), an edited volume that elaborates on an anthropological critique of neoclassical dogmas in development economics.

Peter Loizos is Emeritus Professor at the Department of Anthropology, London School of Economics and Social Sciences, UK. He is currently teaching at LSE, SOAS (School of Oriental and African Studies), and Intercollege (Nicosia). He has authored four books and numerous papers researched in Cyprus. He has also done development work in Sudan, Sri Lanka and Bangladesh, and films in Cyprus, India and Bosnia. His publications include *The Heart Grown Bitter: A Chronicle of Cypriot War Refugees* (1981), and in 2008 the series Berghahn Studies in Forced Migration will publish his *Iron in the Soul: Displacement, Livelihood and Health in Cyprus*.

Swanie Potot is a sociologist, researcher at the URMIS (Unité de Recherche Migrations et Société), University of Nice Sophia-Antipolis, CNRS, France. She works on the diverse forms of East–West migrations and their economic implications in Europe. In 2007 she began new fieldwork on foreign agricultural workers in the South of France.

Finn Stepputat, trained in geography and cultural sociology, is Senior Researcher at the Danish Institute of International Studies, Denmark. He carried out fieldwork among Guatemalan refugees in Mexico for his doctoral dissertation and in Guatemala on issues of refugee return and post-conflict dynamics. He has since widened his geographical scope to include Peru, Colombia and Afghanistan, where he studies forced migration in relation to armed conflict, state building and the security/ development nexus. His publications include (with Thomas Blom Hansen) *Sovereign Bodies: Citizens, Migrants, and States in the Postcolonial World* (2005).

Sharika Thiranagama is ESRC Postdoctoral Fellow in Social Anthropology at the School of Social and Political Studies in Edinburgh University, UK. She received her Ph.D. in Social Anthropology from Edinburgh University in 2005. She is currently working on a monograph based on her doctoral dissertation on issues of home, return, generation, memory and displacement for war-displaced Northern Tamils and Muslims in Sri Lanka.

INDEX